Roger Horchow

❧ ❧ ❧

LIVING IN STYLE

❦ ❦ ❦ ❦ ❦

LIVING IN STYLE

In a Time When Taste
Means More Than Money

❦ ❦ ❦ ❦ ❦

by

ROGER HORCHOW

with PATRICIA LINDEN

RAWSON, WADE PUBLISHERS, INC.
New York

Library of Congress Cataloging in Publication Data

Horchow, Roger.
  Living in style.

  Includes index.
  1. Conduct of life.   I. Linden, Patricia.   II. Title.
BJ1581.2.H643   640   80-5992
ISBN 0-89256-166-1   AACR2

Designed by Jacques Chazaud

First Edition

For Carolyn,
the essence of style

⚜ ⚜ ⚜

Contents

❧ ❧ ❧

LIVING IN STYLE

❧ ❧ ❧

1
THE MEANING
OF STYLE

Years ago, before Carolyn and I were married and I was still young enough to puzzle over the questions that perplex our three daughters today, I had the good fortune to know a wise and discerning woman with a taste for philosophical discussion. Margaret was then in her sixties, passionately youthful in her outlook and as vital as she was voluble. We became instant friends on the day that fate, with the aid of a hostess at Schrafft's, seated us at the same table for lunch. Margaret made a comment to me, I answered her with a question, and that was the start of a fascinating conversation that continued until her death a quarter of a century later. In those twenty-five years we explored every topic imaginable, from the world's weighty mysteries to her recollections of frivolous escapades. I wish I had kept a notebook of the stories Margaret told about her early years: the fabulous life she led and the legendary people she knew. It would be like reading the diary of Auntie Mame.

During one of our serious conversations, Margaret said something that has been a touchstone for me ever since. I had posed the eternal riddle, "What is life all about?" My dear friend replied, "The answer is simpler than you think. You will find, when it is all said and done, that life is nothing more than a survival contest." Then she sat up very straight, looked at me intensely, and added, "The thing is to survive in style."

The longer I have thought about what Margaret said, the clearer her wisdom becomes. Whatever definition you give to "style," in the end it is the ability to select the best of everything that is available to you, in order to lead a happy life and give pleasure to the people around you.

Some people, like my wife Carolyn, seem to have been born with style. They create an atmosphere of beauty and harmony around them: in their homes, their dress, their manner. But the truth is, style is not an inherent trait. It is an acquired characteristic: a combination of abilities that we learn as we mature, just as we learn to speak French or repair faucets. The other truth is that the basis for style comes from within. It is a quality that we develop in ourselves by learning from others, then editing their ideas to fit our own needs. Style is a very personal acquisition, a quality that cannot be bought and in fact has nothing at all to do with money.

It has been my observation that personal style is a composite of six main ingredients:

1. *Proportion* Balance, restraint. Knowing what to add and when to stop.
2. *Attention to detail* Thinking things through to create comfort and satisfaction.
3. *Consideration* Alertness to other people's needs and sensitivity in response to them.
4. *Poise* Self-confidence, grace, serenity. Self-knowledge without vanity.
5. *Discernment* Ability to make good choices through a knowledge of excellence.
6. *Individuality* The distinctive, tasteful expression of personal preferences. Identity. A point of view.

In sum, to possess the ingredients of style is to know how to live pleasantly, and give pleasure to others.

Yet I know of no time in history when it has been more difficult to "survive in style." We are faced with a shortage of everything that we grew up expecting to have in abundance: money, time, space, and the vigor to accomplish everything we dreamed of. We are confused by the new economics and world politics, frustrated by the general depersonalization of life and our own daily tensions. What is more, yesterday's black-and-white rules and traditions have vanished. We no longer have rituals to guide us through each situation, or patterns to tell us what will come next. For the first time ever, we are unable to promise our children that their future will be better than ours; we are lucky if we can hold our own. I sometimes think that the late humorist James Thurber's witty prediction of imminent doom is about to come true. He said, "Man is moving too fast for a world that is round. Soon he will catch up with himself in a great rear-end collision and man will never know that what hit him from behind was man."

Thurber's humor helps. What is more useful is the realization that the very problems that plague us also create opportunities to lead an easier life:

• The disappearance of ritual frees us to explore fresh ideas and express ourselves honestly. Without other people's rules imposed on us, we can choose for ourselves how to decorate our homes, entertain our friends, and use our time.

• Technological advances depersonalize life in some ways. They also provide almost limitless, instant access to information on nearly every aspect of life, from shopping at home to travel reservations, astrological calculations, and the latest thing in cooking equipment.

• The absence of service people forces us to be self-reliant: prompts us to uncomplicate daily tasks, conserve our energy, and discover a simpler way of life.

• The problem of reduced living space expands the variety of ways in which we make our homes comfortable, spawns imaginative new products, reveals alternatives and solutions we might otherwise fail to see.

• The unstable value of money challenges us to reexamine the meaning of worth. We demand fewer fads and better quality, possessions that last, efforts that matter.

I don't mean to sound like a Pollyanna who sees only the bright side of disaster. Heedless optimism is no more rewarding than long-faced pessimism. But I do think that the New Reality offers freedom and the excitement of discovery. It is a chance to make choices, develop your tastes, make changes that you may not have realized you are ready for.

Some things do not change. Invariably I have found that the people whose style I admire practice the Golden Rule of manners. They are considerate, courteous, pay close attention to what other people say, are generous with their time, and warm and helpful in their relationships. As you will learn in some of the stories in this book, Letitia Baldrige, the busy publicist and former social secretary to the White House, is never too busy to remember a friend's birthday or to find five minutes for a phone call. Jim Lehrer, of the McNeil-Lehrer Report on television, is another friend who tries never to lose sight of the personal, despite the fact that his days and nights are a constant race with world events. He once took time from his television assignments to guide Carolyn and me around a White House reception so we would know with whom we were visiting. He pointed out Zubin Mehta, Leontyne Price, the Supreme Court justices, senators, and a glittering Milky Way of celebrities. When we got to the presidential receiving line, the First Lady said to me, "How do you do, Mr. Horchow. The President and I admire your catalogs very much." You can imagine how pleased her remark made me feel, and how impressed I was by her knack of singling me out in a roomful of famous people. Her words struck a chord I could respond to comfortably.

It has been my experience that the people we think of as "charming," the people we want to be with again and again, all share the ability to put others at ease. It is their signature. The famous fashion designer Pauline Trigère is like that. She says that whenever she entertains, all the worry and arrangements must take place beforehand. When guests arrive at her home, Pauline says she is "cool as a coo-cumber," has a drink in her hand, and is ready to give full attention to each person. Carolyn is the same way: all the planning and preparations are backstage and the effort never shows. Gracious entertaining has become the trademark by which people identify her, and you will learn some of the nuances of her style in later chapters.

People tell me that the distinguishing characteristic of my style is friendship: keeping in touch, adding to the chain, building a continuum of shared interests and experiences. In my opinion, friendship is what pulls everything else together. It is the mortar that gives structure to the material symbols of life. For me, real happiness lies in the warmth of human relations.

That is my style. It is not for everybody. You have to decide for yourself what makes you comfortable and what you want out of life. Some people are happiest with just two or three close friends. Some take pleasure in contacts with large groups of people, and others enjoy friendships with colleagues who can further their careers in some way. To each his own. The point is to gain enough experience so you can evolve the style that suits you best.

I have been exceptionally lucky in the experiences and knowledge I have been exposed to over the years. From the start I have been surrounded by people who are informed, tasteful, and willing to share themselves freely. My parents, teachers, friends, business associates, and certainly my wife have been the experts from whom I have gained what I consider the world's finest education. I am lucky, but I am not unique. I believe that everybody has a similar opportunity.

You can learn, as I have, by observing leaders and listening to famous, successful people such as the celebrities whose stories are in this book. You can gather ideas from your neighbors, friends, and family, as have I. You can add to your knowledge through the magazines, newspapers, and films that you see every day, and through formal studies. Whether formal or informal, education is a never-ending experience that continually broadens your horizons, so you have more and more ideas to draw from.

I hope that you will find ideas in these pages that you can use to make your life more pleasant: ideas you can reshape to fit your particular needs. Perhaps some of our experiences that you read about, or some of the things that have happened to our friends, will stimulate you to experiment with new ways to give and receive the pleasures of Living in Style.

2
ENTERTAINING
IN STYLE

Usually when the girls wander into our bedroom to talk with Carolyn and me before they go to sleep, the conversation centers on things like homework or permission to go someplace special—the logistics of teen and preteen life. Every so often, though, we get into deeper, more cosmic topics. On one particular night we had a family discussion that I find hard to forget. It had to do with the changing values in contemporary society. Sally, who was ten years old at the time, had asked Carolyn and me to explain something she'd seen in the newspaper. It was an interview with Geraldine Stutz, president of the famous Henri Bendel store in New York, in which Ms. Stutz had said, "The eighties will be more focused [than the seventies], with time increasingly seen as the most valuable of valuables, to be spent carefully on real interests and real friends." That was clear enough, but the part that puzzled Sally was, "I intend to know more and care more about everyone's value, including my own."

I thought that was a valid and profound commentary on the hectic, complex, fragmented existence that seems to confuse so many people these days. Just to get through an ordinary day now requires responses to such a welter of disjointed demands on our time and emotions, we are losing touch with one another. And getting edgy about it. It seems to me that we need to make a real effort to find ways to focus on the personal. I wondered about our other daughters' reactions, and asked Lizzie and Regen what Ms. Stutz's remarks meant to them. Lizzie, who was sixteen, replied, "I think she means you should see fewer people and do less things so you can get to know each one better, instead of trying to do everything all at once. But how can you follow that advice when everything and everybody interests you, and you want to try them all?"

Eighteen-year-old Regen said, "I know how Lizzie feels. But maybe Ms. Stutz means you should experiment with everything you're curious about when you are young, and then begin to narrow your interests when you grow up. I don't see how you can 'know your own value' until you have explored enough to know what you do best."

Carolyn and I smiled at each other, pleased by our girls' thoughtful answers. Then Sally asked, "What do you think, Daddy?" I told her, "As it happens, this is a subject your mother and I have talked about often. We agree with all of you, that curiosity about the world around you is a wonderful quality to encourage in yourself, and that you also have to spend precious time building genuine friendships and pursuing real interests. But there is such a shortage of time these days—time, energy, and money, too—that people feel frustrated and nervous because they never can quite catch up. As a result, they don't take the trouble to make themselves and other people happy, and lose sight of the value of graceful, personal touches because the small things seem to take too much time and effort.

"I think one of the most important things in life is to respect the value of friendships, and not to be so frenzied that you let people vanish from your life. You've noticed how each of you always gets a birthday card from Stanley Marcus, or a postcard from wherever he is in the world. And how our friend Tish Baldrige, as pressured as her busy life is, always finds a minute to telephone. And how we manage to have people in our home all the time, even though we both work. It may be just for a drink or a cup of coffee, rather than a full-scale sit-down dinner. The point is, we are very conscious of the need to maintain the links we have forged with people we like, so we find ways to manage. No matter how simply we entertain, even when we ask friends to join us at the last minute, we feel that we are strengthening the quality of our lives. When you get down to it, that is what has 'lasting value.' "

Entertaining with Serenity

I call this the Nervous Decade: people are edgy about so many things. That is why it has become important that we create an aura of grace and simplicity for ourselves and for the guests in our homes. With entertaining an essential part of Carolyn's and my life, we have learned that a little forethought can make a big difference in the pleasure we give, whether we are giving an organized "party" or having a couple of friends in for a casual, impromptu get-together.

Even for casual drop-ins, a certain amount of planning creates a warmer welcome for our guests. In our home, there is always a collection of assorted cocktail foods on the shelf, and packages of Carolyn's homemade entrées in the freezer, "just in case." It seems to me, though, that the most important ingredient of a successful party is not the food you serve, it is the mixture of people you invite. It has been our experience that you have to mix and stir your guest list as artfully as you do a soufflé. A pinch of this, a dollop of that, and pouf—a delectable concoction that captivates everyone. Nothing is as flat and as tedious as a party where the guests are all of an age, all of the same background, all acquainted with one another, and all of the same general interests. You might as well be at a PTA meeting, with the participants doing nothing more than comparing notes on teachers and children's grades.

Minding Your Guests

You need young people mixed in with older and in-between aged people. Artists and writers shuffled among the bankers and businessmen. People who have never met before and will have new things to discover, different ideas, fresh conversational paths to tread. As a matter of fact, a judicious mix of guests will increase the odds of their finding things in common to talk about. I remember one rather remarkable time when that happened to me, as a guest.

I was on a buying trip in Milan and the well-known interior designer and architect, Count Filippo Perrego de Cremnago, invited me to an informal party with his friends. He calls all his parties informal and indeed many of them are, despite the fact that he is constant host to the most elegant and celebrated people in Italy and America. That night he had included me in a group he had invited to a neighborhood restaurant, where he had planned the seating so that strangers, celebrities, and his own close friends were all shuffled in checkerboard fashion. He used place cards, which I think are a must, no matter how large or small your party is. Otherwise old friends are apt to sit and hobnob together, and side-by-side married couples will spend the meal repeating conversations they had the night before. There is only one time when I do not insist on breaking up husbands and wives at the table—when they are obvious swooning newlyweds who would rather have poison ivy than lose one hour of conjugal joy.

Seated as we were at Filippo's dinner table, we had no choice but to ask exploratory questions of each other. I introduced myself to the woman on my left and before I could catch her name, she was off to the races. "Oh, you must be the man who does those catalogs," she said. "I just love shopping by mail. It saves so much time and energy, don't you think?" I said I certainly did think so, and there was also a great advantage in being the person who puts the catalogs together. "Traveling on buying trips, like this, gives me an opportunity to discover restaurants all over the world. The food here is superb, and I hope I'll be able to match it when I get back to Dallas." My table mate exclaimed, "Dallas! Why, my husband just donated a painting to your Dallas Museum."

I was in the process of explaining that I am on the board of that museum, and delighted to find a table mate who is also interested in art, when I realized that I did not know her name. I said, "I'm sorry, could you repeat your name, please? Then I'm sure I will know the painting your husband donated."

The woman identified herself as Mrs. Vladimir Horowitz, the

wife of the famed pianist. She then introduced me to the woman across from me, seated between Geoffrey Beene, and a beautiful woman with jeweled combs in her hair. The woman opposite was Mrs. Horowitz's sister, Wally Toscannini, who also shares an interest in the arts, a legacy no doubt, from their gifted father, Arturo Toscannini.

There I was, a businessman from America, having dinner in a foreign country with strangers with whom I suddenly found common ground. For the next quarter hour, the three of us chatted like old friends, swapping opinions and stories about the subject that linked us together. The experience was an engaging surprise for me, and the reason I am telling you about it is to point out that when you are hosting a party, it doesn't matter whether you are the Count de Cremnago or a plain Mr. or Mrs. Everyday, in Anytown, U.S.A. If you want an evening that sparkles with stimulating conversation, the first essential is to make sure it is cross-fertilized with a mixture of people who have a variety of interests—some of them are sure to spark together and make the evening go.

Small Talk

At the Count's party, we had all arrived at table separately because we met in a restaurant. When you entertain at home, however, the curtain raiser usually is the cocktail hour. This is the time when skilled hosts or hostesses employ their talent for getting conversations going. I have noticed that those who are good at it most often use a technique I call Instant Biography. They brush up beforehand on each person's occupation, or something that person is noted for, and use that information to get talk going when they make introductions. For example, "I'd like you to meet Vona McDonald. Vona is famous for her delicate watercolors—some of her paintings were shown last month at the Lakeway store. We are proud of our new celebrity."

Almost always, someone in the group will race through the door you have opened. They'll exclaim, "Oh, I just saw the display, Vona. How wonderful to meet the artist. Tell me, do you always paint children, or do you like to do other subjects as well?" Another person might add, "I paint a little, too, though

I'm not very good at it. A lot of my friends have taken up painting lately. Do you think there is a movement toward more amateur painting, as a kind of therapy to take our minds off our
troubles?"

If you are unlucky and everyone just says "How do you do,"
and then stands around mute, you can ask the leading question
yourself. Something that will give your guest a chance to pontifi-
cate a little, and inform the others. "This is my friend Lew
Brown. He has a computer manufacturing company in Houston.
Lew, how long do you really think it will be before we will all
have computers in our homes?" You don't have to worry about
coming up with profound or snappy questions, anything that
will get the ball rolling is fine. And remember, you can always
fall back on an old reliable: "You've been a noted decorator for a
great many years, Mr. Baldwin. Tell us, if you had three pieces
of advice to give the world, what would they be?"

A Challenge to Short Budgets

An effective party is mainly a matter of using your imagination, planning well, and making the most of what you already
have. It would be unrealistic, however, to claim that you don't
have to spend anything when you entertain. But these days we
all try to keep the expenditure down, even as we entertain with
grace. Here are some fundamental tricks of the trade, techniques
that have been tested and proved, ideas you can mold to your
own pattern of living.

Menus

Over the years, Carolyn has developed a repertoire of menus
that she knows will please people and that don't require a great
deal of money or effort to prepare. They also lend themselves to
variations, so she doesn't keep repeating herself. You lose out on
zest when there is too much predictability. It's like staring at the
same wallpaper, year after year.

Keeping Track

One of the ways Carolyn prevents repetition and keeps her good ideas flowing is with a hostess book that she can refer to through the years. It is a simple system, and it saves having to reinvent the wheel, so to speak, each time you entertain. You can set up your hostess book any way that is practical for you. What Carolyn uses is a loose-leaf notebook with alphabetically tabbed dividers in front and blank divider tabs at the back. Carolyn's blank dividers are marked:

> *Recipes to Remember* (in which she notes the name of the recipe, the cookbook in which it can be found, and the page number)

> *Annual Affairs* (New Year's Eve, Office Parties, Nantucket Reunions, etc.)

> *Old Faithfuls* (seven sections of a page or two each, reminders of basic tried-and-true dishes. Pages are headed Hors d'Oeuvres, Entrées, Casseroles, Vegetables, Salads, Desserts)

The important part of the book is up front, in the alphabetically divided part. This is where you write in the names, dates, menus, and special notes for each party you give. For example:

> *Roberts, Al and Diane*
> 2/26/80 with Allen Rushing, Margaret Anne Cullum, Pam and Jere Mitchell. Crudites, Havarti cheese, and stoned wheat crackers.—C. Claiborne's spareribs (p. 256), Swedish potatoes, hot curried fruit. Green salad/vinaigrette. Coffee: grapes in sour cream w. brown sugar.
> *Note:* Al likes a martini before dinner. Coffee with cream. Diane: white wine only. No mayonnaise.

Then under Rushing, Cullum, and Mitchell, you would have entries like this.

> *Rushing, Allen* 2/26/80 w. M. A. Cullum, Al and Diane Roberts, Pam and Jere Mitchell. See Roberts.

If the Roberts are people you entertain often, you will probably devote separate pages to them. You may want to add preparation and cooking times along with some of the menu items in your hostess book, and scribble notes in your cookbooks, too. Carolyn's are filled with comments such as "Great! Use less garlic. Served 2/26/80 to Roberts, etc. 1 lb. coffee makes 45 cups in large pot."

Shopping

Obviously, the first thing you have to do after you decide on your menu is check to see what ingredients you have in the house, and what you need to buy—right down to butter, onions, salt, and soda for highball mixers. It helps to do some visualizing. For instance, if you are going to serve cheese and fruit for dessert instead of a sweet, because so many people are watching their diets, you may want the fruit to double as a centerpiece. If so, you will probably add to the types and amount of fruit on your shopping list. Perhaps a pineapple, melon, extra grapes and some whole walnuts—with nutcrackers.

Marketing

Carolyn likes to write her marketing lists in sections according to the stops she will have to make, and also according to how our supermarket is laid out. On a photocopier we run off a bunch of master lists with headings that read: Meat and Fish, Produce, Canned Goods, Freezer, Bakery, Dairy, and Household (for cleaning things and paperware). She says this method saves her time and energy and cuts down on the chance that she will have to retrace her steps because she has overlooked an item buried in the list.

Preparing for the Unexpected

Carolyn has another hostess trick that I notice our girls have begun to adopt. When she is going to make something like beef stew, pesto sauce, chili, or a casserole, she buys three or four times the amount of ingredients the recipe calls for and cooks up the whole batch all at once. Then she packages the extra in individual portions and freezes them. When we have unexpected guests or if we feel like inviting people over on the spur of the moment, we are ready to serve in as much time as it takes to defrost the entrée or hors d'oeuvres. We like to freeze small packages of cooking ingredients, too, so we can reach for them in a hurry. Grated lemon peel, chopped onions, chives and parsley, whole or chopped ginger, bread, rolls, and butter all tuck into small spaces in the freezer, and keep for a month or so until you need them.

Visual Appeal

Grated peel, chopped chives, and such add piquancy to the taste of foods, and condiments for the visual sense as well. It is bromidic but true: we eat with our eyes as well as our taste buds. You can take the simplest dish, dress it up with a little glitter, and win raves for the enticing, inventive meal you prepared. Plain jellied consommé becomes a celebration when you spike it with a dash of sherry and a sprig of fresh parsley, then present it in a colorful bowl centered on a contrasting plate. Ice cream is just a bowl of ice cream, until you pile a rainbow mix of colors and flavors into a tall, stemmed crystal goblet. Then it becomes glamorous.

Once, when I was at Neiman-Marcus, Mr. Marcus asked me to take Helen Hayes to see the store's weight-loss resort, The Greenhouse. The late Helen Corbitt was in charge of the cuisine, and her challenge was to make each day's 500 calories look as appetizing as the glorious double-fudge sundaes all the guests were dreaming of. Miss Hayes and I both were astonished at the culinary coups Helen Corbitt pulled off. Every meal was a *trompe l'oeil* delight.

The dinner we attended was properly skimpy, an ounce of sole, a flick of lettuce, a quarter of a cut-up apple. Yet it seemed positively luxurious because of the way it was presented. On each opulently embroidered, lace-edged linen place mat was a magnificent Royal Crown Derby service plate, its regal reds, blues, and gold a dazzling lining for a crystal dish so luminous it made the smidgeon of sole look like a 40-carat diamond. Above the ornate sterling fork, a glistening crystal bowl cupped its nibble of salad as if to proffer the first precious dew of morning. Dessert, which consisted of all of five bites of no-calorie gelatin crowned by a single green grape, was served in a halo of Baccarat intended for vintage champagne, and underscored by another Royal Crown gem. The guests were ecstatic and Miss Hayes even applauded. She said she had never seen prettier dishes set before a queen. The phrase was apt: the elegance and care lavished upon them made the women at the table feel they were privileged royalty, not calorie-starved overweights.

It doesn't take eons of time or a treasure in Royal Crown Derby to make a table memorable. Just ingenuity and an eye for the unusual. Instead of a traditional dining room table, we use a stainless steel frame topped by an inexpensive, stock-size 48-inch by 84-inch mirror. If the top breaks or becomes scratched, we can replace it quite cheaply with another mirror or, for a change, clear or tinted glass. Another advantage is that we don't need to use and launder tablecloths or place mats if we don't want to.

When it comes to table coverings, there is a great deal of leeway these days. I have seen Marimekko sheets used instead of traditional tablecloths, or hemmed or fringed remnant material. I find the effect refreshingly original. Another stroke of individuality is to mix the colors of your napkins and then showcase them in the napkin rings that are idling in a drawer, or pop them into wineglasses or plant pots. Carolyn likes the bright festive colors of bandannas as napkins, and often uses them as a foil to solid-colored place mats.

With matching tableware no longer the only thinkable option for proper dining, almost anything goes—within the bounds of suitability and good composition. A "set" of china or linen used to be the full complement of everything from soup through coffee, duplicated to serve twelve. Now a "set" can mean three or four different services for four, coordinated but not matched. The result is that your table becomes your personal signature. Experiment. For instance, one Christmas we received a gift of eight octagonal salad plates in black, of all things, that matched nothing we had. We were delighted to discover that the black plates set off and complement every other piece of china we own, both contemporary and antique! White is another good basic. It might be just the dinner plates, or the bread and butters, but the neutral white—like our black salads—is a thread that lends harmony to other odd pieces of china.

Style in Everyday Dining

You have to create your own style, whether it is informally original, formally traditional, or a blend of both. If it happens that you are blessed with fine china, crystal, or flatware, identify with them. Make them your style. As far as I am concerned, there is just one thing to do with very fine tableware—use it all the time. I told this to a cousin of Carolyn's, and she was horrified. "What if something breaks!" she gasped. I answered, "Jean, it's either going to break, or, if you're careful, not break. But what's the use of keeping it in the closet? Think of the mathematics. If you keep on using your Sevres for Thanksgiving dinners only, and you live till you're eighty-five, you are only going to get to enjoy that lovely china thirty times. It's not fair. You have to learn to think rich. People who are accustomed to great wealth always spend their riches in the way that will give them the most pleasure. They know that they can't take their china and limousines with them. They enjoy what they own whenever they please, which is all of the time. It makes life so much nicer. There is no reason on earth why you shouldn't loosen your thinking and enjoy what you have the same way."

Your Kitchen

We entertain so frequently, our kitchen often seems to be a torrent of industry. About two years ago we decided that it was time for some streamlining. The kitchen was then thirty years old and not geared for today's Cuisinart-microwave-electronic cooking. Our major need was storage. We had to find space for all the equipment we use constantly, and allow room for growth as well. In addition, we needed a dishwasher, a new range and oven, cabinets . . . everything. Including the kitchen sink.

Our first move was to take a diagram of the kitchen to an appliance dealer and ask the advice of their professional planner.

This is one of the free services offered by many companies that want you to buy more of their products. The electric company will send you a consultant on lighting, free of charge. Department stores supply decorators. Audio outlets provide free, expert advice on equipment, placing your speakers, and so on. The kitchen planner told us that the sink, range, and refrigerator should be in a triangle for the utmost efficiency, with the dishwasher on the right or left of the sink according to personal preference. We also learned about new equipment on the market that we hadn't been aware of: residential and institutional ovens, plastic materials for cabinets, area lighting, and new floor materials. In the end, we selected certain installations that the planner suggested and finished the room from other sources. You are never obliged to a supplier just because his selling advice is free.

Here is a bird's-eye view of our new kitchen. It may ignite ideas you can adapt for your own. Kitchens are by nature wellsprings of creativity, so any idea that works for somebody else is an idea you can add to your repertoire.

Notes. To select the size oven our family needs, Carolyn took her largest turkey-roasting pan to the store and made sure it would fit.

An alternative to built-in counter space is a movable butcher block table, fitted with drawers and even removable bowls to catch scrapings.

When cabinet space is tight, stemmed glassware can be stored as it is on shipboard—upside down from a rack that holds each glass by the stem.

A refrigerator space-saver is a U-shaped plastic wine bottle holder that suspends from your refrigerator shelf.

A cookbook space-saver is a computerized viewer with display screen that contains 500 cookbooks and takes only ten inches of shelf space!

Party Storage

You will notice that we store all of our serving pieces but very few dishes in the kitchen, and none of the flatware that we use in the dining room. Those items are stored where they are used, in cupboards and drawers close to the dining room table. By the same token, paper goods, plastic glasses, and other cookout paraphernalia are stored in the poolhouse, our cookout area. And we keep duplicate can openers, corkscrews, cleaning items, and so on in the kitchen, poolhouse, and bar, to save steps.

It is my guess that whoever first invented the kitchen had a bevy of servants in mind, and decreed that all serving and cleaning objects, as well as people, should be confined to that room. The concept no longer makes sense.

Space Shortages

For hundreds and thousands of New York apartment dwellers, a kitchen barely exists. But Manhattanites are absolute wizards when it comes to storing the accoutrements of entertaining. They can cope with kitchens that are doll-size cul-de-sacs with no drawers or counter space to speak of, microscopic appliances, and sinks that look like the feeding cups in canaries' cages. Dining rooms are unheard of, and even a dining area can be merely a longed-for luxury. But that doesn't stop them from entertaining in style. The ebullient, dark-haired, party-loving Audrey Wertheim comes to mind. She is a public relations and special events magician whose clients include well-known non-profit organizations for whom she produces glamorous parties that you read about in the papers. Her apartment is a mere dab of space, two rooms and a closet-size kitchen, out of which float parties for two dozen couples, with not an iota of visible effort. When I asked Audrey her secrets, she invited me to come and see for myself. On a literal cook's tour of the apartment, she told all.

"This entire setup is a series of illusions. The small pine table you're sitting at looks like part of my living room arrangement, doesn't it? It is, and it is also the dining room table and the buffet table, as well. The table is expandable, thanks to a drop-leaf extension on each side. When the extensions pop up, the table becomes large enough to seat six. If I put a round board on top of the table, it becomes a buffet large enough to hold everything needed to serve dinner for twenty-four. I'd like you to notice the windowsill next to the table. It's a Formica ledge attached with metal struts to the original narrow, painted-wood sill. The Formica takes quite a beating and is easy to keep clean. And when the ledge is not in use as a sideboard, it's a decorative base for that handsome piece of sculpture that you see there now."

The Secrets of Living Big in Small Space

At Audrey's urging, I peeked behind the window curtains at each end of the ledge. In back of one is a five-foot stack of place mats, paper napkins, baskets, and other party trappings. The other curtain conceals a vacuum cleaner and, above it, hi-fi components perched on a shelf. Even the hi-fi speakers do double duty in this room. One is a plant stand and the other can hold a platter of hors d'oeuvres, candy, or whatever needs holding at a party. In addition to the vacuum cleaner and hi-fi, the window curtain hides a folded-up tripod of wood with a leather thong laced across the top. Opened, it's a wooden salad bowl or platter stand. Another slender fold-up made of chrome poles is in fact a coat rack, which Audrey places in the hall outside the apartment for wintertime guests.

I began to get the idea. People who live in small spaces can think big nonetheless. And they are marvelous at devising cunning techniques that really work. Practically everything they own leads a double life.

In this living room, for example, on top of a black-lacquered Regency cabinet there rests a large crystal coupe that holds real lemons and limes. The fruit is a decorative touch, a room scenter, a kitchen space-saver, and a practical adjunct to the handsome cabinet which, when opened, is fitted as a bar. Centered on the coffee table is a richly hand-painted basket made of black-lacquered papier mâché that doubles as a server when guests come to call. Sometimes the basket is lined with grape leaves that embrace crudites: radish roses, scallion curls, cucumber spears, and mushrooms, with a champagne glass in the center to hold sauce for dipping. In winter, the tray is usually filled with glistening red apples strewn with whole walnuts and pecans and a handsome nutcracker.

Serving a Crowd

At either side of the sofa, round tables draped with cheerful yellow felt provide secret hiding places for the pots, pans, and what-have-you that spill out of Audrey's snippet of a kitchen at party time. Nestled under the skirted sofa are the oversize platters and trays used for hot and cold hors d'oeuvres. Not an inch of space is wasted, and a system of serving techniques has been thought through with care. As you can imagine, in miniature space such as this, where you cannot serve a sit-down appetizer, generous trays of hors d'oeuvres are a must. Further, hors d'oeuvre trays permit serving all of your guests at one time, and eliminate the fluster of clearing appetizer plates away and then finding a place to put them in the crowded, tiny kitchen.

As for the main course, a dinner plate has to hold everything; bread-and-butters or salad plates would be a cumbersome nuisance. The less tableware people have to handle, the better. Many hostesses prefer to serve finger food only, so there won't be pieces of meat flying off of plates onto the carpet. When the meal does call for cutlery, you have to bear in mind that guests cannot perform juggling acts while they fill their plates. One happy solution is to arrange tall, slim wineglasses on the buffet table and stuff each glass with a colorful cloth napkin, points up, the way you fix a pocket handkerchief. Then you tie a knife and fork together with a slender colored ribbon and stand the flatware straight up in the center of the glass. The ribbon keeps the cutlery from flopping over and adds an attractive "custom touch" to the service as well.

The dessert course at a buffet should also be simple to serve, but not so simple that it looks plain. Fresh sweet strawberries are a nice, uncomplicated finale, but if you want to make the course irresistibly appealing, try piling the berries in a huge basket with a crystal bowl of powdered sugar in the center.

To give you additional ideas, I asked Audrey if she would share some of the buffet dinner menus that she has found work well in small space.

#1 THE ALL-TIME STANDBY

Polynesian chicken (have butcher cut a whole chicken breast into three small parts for easy cutting, and use legs and thighs as finger food) served in a ring around
Golden rice (made golden with turmeric; garnish the casserole dish with a ring of chopped parsley)
Mandarin orange-watercress salad, with mandarin salad dressing
Strawberries with powdered sugar

#2 MARILYN HORNE'S GLORIOUS GREEK SUPPER

Canapés. Taramasalta (red caviar and olive oil), Saganaki (cheese fried in butter)
Grilled red snapper with lemon oil sauce
Salad. Thin-sliced cucumber in yogurt and sour cream
Long loaf of crusty bread
Dessert. Fresh honeyed fruit in champagne glasses (banana, peaches, melon bits, drizzled with honey; serve chilled and top with chopped nuts) and butter cookies

Setting the Stage

You need to think in advance about more than the food of a party. What we usually do when we entertain is project a mental movie of the occasion beforehand and then set the stage for what will take place. If it's going to be a large party, we make sure the living room is arranged so people won't stumble over the piano bench, or find themselves in a traffic gridlock at the doorways. We may slide the sofa or a chair to one side, to make room for an easy flow, and let whoever is serving drinks move around the room readily. If there is an hors d'oeuvres table, we set it up on the opposite side of the room from the bar, so people will have a reason to move around. Wherever the bar is, we make sure it's away from a seating group, since people tend to get anchored there. We want to have chairs open for people who need to sit once in awhile. And we want to give people a reason to walk away from whomever they've been talking with, so they won't be stapled to the same person all evening long.

You have to put yourself in other people's places. Spot plenty of sizable ashtrays and matchbooks around the room, even if you don't smoke yourself. Have coasters and napkins in strategic locations for the guests' convenience and to protect your furniture. Figure out where to put flowers and candles, so they won't be in people's way. Sometimes we skip flowers completely and use candles instead, or move one of our plants to a new position. Kenneth Jay Lane, the jewelry designer, says that he always has flowering plants in his home and they are his party decor. I like the idea because the cost of cut flowers has become almost prohibitive, especially when you consider how briefly they last. Kenneth also told me that the noted clothing designer, Halston, uses orchid plants to glamorize his rooms. If growing orchids, African violets, bromeliads, or any other botanical form happens to be your hobby, you might look at your collection with a fresh eye next time you entertain, and consider relocating the containers so they will enhance the occasion.

Whether we use flowers or not, Carolyn has learned that it is wise to keep a couple of vases where she can reach them in a hurry. There is always a good chance that somebody will come in with a bouquet for the hostess. And she knows just where to put her hands on serving dishes for the unexpected box of chocolates or exotic pâté that a guest might bring. Sometimes guests arrive bearing wine, and there is always a brief moment of discomfort, especially if it is a dinner wine. You have probably experienced the feeling. You wonder what to do with the cocktail-hour wine that you have already opened, or the special Burgundy that you have decanted for service with dinner. I have found that the simplest way to handle the situation is simply to thank our guests, and tell them that we will save the wine to enjoy on a special evening.

It always amazes me how flowers dress up a room. They are also a statement that somebody cares enough about you to do something especially pleasing. And they are a means of expressing your sense of design. For me, a loose, relaxed arrangement is usually the most charming, but I am charmed by other people's inventiveness with flowers. I understand that one famous New

York hostess sometimes makes a garden of her long dinner table by massing its center with clusters of delicate bud vases, each holding a different kind of flower. It's a delightful idea. If your table is large enough, you could use a single bud or a tiny nosegay at every place setting, instead of the conventional low centerpiece. Or you could make a change-of-pace centerpiece out of inexpensive blooms massed voluptuously in a fat goldfish bowl, a silver vegetable dish, or a lined basket. A single costly flower in a slim vase with perhaps a single dramatic spike of green can become a conversation piece. So can a cluster of cheerful blossoms floating in a candy dish in the bathroom, bright petals garnishing a platter, or one tender flower placed on the guestroom pillow. I've seen rooms where a theme is carried out by means of the flowers—Chinese water lilies in a prized Chinese vase; Monet's nasturtiums to accent a Monet painting; an all green-and-white room enhanced by sprays of shiny green leaves and white stephanotis, set in milk-white ironstone pitchers and fine porcelain containers.

It's nice to take a floral cue from your table linens, too. Or you can do it the other way around and select linen to go with your flowers. Picture that green-and-white room with a leaf-green cloth laid on the bias over a pure white undercloth. Or pale peach to complement a centerpiece of amaryllis. Naturally, the first course would be clear of tomato soup or lobster bisque.

By the way, double cloths are one of those disarming tricks that clever restauranteurs and resourceful hostesses use to deliver maximum visual impact with the least amount of effort and contrivance.

You should be aware of the fact that some flowers are too powerfully aromatic for a party, especially when they are in the immediate vicinity of food. I would not like to dine with the engulfing odor of gardenias at the table, for example, nor would narcissus-and-nectarines be my idea of epicurean heaven. The sense of smell, like the senses of taste, sight, touch, and hearing, is an active and involuntary receptor that affects our perceptions of pleasure perhaps more than we realize.

Clearing the Air

You cannot control every odor in your home. But there are ways to sanitize undesirable smells. You can mask offenders such as cabbage, tobacco, or dankness with room sprays, pot-pourri, lightly scented votive candles, or the various Rigaud candles. One thing you cannot spray away or mask is noise, when it is a disturbing intruder. We suffered from undue sound in our own dining room for years until Tonny Foy, our decorator, pointed out that the room was an echo chamber. Its brick floor, plaster walls and ceiling formed a cube of hard surfaces that bounced back every murmur with a bang. His solution was both uncomplicated and inexpensive. He laid a padded sisal rug on the floor and stapled padded linen, as if it were wallpaper, onto the walls. Our noisy dining room quieted down instantly.

The decibels can reach a deafening volume even in rooms that are carpeted and draped. I am sure you have been at cocktail parties where attempts at conversation are futile: you can't decipher a word anyone says to you and they just smile vacantly at your cleverest epigrams. The problem is with the set. Too many people crowded into too little space. The traffic pattern set up so everybody gathers in the same spot, usually near the bar. Music that is overpowering rather than mood-building and in the background where it belongs. Somebody neglected to plan for your comfort and there is very little you can do about it, except to remember to tune into the importance of sound when it is your turn to entertain.

Music

The effect of the sound of music on a party is prodigious. It can be an elevator or a sedative, an intoxicant or relaxant, a mood and theme setter, and a conversational lubricant. To me, music is invisible decor. Combine it with the gleam of candles and you create an atmosphere that is instantly festive. Like everything else, though, music has to be planned according to what you want to achieve. If you want to encourage people to be lively and talkative, you had better forget your favorite Wagnerian opera and choose something peppy instead. I dote on jazz piano above everything else, but I have learned to keep it in its place. Teddy Wilson is fine for the cocktail hour, but apt to be too domineering during dinner. A quiet Mozart symphony, low and in the background, is less distracting at the dinner table and permits conversation to glide. After dinner, I think something like classical guitar sets a good tone, neither ponderous nor frivolous but mellow, the way one likes to feel after a good meal.

It's fun to create a musical program for themed parties: Hawaiian music for a luau, country and western for a cowboy scene, Italian or Greek to tie in with an ethnic dinner. Just don't get too carried away.

One of the best times I ever had was programming a party where I was the guest of honor. It came about when Carolyn and I thought up an audacious way to assemble scores of our friends, give them a good time, and have a good time ourselves. My excuse to myself was that it was my fiftieth birthday. We put together a three-night Roger Horchow Film Festival, for which we rented three terrific 1930s movies with scores by the Gershwins and Cole Porter—my heroes. We sent out invitations that looked like film strips. The invitation didn't mention the word birthday, so nobody would be embarrassed about gifts. Carolyn stocked up with the quintessential movie-party food, popcorn, and saw to it that there were plenty of other snack foods and beverages on hand, too. For afterward, she had several dessert platters heaped with cookies, cakes, fruit, and cheese. With the films as a focal point, we didn't need to get into a costly cocktail-party menu.

My job was to select the music for before and after the screenings, a job I tackled with considerable zeal. Gershwin and Porter were the natural mood-setting selections and for once I got to play my favorite tapes at full volume for hours at a time. Ordinarily, I use a $1 cutoff gadget that confines my music to areas where only I can hear it, so as not to impose my fetish on the rest of my family. I am grateful that they are just as considerate of me, especially when the girls go through periods of dedication to rock 'n' roll, disco, or some other style that I am not particularly fond of.

Dancing

Records and tapes are a must in our house, and so are speakers upstairs, downstairs, and "in my ladies' chambers." I have been very happy to note that in addition to the popularity of the stereo and tape players, live music has made a comeback at parties. Especially music from the 1940s, that you can dance or sing to. For dancing, all you really need is a bass for rhythm, a piano for melody, and some local college musicians or neighborhood friends who can play. What a difference it makes at a party.

I know of a lively couple in New York who got their live music from a professional entertainer, and it didn't cost them a cent. Mary and Bob had asked eight friends to their apartment for a New Year's Eve celebration, and then invited a ninth: the stroke that made the evening gala. The extra guest was the piano player at their favorite neighborhood cocktail lounge. They had gone in for a drink earlier in the week and asked him to join their New Year's group when he got through work at 10:30. He did, and by 11:00 P.M. the somewhat subdued tone of their party had become rollicking, with everyone clustered at the piano having a very good time. Mary says she thinks the pianist had the best time of all; people love to be asked to show off their talents and be the center of attention. Her husband Bob swears that attention is the only reason Mary ever gives a party or cooks a meal; she's a ham and loves the applause.

The opposite extreme from Mary and Bob's party was the one we went to at the Kimbell Museum in Fort Worth. Kay Fortson, who is the niece of the late Kimbell benefactor, and is therefore privileged to have access to the museum, arranged for the Fort Worth Symphony to entertain at a special dinner there for a visiting international art group and a few of Kay's close friends. Richard Oldenberg, director of the Museum of Modern Art, publisher-now-art-dealer Charles Cowles, Mrs. Lily Auchincloss, Prince Von Bayren of Bavaria, and a society column-full of resounding names were enchanted. So, I might add, were the Horchows. I learned later that one of the guests adapted Kay's idea on a more modest scale. She hired a chamber music group whose members she knew to come to her home, where they joined fifty guests at a candlelit dinner, then beguiled everyone

everyone with an hour and a half of fine music. I don't think the chamber music idea would have worked out as a before-dinner entertainment. You need to give people something with a bit more gusto then. But after dinner is a perfect time to sit back and relax.

Why People Entertain

Whether you choose to give a dressy sit-down dinner, cocktail party, or casual outdoor buffet depends on your objective. You may want to pay off social obligations, reunite old friends, introduce a newcomer to the community, celebrate a birthday, entertain as a means of inserting yourself into the social stream, or just plain have fun. I think that most of us, most of the time, entertain for no more calculated a purpose than to share the pleasures of being together with a coterie of friends.

There are times when you feel that you need a specified reason for a party. Any excuse is fine. You can invite people in to celebrate Groundhog Day, Millard Fillmore's birthday, Christmas in July, the first day of autumn, or the fact that it is time to celebrate. We have a friend in Houston whom we wanted to inveigle into visiting us more often, so we invented a weekend party he couldn't refuse, The First Annual Bubba Levy Festival. It worked out so well that we are now planning the Fourth Annual B.L. Festival, and all of our friends are looking forward to welcoming Bubba to Dallas again.

A Weekend Round

The first year set the pattern. Carolyn made up a huge red-and-blue poster for the front door, "First Annual Bubba Levy Festival," and garlanded the entrance hall with red and blue streamers. Bubba and his wife arrived Friday evening, and the minute they saw the exuberant setting, they knew they were in for some special goings-on. We eased them into the weekend with a relaxing family welcome at home: just the two families becoming reacquainted over drinks and a casual supper of barbecued spare ribs and corn pudding. Saturday and Sunday were for hoopla, with a schedule of events that we had planned weeks in advance. Knowing that Bubba is an attractive, energetic, well-traveled person who makes friends readily and is notably athletic, we had arranged Saturday matches for him with the best tennis player we knew. Since we are not sports enthusiasts, that left us free to drive home and put the finishing flourishes on the cocktail party that we had announced for six to eight o'clock.

Carolyn had sent out invitations, with stamped addressed return postcards so people could respond easily, and we expected about forty-five people. The idea was to introduce Bubba and his wife to a comfortable group of our Dallas acquaintances in a setting where they could chat and find things that they like about each other. Those who struck up a rapport with the Levys and wanted to see more of them were sure to extend invitations for a drink or meal. It was part of our plot for getting the Levys to visit Dallas more often.

When the party was over and the last cocktail guest had said good-bye, the four of us drove to our friends, the Smiths, home for dinner and conversation. The Smiths had invited two other couples, good friends of both theirs and ours, deliberately keeping the group small so everyone could really talk with our visitors.

By Sunday, Bubba had received an invitation to play tennis and I drove him over for a doubles match. After the game, the foursome came back to our house where we had invited some other couples for brunch. Carolyn had asked one couple to bring the garbanzo salad they were famous for, another to supply a casserole, and the third to bring ice cream. She had also asked Sally and Regen to help out with serving, and Lizzie was assigned the job of official photographer. It's fun to take snapshots at a party so everyone can have a memento. Lizzie was using a Polaroid and handed out the pictures on the spot, which guaranteed that there was never a lull in the conversation. Another way you can use a party camera is to tuck one of those small pocket-size cameras into your purse or pocket when you go visiting. A week later you will have prints you can give to the people you photographed: a nice way to keep in touch with them, and a uniquely personal thank-you gift for your host or hostess. Something nobody else could possibly duplicate.

Reunion in Nantucket

Last summer in Nantucket we did something similar to the Bubba Levy weekend, but there are so many outdoor things to do on the island that we knew people wouldn't want to be tied to so tight a schedule. We invited fourteen of the friends we had known when we lived in Cambridge, back in 1968, to come stay for the weekend, and to give the event a raison d'être, we went back to their early days and called the party the 1980 Street Gang Reunion. The motif gave focus to an otherwise meandering weekend.

Themes Give Cohesion

Carolyn carried out the Street Gang theme throughout the house. There was a poster on the door to greet our guests, and more posters in the downstairs hall and in each bedroom. The signs announcing "1980 Street Gang Reunion" were glorified with photo blowups of "the kids" when they were very little, like stills from an *Our Gang* movie. We gave each of the visitors a tee shirt stamped in blaring colors, "1980 Street Gang Reunion." Carolyn had bought paper dinner and cocktail napkins in bright red, green, and yellow and had them stamped with the weekend motto as well. Aside from food and drink, the whole thing cost very little; a very inexpensive weekend indeed, with fourteen guests in the house. I think the fact that we gave it a theme went a long way toward making it a huge success.

Birthday

I keep repeating that parties and places don't need to be deluxe and expensive to be top-notch. Regen's eighteenth birthday is another illustration. Instead of an all-out gala, we had a predinner champagne fete. The peg was that in Texas you are allowed to drink when you turn eighteen. Regen invited twenty of her friends to the house and we served the champagne from a silver cooler on a silver tray, which immediately made the evening more festive. The food was simple rather than haute cuisine: cheese, fruit, crudites, and a dip. You can be sure that there

wasn't a nibble left over. To surround the guest of honor with
sparkle, we blew up a dozen balloons and tied them to the backs
of chairs and let a few drift up to the ceiling. We encircled the
plants on two of the tables with small round candles, all white,
and placed eighteen of Carolyn's crystal candleholders, with
eighteen lighted white candles, on the piano top. Regen's date
had sent flowers in the morning, and Carolyn arranged them on
the round table near the champagne glasses. It was a gala eighteenth birthday party, and probably would not have been more
gratifying if we had rented the Astrodome and hired the Dallas
Cowboys to turn cartwheels.

Parties in Public Places

You don't always have to entertain at home. The group may
be too large, the occasion too public, or you might be in the
middle of having your home repainted. Almost every town has
several inexpensive restaurants that are fun to take people to. I
have found that the least expensive way out is to find a restaurant that has no wine and spirits license, but does have permission to serve setups for the bottles you bring from home. You
save the restaurant markup. Jo Marie Lilly, one of Dallas's most
talented advertising directors, sometimes invites a half-dozen
friends to be her guest at the Dallas Museum. She arranges beforehand for one of the museum docents to be her group's private guide, which makes it a very special occasion. As a final fil-
lip, she presides over a tea-and-sandwich hour in the museum's
small dining room. For the price of the refreshments, which is
nominal to say the least, she is the gracious hostess of a memorable and stimulating afternoon.

One of the best times we ever had was when our friend Bob
Alpert hosted a football game. He asked us and fifteen other
couples to meet at a downtown parking lot, leave our cars, and
board a bus he had chartered. Before we arrived, he stocked the
bus with four large Styrofoam coolers heaped with drinks and
sandwiches, which we consumed with great enthusiasm en route
to the Dallas stadium. What we didn't finish on board we
brought to the game, to enjoy while we rooted the Cowboys to
triumph. Then, when the game was over and all of us were ex-

hausted from the day's spectating, the bus took us back to the parking lot.

At Home when You Don't Have a Home

A friend of ours who is now a well-known Washington hostess used to dread entertaining at home. That was twenty years ago, when Louise—the alias I'll give her—had practically no furniture or accessories to her name. That doesn't bother some people. Our friend Pam Mitchell, who used to be Connecticut Senator Dodd's secretary, has a genius for throwing a party together out of nothing, in what seems to be helter-skelter, last-minute fashion. It always comes up glorious. We are still reliving the time when she and her doctor husband, Jere, were building a house near us in Dallas. Before it was two-thirds finished, Pam got the urge for a party. She phoned a dozen good friends, and invited them to a picnic on her very unfinished porch. Then she raced out and bought gaily colored paper plates, napkins, and plastic glasses. By four o'clock we were all perched on a quilt that she'd spread over the portion of the porch that was finished, having the time of our lives.

Louise, however, was hung up about the sparseness of her belongings. At the same time, a diplomat whom she wanted to impress was coming in from France, and Louise was determined to entertain him in style. She thought fast. And cheap. Before you could whistle *La Marseillaise*, she had waved a wand over her naked little apartment and turned it into a charming French bistro. First, she went to a lumber company and bought four round poles, tall enough to stretch from carpetless floor to ceiling. Her next stop was a paper party-ware store, where she bought a 10 foot by 10 foot red-and-white striped paper awning, which she hung from the poles to form a French Bistro awning. Then Louise borrowed three sets of bridge tables and chairs from her family, plus a selection of French phonograph records. Finally, she prepared up a *boeuf bourguignon*, which she served to the diplomat and eight guests along with a salad, fresh French bread, and a modest Burgundy wine. She had created a stage set and a fabulously original evening out of next to nothing. Louise still has the poles in her closet. She says if she ever buys the country house of her dreams, her first patio party is going to be stage-set as a Paris sidewalk cafe.

Invitations

I think invitations are a third of the magic of a party, and Audrey Wertheim, who gives many parties professionally, concurs. "They set the scene, whether they are written, verbal, sent by Western Union, carrier pigeon, or printed with a felt pen on one of those giant paper napkins," she told me. "They should be clever, inexpensive, and strictly *you*—not something you just go out and buy from a rack. I often use the larky new notepaper they sell in stationery departments. For example, one of my clients, a hotel, was putting on a jazz night. So I went to a store and bought notepaper shaped like a piano keyboard. Then I got music manuscript paper and made up a funny little poem to print under the staffs and clefs." Nobody on the invitation list could doubt that they were in for a musical evening where the bottom line was to have a good time.

A Nostalgia Motif

A friend told me about a benefit she had been to at New York's Radio City Music Hall. It was held around Valentine's Day, and keyed to play up the sophistication and elegance of the Music Hall's 1930s decor, the era when potted palms and silver cocktail shakers were all the rage. The huge stage was lined with potted palms and mirrored panels, against which Lester Lanin's society orchestra, with twenty-two violinists, poured out tea-dance music. Two long buffet tables shimmered in the gleam of rows of gigantic candelabras, which also helped create a room atmosphere. Kitty Carlisle Hart, who was a co-chairman of the event, said that even though the Music Hall has no kitchen, she had never been to a benefit where they served better food. The meal, catered by Basil Rathbone's granddaughter and her husband, was simple, since cost was a factor, but embellished with fancy names to make it seem dressy. Codfish casserole became "Cabillaud Andalouse" for example.

You probably would not do things on quite so grand a scale in your own home, but you can modify the basic ideas. Instead of hiring Lester Lanin and twenty-two violinists, you might ask a quartet from your local symphony orchestra if they would perform at your party in return for a modest fee and the opportunity to help popularize the symphony. Or you may know some young people who would like to "showcase" their talents as musicians, magicians, or quick-sketch portrait artists, and would welcome your party as a way to do so. Just be sure they are good at what they do; nothing slows down a party like a bumbling entertainer.

Rentals

When you can't beg or borrow the furnishings for a party and you haven't the cash or storage space for things you use only occasionally, the most economical thing to do is to rent. You can rent things, people, places, atmosphere. Most common are dinnerware, food, waiters and bartenders, music, entertainers, limousines, boats, and buses. Besides the professional caterers and party planners listed in the phone book, you can find platoons of helpful people in your own backyard who can be rented inexpensively. College students are always eager to hire out for a stipend and most universities have a student employment agency that acts as recruitment headquarters. Young people will abandon their books to tend bar for you, clean ashtrays, take coats, park cars, pass hors d'oeuvres, wait on tables, wash dishes—in short, free you to concentrate on your guests' enjoyment instead of darting from kitchen to living room like a nerve-wracked hamster. It is a worthwhile investment.

You can cut down on your outlay by leasing neighborhood teenagers or your own children as helpers. We have found that they enjoy the responsibility as well as the opportunity to be in on grownups' parties. In fact, we have developed quite a retinue of "staff," and Carolyn always has somebody to call for party help. She uses them on workdays, too, when she hasn't the time to run around to the cleaner's, the post office, the hardware and grocery stores. Some of our favorite askees are Sally, Lizzie, and Regen Horchow. Remember the cookout, where Lizzie pitched in as photographer? For that affair we also put Sally in charge of answering the front door, and later on she helped Regen heat and serve the hors d'oeuvres. All three were charged with playing detective, too. They were to keep an eye peeled for empty glasses and let me know who needed a refill.

Entertaining Alfresco

The menu for an outdoor party is one of our favorites. Besides the fact that it is very Western, much of it can be prepared in advance: an important consideration for a smooth-flowing party. I think it a good one to keep in the hostess book under *Old Faithfuls.*

CAROLYN'S BASIC BACKYARD BARBECUE

Spicy guacamole and tortilla chips
Barbecued spareribs
Gertie's jalapeño rice
Raw vegetable salad with sherry French dressing
Mrs. Taylor's three fruit sherbet
Oatmeal chocolate chip cookies

When it comes to setting the stage for alfresco entertaining, it is best to work from the outside toward the center. What I mean is, start with the peripheral things, then work your way toward the food. Will there be mosquitoes? You'll need cans of spray here and there, and bug-repellent candles. How about lighting? You might stick hurricane lamps in the ground to outline the party area. Outline a tree with twinkling bee lights. Bob Floyd, who is responsible for the striking Fitz and Floyd dinnerware that we admire so much, always has scores of votive candles on his outdoor tables, and a background of lively music. You can use hurricane lamps to light the night. For soft romantic lighting at practically no cost, do as the Southwesterners do and make *luminarias:* small brown-paper sacks partially filled with sand into which you plunge a short, stubby candle. To make interesting shadows, cut a sunburst design in the paper above the sandline. To further the festive atmosphere, you could hang a tree or the eaves of the house with colored streamers made of crepe paper or felt.

Consider where people will sit and provide stools, director's chairs, small tables, or quilts on the ground. What about ice and cold drinks? We like to use giant-size plastic trash containers or large washtubs, one filled with ice, the other with ice plus cans and bottles of chilled drinks. We conceal additional trash containers behind trees and shrubs, to catch our guests' paper plates and food discards. Finally, you will want to set up a bar someplace, preferably away from the seating and food-serving areas, the same as if the party were indoors, so people will have to circulate.

Stocking the Bar

How much wine, beer, spirits, and mixers to stock can be puzzling. Haven't you ever prepared for a hot August night when you are certain there will be a heavy demand for vodka and tonic, and for no reason on earth everybody troops in parched for bourbon? Danny Zarem, who presides over the smart New York shop, Andre Oliver, and is on the *Gentlemen's Quarterly* list of best-dressed men, says he has been caught short many times, despite the fact that over the years he has developed certain rules of thumb, such as how many glasses a bottle contains and how many drinks per hour are likely to be consumed. Danny adds, ruefully, that rules and reality do not always match. I certainly agree. What is more, rules of thumb keep changing. You have to keep up with the tides of fashion in food and drink just as you do in clothing. In the thirties, any respectable bar displayed bottles of applejack, gin, and pink grenadine. In the forties and fifties, people were drinking scotch and bourbon, along with soda. Then there was a trend to vodka drinks, and by the time we got into the seventies, people had begun to use wine instead of spirits for predinner drinking. That meant we had to figure out how much wine to stock for the bar, as well as which wines to provide with our meals. And I haven't even mentioned what has happened with brandy and after-dinner liqueurs.

Not only are there changes in general drinking fashions, there are regional and seasonal differences. Those factors, the time of day, and the type of party make a difference in how you stock up. The best approach, it seems to me, is to keep a running supply on hand of everything you will ever need, and give your bar a concentrated checkup just before each particular party.

BASIC BAR CHECKLIST

White Wine   Inexpensive or medium-priced dry white wine in jug sizes that you can decant into carafes for easier pouring and pleasing appearance. We like to buy by the case, for which dealers give you a ten percent discount.

Red Wine   One or two regular-size, medium-priced bottles is plenty. Most people drink red wine only with meals.

Aperitifs   A bottle of dry sherry and a bottle of either Lillet or Campari. Dry vermouth for cocktails.

Beer   We keep a dozen each of American and imported brews, to satisfy different tastes, and light beer for calorie counters.

Spirits   Vodka, gin, light rum, scotch, bourbon, blended whiskey.

After-dinner   One brandy and one sweet liqueur.

Mixers   Soda, Perrrier, quinine, fruit juice, regular and low calorie soft drinks. Lemons and limes.

Equipment   Corkscrew. Bottle opener. Stirrer. Paring knife. Ice bucket and tongs. Water pitcher. Large-size wine and highball glasses. Cocktail napkins. Serving tray.

New Year's Eve Parties

One of the biggest and busiest drinking nights of the year is December 31st. Huge, hectic New Year's Eve parties are a national rite, and too often the sprightliness runs to excess. Carolyn and I used to abhor New Year's Eve celebrations so much that we would tune out, invite a few close friends to stop by for an early drink, and then scuttle to our beds by eleven o'clock, while our children moped around wishing they had selected a livelier set of parents. A few years ago Carolyn decided that the Horchows' New Year's Eve ritual was unnecessarily depressing, and that there was a pleasant option to either going to bed early or whooping it up until dawn. Her idea, which has since become an almost annual pleasure, was to make New Year's Eve a joyous gathering for all of our friends, their friends, and their families. Most people don't think of inviting whole families, including children, to a New Year's Eve party, and grownups often have to go through the agonies of finding suitable sitters or else missing out on the fun. Or they have to sit home with their holiday houseguests whose attractions began to fade two days after Christmas.

Carolyn's invitation made it clear that the evening would be from 8:00 until 1:00, with drinks and hors d'oeuvres, so people would know how to gear their evening. She addressed the invited children by name, so the party wouldn't be burdened by babies, or youngsters nobody in our group knows. One thing I especially like about Carolyn's family idea is that it gives the young people a chance for intergenerational mingling, a social advantage they need and often cannot find.

We didn't have to worry about overflow. Our guests arrived in waves, as we had anticipated they would. Those who were going on to other parties came at about 8:00 and left a couple of hours later. At about 10:30 they were replaced by a second wave of people who had already been out to dinner somewhere and then came to see us. After midnight we welcomed a crowd who had traveled a circuit of earlier parties and were ready to toast New Year's Day.

All night long the dining table was laden with food. Nothing fancy or glamorous; reliable fare that we know everybody likes, that is easy to fix, and that doesn't leave trails of debris in the kitchen and elsewhere. We placed large trays of cheese at strategic places throughout the house, and did ourselves another favor by making sure the post-party cleanup would be minimal. We used only disposable plastic glasses, paper plates and paper napkins. We had the plastic glasses inscribed "Happy New Year—Carolyn, Roger, Regen, Lizzie and Sally" to make them special. Our "hired help" consisted of teams of willing teen-agers—one to park our guests' cars and, not incidentally, keep the cars off our lawn. The second team circulated inside the house, emptying ashtrays and passing champagne.

In addition to the dining room table and cheese trays in the house, Carolyn set up a buffet table in the poolhouse, where the younger set inevitably winds up. The sun-room table was laden with sweets: all kinds of holiday cakes and cookies, along with coffee and cola. She decorated the tables with bright red tulips in silver mint-julep cups: a nice change from the Christmas poinsettias that had lost their bloom. The youngster's poolhouse buffet consisted of cocktail franks, heaps of popcorn, and hot cider punch. The grownups' table was slightly more ambitious. You might like to make note of the menu, and perhaps use it as the basis for a party of your own.

Barbecued pork roast with thin biscuits
Sliced smoked salmon with pumpernickel bread
Large wheels of Brie cheese
Glacé apricots to spread with Gourmandaise cheese
Large silver bowls of roasted pecans

Assessing the Results

When New Year's Day dawned, Carolyn and I sat down to critique the party. Our mutual assessment was that it had been a great success from the first tray of cocktails to the final urn of black coffee. Carolyn got out her hostess book and made notes in the Annual Affairs section as to how many guests we had had and how many bottles of wine, liquor, and soft drinks we used. Her notes gave us an automatic shopping guide when we stocked up for the following year's open house. She also jotted down the names and phone numbers of the best helpers, and the taxi companies that had responded promptly when we called them to pick up guests who weren't able to drive themselves home. The minute we started to review that aspect of the party, Carolyn and I looked at each other and burst into laughter. "Do you remember the story Pauline Trigère told us?" Carolyn gasped, nearly speechless with mirth. I tried to help reassemble the story: "There was this stranger at the party and . . ." I went under, too, in a gale of hilarity. Solemn now and with pen in hand, I will try to recount the story Pauline tells so well.

It seems there was a large cocktail party at a lovely home in Connecticut. One of the guests arrived with an escort, a soigné Englishman who somehow overestimated his capacity. At party's end he was quite drunk, and the hostess told her friend, "It would be silly for you to try to get him home in his condition. We'll just put him to bed in the guestroom and let him sleep it off. Then he can join us when you arrive for brunch tomorrow at eleven, and you can take him home afterward." The man was escorted to the guestroom and fell into a prompt, deep sleep. A couple of hours later he awoke, still dazed and in strange surroundings, to find his way to the bathroom. Unable to locate a light switch, he fumbled his way through the room by braille. At one point his hand knocked over a jar and he felt something wet, but continued to grope his way along the wall and eventually found the bathroom. Mission accomplished, he relocated the bed and went back to sleep.

At 11:00 A.M. he was still sound asleep, and the hostess dispatched the troops to rouse him for brunch. As he showered and dressed, the guest, now sober, saw what he had done during the night. The jar he had knocked over was an antique inkwell, a decorative relic of the days before ball-point pens were invented, which had been filled with black ink. In his midnight prowl, he had knocked it over and left a smudgy trail of ink-black fingerprints on the guestroom wallpaper all the way from the desk to the bathroom. Appalled, he went downstairs and began to apologize profusely to his hostess.

She, however, thought he was apologizing for having been drunk at her party. The conversation was a comedy of misunderstandings.

> HE: I cannot tell you how sorry I am.
> SHE: Don't give it a second thought. You did nothing unusual and I am sure nobody noticed.
> HE: But I must tell you . . .
> SHE: It's quite all right. We understand. These things happen all the time. Please do get some food and sit down, we have all been waiting for you to join us.
> HE: But you must tell me how I can make it up to you.

SHE: Believe me, I am happy that you had a good time. Now please come and sit down.

The poor man gave up trying to explain and sat down. Hard. On a bench that held a large and delicate tureen of very moist, piping-hot scrambled eggs. There are times when all the good intentions in the world lead straight downhill to disaster.

3

DECORATING
YOUR HOME

Some people bring fabulous heirlooms into their marriages. Carolyn and I did not. We furnished our first rented home in Dallas with a lot of love and enthusiasm, but very little in the way of material goods. Aside from our wedding china and flatware—simple, enduring patterns that we use constantly—we started out with the leftovers of our respective bachelor days. Carolyn's major contributions were a brass hat rack and an antique shoemaker's sign that she had found in a Third Avenue shop when she was a fashion coordinator at Bloomingdale's in New York. What I brought to the household was a pair of seriously green-and-blue Danish-modern chairs, and a white Formica-topped table with a base the color of baseball-park mustard.

It is typical of Carolyn's sensitivity to people's feelings that she never told me how awful she thought they were. Instead, she reupholstered the chairs in a soft pastel pattern, and performed some alchemy on the table so that I never realized it had vanished. The chairs are still members of the family in good standing. They have been covered, recovered, stuffed, and whittled down several times over the years, and now nestle cozily by the hearth where Carolyn and I like to read in the evening. I see them as reminders of how our tastes and needs have evolved over the years, just as we and our family have changed.

Like most young marrieds, we had many adjustments to deal with at first, including the places where we lived. Our first home was a large, five-bedroom house on twelve sprawling acres— quite a handful for two furnitureless people just starting out. We had stumbled onto a bit of luck: the owner was planning to raze the house and was willing to rent his property to us in the meantime for practically nothing, just enough to pay his taxes. We thought we would be there for a year or so. It turned out to be our home for seven years. Ours, and Regen's and Lizzie's, too. Regen was seven and Lizzie five by the time we left Dallas and moved to Cambridge, Massachusetts, where I went to work at a home furnishings store called Design Research. The move brought another adjustment for us to deal with. The house in Cambridge was so tiny that the girls practically had to sleep in bureau drawers and the only place we could store their toys was in the crawl area under the house.

Changing Needs

Those particular Dallas and Cambridge years were the fast-est-changing that either Carolyn or I had ever lived through. We switched environments completely. New business connections and new friends entered our lives. We added one baby, then two more babies to our home, along with social and family responsi-bilities that neither of us had ever encountered before. All I have to do, to remember those days, is look around the house we live in now and see the collected footprints-in-time that have trav-eled with us over the years.

Upstairs in eleven-year-old Sally's room are the modular cab-inets, doing duty as night tables, that we bought for Regen's and then Lizzie's baby clothes. Beside my easy chair in the poolhouse is a hand-painted box that holds correspondence; I remember when it first stood on our bedroom bureau in Cambridge. The box rests next to a slender brass lamp that is wearing its fourth shade and is in its fifth setting. It still looks as handsome to me as the day we brought it home to light our 9-by-12 rented living room. Upstairs, of course, are the reincarnated sitting-room chairs, two of the longest-wearing friends we have ever had.

Mostly, though, it's the accessories, like the lamp and the box, that have lived with us so well over the decades. The reason for that is that we viewed our first rented house in Dallas as temporary quarters and concentrated on buying good incidental pieces rather than major furniture that might not fit into our futures. We didn't want to invest in Lilliputian-scaled furniture when we knew that we would soon move on to rooms with larger proportions. Besides, in the fifties everybody was using those wrought-iron sling chairs and do-it-yourself bookcases. We were conditioned to the look and it suited our needs at the time. I think if we were furnishing our first home today, we would buy more of the simple-lined, plastic furniture like the modular cabinets I mentioned; they are durable and blend well with other styles. Then we could mix in some special, more distinctive furnishings that we might buy at estate sales and auctions—carved wood tables, perhaps, or good upholstered furniture that we could restore later on with new springs and covering.

Furnishing from Scratch

I have learned something about furnishing a home when you are first starting out. I no longer agree with the people who advise against buying anything good until you have formulated your tastes. It is true that your tastes will undoubtedly change, and keep on changing for as long as you live. You will never see the world again as you see it today. But that does not mean you should deprive yourself of beautiful objects en route. Even your very first purchases should be things that you really like because, if you are like most of us, you will find that it is difficult to discard personal possessions as you move from home to home. Since you and your belongings are probably going to have a long life together, why not weight the odds so it will be a happy life?

I do agree, however, that you should choose your things with care, especially anything that costs over $200. That is too much money to squander on something that has the life expectancy of a snowflake. Shop around. Take your time. The first porcelain vase you see surely is not the last porcelain vase in the world. Unless you are the type who can make instant decisions and rarely regret them, hold off for a week or so and look elsewhere. Try offbeat places, if you are looking for offbeat things at off-retail prices. White elephant sales, antique shops, and country fairs are full of other people's gems that they no longer want. It pays to remember the smart shopper's axiom: one person's white elephant is another person's treasure.

When you find something you like, take it home and enjoy it to the full. Don't stop to worry that it may not fit into your future; there is no way to predict what your future will be. What you can predict is that somewhere, in some guise, you are sure to find a perfect niche for the object you love. I am thinking of how we have always found a spot for the drum table that enchanted us in an antique shop twelve years ago. It has moved with us from living room to living room to den, and now stands next to my bed, the ideal holder for books, flowers, reading glasses, clock, and other nighttime companions.

I am often bemused by the way people's belongings travel from place to place in their homes. Our neighbor Claire has an antique flower holder that she bought at a country barn in 1957, and I have followed its itinerary for the past quarter of a century. Its first stop was on Claire's desk, as a pencil holder. Then she had the brilliant idea of using the holder for flowers, and I noticed that she often placed it in her bookshelves, where it became a small objet d'art. When that idea palled, Claire put the holder away in a closet for a year or so, until she got to thinking of ways to spice up her bathroom. At this very minute, the flower holder sits on the basin, a charming container for her toothbrushes and paste. Claire once mentioned that the holder cost only $4; certainly it has given her a wealth of pleasure for many years. I daresay that would also be true if the holder were a $400 prize, but money is not the point. When you love something, buy it, if you can afford to. Sometimes, even if you can't afford to. Dollars and cents are not the only measure of the pleasure you will receive.

Money is important, of course, and its scarcity is one of the reasons it has become imperative to find ways to simplify our lives. We have to face the fact that we are in an era where most of us simply do not have enough money, time, or energy, and there is even a shortage of help from the suppliers and service people we used to depend on. If there is one lesson to be learned for the 1980s, it is this: in these times, waste is out and mistakes are unaffordable. We have to discover how to do more with less, and we have to be receptive to solutions that we may once have thought out of the question. As far as I am concerned, when it comes to furnishing a home the very best and most economical solution is to call in a decorator. The idea is not as high-flown as some people think.

How Decorators Can Help You Pinch Pennies

It took Carolyn and me several years to realize that you don't have to be rich to use a decorator. On the contrary, the rich use them to pinch pennies all the time, because decorators can actually save you money. They keep you from making costly mistakes, like buying four acres of wall-to-wall carpeting in a material that will wear out in twenty minutes. They let you spend your time and energy doing things other than run around trying to find just the right fabrics and styles out of the hundreds that are on the market. They are the ones who take care of the time-consuming, nerve-bending arguments that occur when the things you have ordered arrive damaged or in the wrong color. And in general, you don't pay any more for what you buy through a decorator than if you go to a showroom by yourself. Essentially, what decorators do is either buy or have your things made for you at wholesale cost, and then add on a service fee to pay for their time, work, expertise, and editing. Or, if you go to a showroom with them, you pay the retail price and they receive a discount from the manufacturer, which is the decorator's fee. Sometimes they charge you an additional consulting or design fee as well, for planning and advising you on what you should do. Then they will go with you to shop or leave you on your own, depending on what you have agreed upon. There are other variations: some decorators charge a certain amount, say ten percent over wholesale, in return for advising, shopping, or buying for you. I think it is worth paying a design fee to a decorator if you are not one hundred percent sure of what to do.

Finding the Right Decorator

You may find that the decorator you want has an established fee scale that is beyond your reach. Choose an alternative. There are bevies of excellent, modestly priced designers in just about every city I can think of. If you ask your friends who have had happy experiences with decorators and whose homes you admire, you are certain to find somebody in your area whose fees are within your budget. But before you make a commitment, you should meet with the decorator to find out if there is mutual rapport. You need to trust your decorator, and to like him or her, too. You will be working closely together on matters that are of very personal concern. Your intimate lifestyle will be disclosed, because it is part of a decorator's function to help create an environment that will suit your and your family's needs.

You both have to be able to discuss ideas: agree, disagree, be flexible. So much depends on your personalities and the rapport you establish. I have heard of people who dislike the advice they receive from their decorators, but are so in awe that they never express their own opinions. They just go along, paying their bills, and then are uncomfortable with the room schemes they have to live with. I believe that if you don't like the advice you get from a decorator, you should pay for his or her time and turn elsewhere. A good professional should give you alternatives to suggestions you don't care for, rather than say, "This chair should be bottle green and that's it!" Ask for choices, and hold out until you get what you like. Remember, you are the one who will live with the results, and you are the person who has to be pleased. That is why you are paying an expert.

Carolyn and I are great believers in using experts to help give shape to what we want, to winnow out the most suitable things for our needs, to add fresh ideas, and to teach us. If you are attentive, you can learn a great deal from a good designer about workmanship, color, proportion, function; subjects they have studied for years, that you can absorb very quickly. For example, when we added a new living room to our house in Dallas, we asked the innovative young designer Tonny Foy to help us furnish it. He is one of those people who have such style and flair, they look elegant even when they work in jeans and loafers. We knew his work and his touch seemed right for our new room. Besides that, we knew that he had a quick, sure instinct and was not rigid about imposing his ideas on clients. Carolyn and I both have strong opinions about decorating, so we felt Tonny would be able to move our ideas around a bit so they would be workable.

Planning a Room

The living room is quite large, 30 by 50 feet, and when Tonny came in to see it, the first thing he did was start talking to himself. Naturally, we eavesdropped. "Needs good-size furniture, in proportion to the space. Otherwise the room will dwarf what's in it and make your belongings look scraggly. Makeshift. But we'll stay away from massive, heavy-laden things. We'll keep the tone light, to set a casual, simple mood. We'll have a conversation area over here. And we'll separate it from the main area by doing the upholstery in different shades of the same color; the room can take some defining. There ought to be a place for table games and jigsaw puzzles, too, away from the conversation area. We'll need a rug, to absorb sound, something you can roll back for dancing . . ."

That's where we chimed in with opinions of our own. Meantime, though, we had absorbed the following from Tonny's informative first impressions. The size and shape of a room influence the size of your furniture. Mood dictates style. Colors can take the place of room dividers. You should think about what the room will be used for before you decide what to put into it.

There was one thing Tonny had not taken into account: my mother's grand piano. It had to be in the room, and it had to be in a particular place: in a corner near a window, close to the part of the living room where my sheet music is stored. Tonny wasn't thrilled with that at first; he thought the piano should be nearer the center of the room so people could gather around it. That was not the way I wanted it. When he saw that I was firm,

Tonny adjusted his thinking to our needs. I had agreed that his point was well taken, but since we were the ones who would be using the room, my wishes had to be heeded. He then proceeded to develop the entire new room around the piano, and as far as we are concerned, the result is outstanding.

The Advantages of Simplicity

Tonny's philosophy, that simplicity brings pleasure, solved the question of how to have a floor covering for the living room that would satisfy our personal tastes and at the same time accommodate our guests at a dance. He has talked with us often enough to recognize that Carolyn and I lean toward traditional things in some of our preferences, among them, Oriental rugs. When we told him that we had our hearts set on an Oriental in the new living room, his reply was inarguable. He pointed out that an Oriental proportioned to suit a 30-by-50-foot room would consume our entire decorating budget in one gulp. Instead, Tonny gave us an alternative suggestion, and as soon as we heard it, we knew it was right. He said, "Get the Oriental that you love. But get it in a small size, to fit the 10-by-12-foot end of the room where you'll have a sofa and a couple of side chairs for conversation. For the main area, where people will dance and maybe even spill drinks and salad, we'll put down a 12-by-15-foot rug made of sisal. It will be a tightly woven material so women's high heels won't catch in it. And we'll have it treated so you can wipe off spills with no trouble. And to give it the rich, finished look that you like, I'll have the rug edged all around with a two-inch width of dark brown cowhide. This will help anchor the rug to the floor visually as well as physically." The end of the story is, we liked the appearance and practicality of the sisal rug so much that when it came time to redo our dining room, we asked Tonny to order a second leather-bordered, chemically treated sisal floor covering for us. It's a device you might want to file away with your decorating notes, and use the next time you have a room to do over.

Choosing Furniture for Personal Comfort

When we chose the sofa and chairs for the conversation area of our living room, we had to consider not only the scale of the room, but our own proportions as well. Carolyn and I are both taller than average: I am six feet one and Carolyn is five feet eight. One of the first things we learned about buying furniture is that whether you are tall or short, you actually have to sit in a chair and test whether it fits you. If the seat is too deep or shallow, or not the right height from the floor, you will never be comfortable in that chair. The upholstery filling makes a difference in your comfort, too, so it's a good idea to ask for filling material that will provide the firmness or downiness that suits you best.

Decorating by Mood and Use

Another thing we learned, when we did the living room, was how to decide on the kind of look we will be happy with. The key is wonderfully simple. You just have to stop and think, as our decorator did, what mood it is that you want to establish, and what the room is to be used for. That's the approach we used when we furnished our sun porch. This is a multipurpose room that we have fallen into the habit of using for the everyday, informal things families do: sitting, chatting, eating. The sun porch is at the back of the house overlooking the lawn, and has a long glass wall and brick floor that blend with the outdoors and give it an easygoing feeling. The mood is definitely relaxed. We decided we wanted to do three things in decorating it: retain the casual, comfortable, peaceful atmosphere, furnish the room to accommodate the various uses we give it, and create a space where we could spend family time in surroundings that suit our taste.

One thing we had to take into consideration was the proportions of the room. It is 36 feet by 11 feet with a 12-foot ceiling, though it gives a feeling of greater width because the long side is all windows. We were afraid the elongated shape might be a problem, but when we began to work out where to place furniture, the problem solved itself. We started by locating the furnishings for one of the room's major functions, eating. There was no question where the dining area should be—at the end of the room next to the kitchen. We also knew exactly what dining furniture we would like for our everyday use—an ultra-contemporary, Formica-topped pedestal table and simple contemporary chairs of molded plastic. We felt that a round table would contrast more pleasingly with the angular room than a rectangle, and would take up less of the corner dining space, as well. Besides, a round table is somehow more intimate, a characteristic that suits the mood of the room.

With the dining area established, we were left with a 36-foot length of room for the other things we would be using the sun porch for. We talked about how to furnish it, sparking ideas off one another, and pored through stacks of magazines to find ideas we could adapt. On reflection, it occurred to us that the most comfortable, casual furniture that has ever been invented for sitting-around purposes is the wicker garden furniture our great-grandparents used. You can lounge in wicker to your heart's content, wash it down with a hose, and touch it up with spray paint. We began to think through how to place the furniture so it would work best. Starting with the window corner at the end of the room opposite the dining area, and working toward the middle of the room, we laid out a comfortable arrangement of a sofa, two chairs, and a few tables. We anticipated lazy hours there and made sure the tables would be roomy enough to hold magazines, knitting, decorative objects that we love, whatever we might want, at a fingertip's reach.

We weren't through. The Horchows, as you may have gathered, are not likely to overlook details. We realized that somewhere nearby we would want a place to store and serve between-meal nibbles—peanuts, crackers, soft drinks, a supply of my famous Bloody Mary mix, glassware, dishes. There was wall space between the two doors that open onto the sun porch, opposite where the antique wicker furniture would be, that would accommodate some kind of unit. What came to mind was a lovely big armoire we had seen at an antique shop in Nantucket. We talked about painting or wall-papering the inside of the armoire a leaf green, as a backdrop for things on the shelves. It seemed like a marvelous idea at first, but it didn't take us long to discard the notion. It would have appeared pretentious in the kind of atmosphere we were creating. I won't take you through all the debates, but our final solution was to have a convenience bar and shelves built onto the wall. The design of the unit is tidy and unobtrusive, and the style appropriate to the room.

Tying a Room Together

What gives the sun porch cohesion and makes it soothing to be in is that the dining and sitting areas are pulled together by basic design elements. The whole area is painted white. A strip of track lights runs the length of the ceiling. The sweep of windows and the wall-to-wall brick floor unify the room. And the large plants that we added for punctuation and balance are in scale with the room and its contents. By varying materials and textures—wicker, glass, patterned upholstery fabric, chrome, brick—we have kept it from being boring. It is anything but elaborate and, in the scheme of things, cost very little to decorate, primarily because we took the time to think through and plan the room before we ever spent a penny.

A friend of ours in Boulder, Colorado, Betty Weems, recently redecorated her entire house for one basic use: she wanted to create an environment where throngs of people could congregate comfortably and talk. If that sounds a little unusual, let me explain Betty's background to you. The great-great-granddaughter of George Washington's Parson Weems, and the daughter of the late Wharton Weems, who was a prominent Houston attorney, Betty is a vivacious and outgoing ex-Texan who, at the age of about fifty, went back to Rice University and earned her architect's degree. With her heightened interest in architecture as well as in music, and with the University of Colorado almost next door to the mountainside where she lives, Betty decided that what would make her happiest would be to open up her house and surround herself with the fascinating conversation of university professionals. Her goal, in redecorating, was to make each room in her home act as a receptacle for people, and to keep the elements of decor in the background.

The total effect Betty has created is in harmony with nature. When you are in the living room, you feel that it is nestled among the Colorado trees just outside the vast window, beyond which the majestic Rocky Mountains soar skyward. The materials Betty chose for the living room suggest the strength of the outdoors, too. She used broad fieldstone for the three parallel fireplace ledges where people gather to sit and talk. A huge, deep-piled rug of snowcap white pulls the room together and makes it appear more expansive than it is. Beyond the living room and just off the dining room, which is furnished with the traditional Georgian pieces that have been handed down through generations of the Weems family, there is an inviting nook where people often cluster at the small bar and on the sky-blue sofa and chairs. The nook is also home for Betty's extensive collection of all kinds of eggs—porcelain, glass, enamel. I happen to be especially fond of that collection. Not only do I admire the eggs for their beauty, I can always be sure that a house gift of another egg will bring pleasure to Betty.

A Sophisticated New York Apartment

In contrast to the nature-inspired atmosphere of the Weems house, the New York apartment of jewelry designer Kenneth Jay Lane is the epitome of civilized sophistication. His living room, which can seat as many as fifty, is a study in opulence. Kenneth characterizes its appearance as "a cross between a Victorian gentlemen's club and the bottom of a very tall tent." I must say, I gasped when I saw the room for the first time. Kenneth smiled and said, "Everybody reacts the same way, Roger. The reason is that you enter the room through a disproportionately small doorway, so when you see the huge space beyond, it comes as a surprise. I planned the effect deliberately."

I could see that Kenneth has some very original ideas about the use of space, so I asked him to tell me more of his secrets. In response to my comment that the living room succeeds through a bold combination of luxury, comfort, and daring, Kenneth explained, "I think that many people are too timid when they decorate. More people have died of timidity than of bravado. You have to make strong statements, use furnishings and accessories that are important. If a molding on the wall or an ornament on a table doesn't mean anything, I say don't bother. Take the mold-ing in this room, for instance. I chose a decorative style that matches the original late-nineteenth century style of the build-ing, which was designed by Stanford White, and placed the molding to make the high ceiling seem even higher. You'll notice that it extends a full foot from the wall onto the ceiling, so it forces your eye to keep moving upward. Another thing I did was to change the sash windows that face onto the balcony and in-stall French doors instead. They create a vertical line, which is more suitable to the room and more aesthetically pleasing. I lined the wall space between the windows with mirror, for conti-nuity and to play back the light from huge hanging lamps as well as the rest of the contents of the room."

Kenneth says he was tempted to mirror the entire room from the dado up, the dado being high enough so when people were seated they wouldn't find themselves gazing at their own reflec-tions. He refrained because mirror is a hard surface and sound ricochets from it like bullets bouncing off metal. The din from voices and music would have been distressing. Kenneth says, "Sound is absolutely as important to your physical comfort as the contours of the chair you sit in. That's why I used fabric on the walls, so voices wouldn't echo within the room. And since I own this apartment, I insulated the walls so there would be no leakage of sound from the neighbors next door. It was worth it to me to give up an inch or two of space. I had a sound engineer come in and decide the method that would work best here. If you don't want to go to that expense, the least you can do is in-stall double windows. You'd be amazed at how much street noise they keep out, not to mention the fact that they make your heating and air-conditioning system more efficient."

Not all of us are able to do as Kenneth Lane did. While he could gut his home from floor to ceiling and replace all the be-longings he had tired of, we are more apt to have to recycle things that we already own. You might even say that recycling has become a watchword of the 1980s. Actually, Carolyn and I like to decorate that way. It is how we have always fixed the places where we have lived. To us, decorating with an eye to economy is not so much a challenge as it is the natural course in which we have moved with the tides of our life.

Move Things Around to Create a New Look

One of the first things we do when we look at a room we have grown dissatisfied with is ask ourselves, what if we moved some of our things around? Could we reinvigorate our living space that way? Relocating furniture and accessories is such a simple device, but like so many obvious answers that sit on the ends of our noses, it is a solution we don't always see unless we really look for it. Once you open your imagination to the possibilities, though, you can find a kaleidoscope of "moving ways" to take the staleness out of your rooms, and to escape the money bind we are all trapped by.

A friend of ours, whose name it would be indiscreet to mention, used the relocation technique to overcome a decorating problem that involved more than a limited budget. She had a situation that was fraught with potential emotional danger. She had married a man who was not completely recovered from the death of his wife two years earlier, and moved into the suburban Chicago home he had shared with the former Mrs. D for something like fifteen years.

Immediately, the second Mrs. D could see that she had dilemmas to conquer, if she wanted to launch the marriage happily. The place was basically well furnished, but after fifteen years many of the things were in shabby condition. With some fixing up, she could live with most of the furnishings, even though not all of them were to her liking. The new Mrs. D also had to think about the things she had had in her former home. She had to be selective about what she brought with her, so the house wouldn't become a hodgepodge of His and Hers.

The element that made her most nervous, however, was the fact that she knew, whatever she did to redecorate, she would be walking over emotional land mines. The second Mrs. D felt certain if she were to make a clean sweep of the furnishings, consciously or not Mr. D would take it as a signal that she was critical of her predecessor's taste. Besides, although the D's are both in comfortable income brackets, they are not so wealthy that they could afford to get rid of everything. Mrs. D had the wit to bring in an expert, a decorator whose touch she admired, to help solve her problems. Here is how Mrs. D describes what they did.

"Our aim was to change the look of the house without chang-ing much that was in it. We started by taking stock of what we had to work with: my husband's furniture and accessories, mine, and the spaces they could fill. Susan, the decorator, is one of those creative people who can go into a trance and envision seemingly unrelated things in new combinations that achieve a completely new effect. We shoved as many of the belongings as we could manage into the center of each room. That freed my mind from the existing pattern—and I could think fresh about shifting things from one place to another. One of the first moves we made was to take a 36-inch round table that had been in the dining room and move it up into the bedroom. The design of the table is rather indifferent, so we threw a batik cloth over it and covered the surface with a collection of framed photographs. It emerged from being a lackluster oak nothing to a piece with real decorative panache.

"In the library we found a huge hulk of an easy chair with a matching ottoman. I was all for getting rid of them, but Susan suggested that we forget the idea of chair-with-ottoman and use the chair and the ottoman separately, as individual pieces. The chair would go in the living room and the ottoman would stay in the library as a perch for TV viewing. As Susan explained this, she taught me a principle worth remembering. She said, 'When you have a piece of upholstered furniture that was well made in the first place and that has a good strong frame, don't let a frumpy appearance throw you off. Hang on to your good things and work with them. You are very apt to find that it's cheaper to rebuild the springs and cushions of rump-sprung chair or sofa, and change the shape if you want, than to go out and buy some-thing new. At least you should get an upholsterer's estimate so you can compare the alternatives.'

"Susan did change the shape of the easy chair. She had the arms and the back slimmed down so it no longer looks like a brooding elephant. She had the seat cushions filled with polyes-ter and down, which makes it both firm and pliant, comfortable to sit in, and not messed up and squashy when you stand. For the covering, we chose a tightly woven beige wool rather than the Fortuny fabric I'd been enamored of. The fact that the Fortuny was cotton eliminated it. Cotton simply would not withstand the use and wear that an easy chair gets. Susan ordered extra yards of the wool fabric, so she could have deep covers tailored to fit the arms of the chair, the part that gets soiled first and needs cleaning most often. By deep, I mean the armcovers reach to the bottom of the seat cushion on both the insides and outsides of the arms and all the way to where the back of the chair begins, so they blend into the chair and don't look like slipcovers or doilies.

"Susan also told me she had specified that the fabric be ScotchGarded by the manufacturer so it would resist grease and dirt, and she gave me another useful tip. She said, 'As soon as the chair and other upholstered pieces are delivered to you, give them another protective spray treatment to beef up the fabrics' resistance to dirt. It wouldn't hurt to spray the dining room chairs, too, even through we're doing the seats in washable Ultrasuede. As a matter of fact, it's a good idea to keep a can of spray in the house all the time. I use mine on all my new clothes, and on clothes that have just been dry-cleaned. It helps cut down on cleaner's bills. Just remember to test the spray on the fabric, on a small patch on the wrong side, to make sure the colors won't run or stain.'

"I thanked Susan for the advice, and I thank her to this day for the Ultrasuede dining-chair seats. I adore the deep salmon color. But the best part is, even when my husband's grandchildren come for dinner, I don't have to hold my breath every time one of them spills a glass of milk."

I asked Mrs. D to finish telling me about the living room, and she said, "When Susan and I took a look at the sofa we decided that it was far too low. Even people who aren't as tall as I am had to struggle to get themselves up and out of the sofa. Correcting that defect turned out to be a simple operation. Susan had taller legs attached to the sofa, and concealed them with a tailored skirt that reaches the floor."

Mrs. D went on to tell how she had integrated her own possessions with Mr. D's. A favorite pair of Biedermeier chairs were given new seat coverings to match the upholstery on the sofa, and included in a conversational grouping near the bay window. Her collections of Zuni fetishes went onto the shelves of an antique medicine chest that had been in the dressing room of Mrs.

D's former home. She placed the chest on top of Mr. D's dining room sideboard, where it added interest to the traditional furnishings. She removed the coarsely crafted doors, which she had never especially liked and which looked quite out of place in their graceful new setting, and painted the inside of the chest a glazed-fruit watermelon, the better to show off her collection. She could have papered the inside or lined it with fabric, but paint seemed to lend just the right feeling. Besides, it was easier and less expensive to apply.

Probably the largest single purchase Mrs. D made in redoing the house was a carpet. With the new color scheme downstairs, the dining room and library rugs were jarringly wrong. And the guestroom upstairs needed more than the pair of small hooked rugs next to each bed. So they moved the dining room rug, a Chinese antique, up to the guestroom, where it covered all but a pleasing two-foot border of wood flooring. They had the library rug dyed rosy tan to neutralize the reds and blues in the upholstery. The living room rug was so worn and stained, in addition to being a shag that was out of place in the house, it defied their recycling efforts. So Mrs. D and Susan took a deep breath, rolled up the rug, moved it out, and replaced it with a classic dhurrie rug that they both had coveted ever since they had spotted it in the back room of a furniture shop. Mrs. D says that even though it was the major item in her decorating budget, it was priced fairly. Besides, she and Mr. D both love it so much, she feels they will receive years of pleasure for every dollar they paid. Sometimes, even when you are working within the constraints of a penny-watching budget, it is right to invest in something that pleases and comforts you—a special rug, a good easy chair, an air-conditioning system. Especially if the object is something that you will have for a long time, you can snuff out your guilt feelings by mentally amortizing the cost over the years.

Not everyone has such a complete or complex redecorating project as Mrs. D. You may want to change just one or two rooms, simply because you are tired of them. Try changing the lighting, to create a different mood. Can-lights aimed at the ceiling or silhouetting a plant, for a theatrical look. Standing votives for drama plus romance. Sixty-watt pink bulbs instead of hundred-watt white, for tranquility. Hundred-watt white bulbs instead of sixty-watt pink for an energy boost. Rheostats—on everything. They are the fastest, least expensive device ever created to elevate or subdue moods at will.

Graphics Are Portable

Sometimes all it takes to create a fresh look is to move pictures and other graphics from one wall to another. Not only can you relocate wall hangings from room to room, you can move them from your home to your office. Or from your office to your home, for that matter. The only restriction to bear in mind is that the proportions must be right—the relationship of the picture with the furniture it is near, or the wall area it occupies. Experiment. Sometimes when a table and picture are not quite right together, you can link them by an entirely new tabletop arrangement.

Some people are timid about moving pictures around because they are afraid they will have rectangular ghosts on the wall where the pictures used to hang. They probably will have ghosts, but the problem can be remedied quite simply. All you have to do is hang another picture over the area, assuming you have one the right size. Or you can wash the wall. Sometimes it is easier to give the wall a fast coat of paint than to wash it. I like paint because it's a simple, inexpensive way to make big changes. If you do just the wall where you have removed pictures, and choose a color that complements the other three walls or else contrasts with them, you can make a truly dramatic difference in the mood of the room. You will also avoid the difficulty of matching existing paint. And perhaps best of all, the big change will cost only a few dollars.

Pictures can make an extraordinary difference in the personality of a home. I can think of at least one couple, Mildred and Edwin Knopf, who gave a new house intimacy and charm by making a photo album of their halls and study. You probably know who the Knopfs are: Mildred is the author of several enchanting cookbooks, including *Cook, My Darling Daughter*, and Edwin is the famous movie producer who worked with such stars as Ronald Reagan, Audrey Hepburn, and Greer Garson. Among the reasons Edwin is practically a legend to me is that besides being able to play a mean piano concerto, he was actually present when his friend and my hero, George Gershwin, wrote *Rhapsody in Blue.*

Some years ago the Knopfs moved from their large Hollywood home into a much smaller place on Mandeville Canyon Road. Naturally, they couldn't take all their possessions with them, but they did want to have reminders around them of the many pleasant years they had lived in the other house. So they took Edwin's piano and Mildred's favorite Italian bowl and Sevres dish and placed them in the living room, amid the other furnishings they really loved. They selected as much of their cherished bedroom, dining, and study furnishings as would fit in the new house, and reupholstered and arranged them to suit the smaller quarters. When they were all finished, they felt that on the whole, the house was lovely and accommodated their needs very nicely. Yet, something seemed to be missing. The house lacked that certain quality that comes when you live in a place long enough to give it a personal imprint.

Creative people that they are, Mildred and Edwin found a solution in no time. They sorted through the stacks and stacks of framed photographs they had acquired through the years: pictures of the film stars Edwin had been closely associated with as a producer, and photos of the scores of other friends they had made during their careers. Then they simply lined the entire study and the downstairs halls with photograph upon photograph of the people who meant so much to them. Instantly, the house came alive: a very personal home filled with the familiar faces the Knopfs have known for so long.

"Less Is More"

Many times you can change the look of a room for the better by subtracting an object rather than relocating it. The perfect improvement may be to remove that picture you're not really fond of, the lamp or chair that has seen better days, a rug that is weary and worn. If the rug is in a room where a bare floor is acceptable and the flooring is basically decent-looking, play it up. Scrape the wood, buff it, stain it pine or teak. Think about using an area rug. In a small space, however, especially in an apartment where sound and dirt are problems, I think that wall-to-wall carpeting usually works best. Its even expanse makes the room seem more spacious. It soaks up sound. You never have to dust-mop. In fact, you can throw your dust mop away if you extend the carpeting all the way into every closet, and thus put an end to one of the biggest housekeeping nuisances of all time. To keep the cost as well as the dust down, try to shop when the carpeting sales are on. Traditionally, that is in January, though in some places the sale month varies. You could save even more money if you buy what they call commercial or industrial carpeting: the sturdy kind used in hotels and other institutions. Commercial carpeting is significantly less expensive than residential carpeting, and comes in a great variety of textures, patterns, and shades. It does not look "industrial" at all, and it wears and wears and wears.

It could be that everything in your room is in perfectly good shape, but you are tired of how it looks. Or you have a feeling that something is wrong, but you cannot quite put your finger on it. A long time ago, we learned how to approach that kind of problem; a decorator gave us his secret and we have used it ever since. What you do is walk into your room as if you were a stranger and ask yourself, "What does this room look like?" It's a sort of mental acrobatic trick that helps solve puzzles instantly. The last time we played Stranger-in-the-House, we asked ourselves what our living room looked like. Our answer was, "Cluttered." We knew what we had to do: pare down the excess things that had accumulated. To start, we cleared away all of the Steuben glass animals and snuffboxes that Carolyn had collected over the years, and stored them away in a box. Then we edited the number of photographs that, we could see now, were elbowing each other off the various tabletops. We had a few too many bowls and other accessories around that we weeded out, too. When we finished, we were rid of the clutter and the living room was accessorized with the things that we felt we wanted to live with every day, at this stage of our lives. All we had to do then was to regroup those objects, so they would resume the significance they had lost in the jumble.

Paraphernalia has a tendency to creep up on you, like the ivy that clings to brick walls. You keep adding things that you like to what you already have, and you don't realize that in the process your room is becoming a jungle. That is why the Stranger-in-the-House trick is so helpful. It forces you to really see what your surroundings look like, and to critique the place almost as if you were reviewing it for a design magazine. You become conscious of whether it is comfortable or nerve-jangling, whether it reflects your personality and your present way of life, if it is a copycat of fashions you have seen elsewhere, or if it expresses your personal taste. I think the most successful room is the one whose owner anybody can identify, even if nobody says to whom the room belongs to.

Personal Preferences

I'll make a confession to illustrate what I mean about expressing personal taste. Five or ten years ago I was swept up by the vogue for abstract expressionist art. I would have killed, then, to furnish my home with paintings from Picasso's cubist period, or art by Helen Frankenthaler or Willem de Kooning. As time went on and I acquired more knowledge about contemporary art, I realized that abstract art is not a style I care to live with. I don't understand it as well as I do a sunny Matisse. By now I have admitted to myself and the world that I honestly do not like abstract art, and I no longer yearn to fill my home with it. The paintings I buy are the paintings that I truly like.

That doesn't mean that I am right and the museum curators are wrong. What it indicates is that I have become secure enough, by virtue of time and experience, to have the courage to follow my own convictions. It takes seasoning to reach that point. I think that the people who stand around and cast sarcasms at things they know little about merely defeat themselves. When you hear somebody comment, "Those Jackson Pollock paintings are nothing but aimless splashes of paint; my pet poodle could do better," you are listening to a person display his or her lack of knowledge. It is perfectly valid not to want to live with Pollock's art, but I would prefer to hear the person explain, "I think I understand what Pollock was trying to express. I have studied the techniques he used and admire his ability. However, his work is not to my taste." People have to earn the right to criticize somebody else's work, and the way to earn it is to accumulate knowledge on the subject. It is knowledge and experience that confer the power of discernment.

It is all well and good to clear away things and freshen up your environment, as we cleared the clutter from our living room, but an excess of fervor can carry you too far. It is better to stop and think: can you repair that tired chair or the battle-scarred desk? Or fix it up so you can use it in a new way? Maybe the lowly camp trunk you have been harboring will take on panache if you gloss it with a coat of bright paint and move it to the den, to use as a storage bin and table. Think ahead. If you find a place to squirrel away the piece of furniture or the accessory that you don't need right now, you may give yourself a very useful bonus when you move to another home. The bookcase inside our Sally's closet, that holds her shoes and games, stood for three years in our attic, biding its time between homes until we found a new use for it. And I cannot tell you how many of our lamps, ashtrays, and other miscellaneous pieces have served time in storage cartons, waiting until we were ready to bring them out and recycle them in another of our decorating eras.

Some people never store anything away. They live forever with the belongings they acquired on Day One. My cousin Rose Rich was like that. She seemed to have a need for continuity in her life, which she achieved through the constant presence of her own past. Until the day she died, in 1960, Cousin Rose lived with the same possessions she had had when she first set up housekeeping. I remember the 1890 Tiffany lamp, the black leather "psychiatrist's" sofa, her rocking chair and her Oriental rug.

I regret to say that when Cousin Rose died, her daughter, overwhelmed by emotional impulse, threw away all of those wonderful vintage treasures. To her, the lamp, the sofa, and so on were worthless junk. You can be sure that somebody else bought them in a minute and is now enjoying their use. I wish Cousin Rose's daughter had stopped to think about the furniture before she disposed of it. Perhaps with a little reshuffling of her own possessions and a little refurbishing of her mother's, she could be enjoying those old things right now.

More Imagination than Money

It may be that you have no past to fall back on. No possessions or household memories. How do you get ideas for decorating? I'll tell you what we do. We avail ourselves of all the free and inexpensive sources we can find. We check the home furnishing magazines constantly: *Architectural Digest* for avant-garde ideas, *House & Garden* for somewhat more conservative design, *House Beautiful*, *Town & Country*'s architecture and design section, and all the rest. We go on house tours, go to see the room setups at retail stores, analyze the settings in films and on TV. And we keep an ongoing file of the decorating ideas that we cull from these sources, which we consult frequently to refresh our thinking.

A good way to put ideas together is to let your imagination float free. Start with the attitude, "Anything is possible. What if I did so and so." Think big at first. Then if "so and so" turns out to be too expensive or difficult to accomplish, you can almost always whittle down your big idea to manageable size. It helps, too, to keep your imagination active. Sometimes, just for the creative mental exercise of it, I go into a hotel room and think, "How could I change this room into something more exhilarating, in just one move that doesn't cost a lot of money?"

• I'd relocate the furniture: put the sofa in the middle of the room, move the chairs and a couple of tables near it, and create a conversation area close to the fireplace instead of huddled along a wall.

• I'd get rid of that nondescript mantel on the fireplace and put up a large mirror instead. I wouldn't even frame it, I'd just have an oblong ocean of glass. That would smooth out the lines, give an illusion of more space, and add a slightly theatrical touch. Maybe, instead, I'd sheath the front of the fireplace with a stroke of shiny black glass. And top it with a single bold streak of glass or some other sensational material.

• I'd bring in a huge plant for the vacant space between the credenza and that side chair. The plant would tie the two pieces together and make them a design unit. It would be glamorous. It would add life to this otherwise static room.

• I could bank the window corner with plants and flowers, and change the flowers with the season. Flowering plants, like chrysanthemums or bromeliads, would cost less and last longer than flowers. With just one stroke, I'd have added the color, shape, and movement that my senses seem to need.

• If we were having a party, I'd tie enormous bunches of multicolored balloons to the drawer handles and chairbacks, where they wouldn't be in the way. The minute people came in, the room would shout, "Instant Party!"

• To lend architectural diversity, I would use a sheath of mirror on that straight wall, and create the appearance of a column.

• I would paint one wall in a color that blends or contrasts with the others.

• I would "paper" the walls with an interesting fabric. To save money, I would do it myself, by stapling the fabric onto the wooden moldings and chair rail.

• I'd get a folding screen and staple a swath of fabric onto each panel. Or else I would paint the screen. Or make one of mirrors.

• I would paint that wooden bureau a bold Chinese red, to give the room snap and dash. And I would replace the wooden drawer pulls with brass handles or ceramic knobs.

• I would slipcover the sofa, rather than reupholster it, and add an armful of huge throw pillows covered with sari cloth. For opulence, I would tie the cloth in a Turkish knot at each corner.

• To rejuvenate that weary round table, I'd drape it with one of those designer sheets they sell in department stores.

• I would buy one sensational new lampshade.

Decorating Themes

Another approach to decorating that takes more imagination than money is to give your home a theme, as we have. What we have done suits us very well, although I must admit that not everybody likes it. As a matter of fact, my mother once told us that while she thinks our house is perfectly lovely, she would strangle if she had to live in it. We were taken aback, until she explained. "It's all those plants hanging from the ceiling, growing from the floor, sprouting out of tabletops, and bursting from every tub and sink. It's like living in a greenhouse, which is all right if you're mad for foliage. But I keep thinking, 'The shrubbery is taking over. What if some of those leaves turn out to be man-eaters?' " We laughed. Mother is well known for her quick sense of humor, and an imagination that will sometimes take a fanciful turn).

It is true, though, that there are so many plants wherever you turn that I guess you could say they have taken over. One thing is certain: they are the theme that runs throughout the house. We're happy with it. It is the evidence of our special interest, and it gives our home an identity.

Personal Trademarks

Carrying out a theme works well for a good many people. I have seen a number of interesting rooms that were decorated from special, personal points of view. Roy Chapin, the retired chairman of American Motors, expresses his enthusiasm for sports in the upstairs library and basement office of his home in Grosse Point, Michigan. They are his private rooms and his wife Sis says they are covered with prints, paintings, and woodcuts of the outdoors. Roy's library, which is painted dark blue, is completely lined with books on fishing, and his office is a lair for stuffed fish and birds. Even the heating vents are hung with Roy's mounted trophies. The rooms certainly bear his particular trademark, yet they do not clash with the rest of the house. The dark blue of the library picks up the blue that threads the coral-and-white walls and upholstery of the downstairs rooms, which are deliberately bright because the weather around Grosse Point is so often gray.

Another sportsman friend of mine, Wesley Dixon, the vice-president of G. D. Searle pharmaceuticals, is married to a sportswoman. Wes and Sue have confined the expression of their mutual interest in game hunting to an octagonal house that they built in the rear of their home in Lake Forest, Illinois. "The zoo," as their family calls it, definitely has a signature theme. It is a jungle of trophies from their big-game safaris for unendangered species. I mention "unendangered" because Wes is an ardent conservationist as well as a sportsman. He is past president of Boone and Crockett, the conservation club founded in 1887 by Theodore Roosevelt, and was conservation chairman of the

Shikar Safari Club International. The Dixons' game house was designed as a showcase for their trophies. It has a Venetian stone fireplace, a skylight, and gleaming copper doors: a dramatic contrast to their house, which is decorated in traditional style.

Color

The theme you choose can be something as general as color. A woman I know has a living room that she says is furnished à la Heinz ketchup: it is a mongrel mixture of fifty-seven varieties of style. The pieces are good, but they are unrelated. She has two 1930s chairs that belonged to her parents, a contemporary black coffee table, fruitwood end tables that once were night tables in a French Provincial bedroom, and a pair of sand-colored lamps that she bought with trading stamps. Yet the room works. What ties it all together is a theme: green. The major expanses, her carpet and sofa, are a soft leaf-green, and the two occasional chairs are upholstered in a yellow-and-green pattern. The other large areas are neutral. The walls, window blinds, and lampshades are off-white. Her ashtrays, bowls, and other accessories are either crystal or colors that melt into the greenness of the room. This living room succeeds because its owner gave some thought to the fact that it needed a unifying point of view. What is more, by selecting color as her device, she gave the room style without having to buy new furniture. She probably saved herself thousands of dollars.

Color has extraordinary properties. It can soften or crisp up a room, make it look more masculine or feminine. It arouses you, calms you, and even changes the atmospheric temperature. Color definitely has thermal qualities. The shade you choose can transport you instantly from one climate to another, and change your mood as well. People who live in intensely hot places like Morocco, Mexico, or Peru have known about color's effect on heat and cold for centuries. That is why you so often see homes there with the walls coated stark white. White is notorious for making you feel cool. So are blues and greens. You could practically air-condition a ninety-degree house for the price of a few cans of blue, green, or white paint—at least as far as how the colors make you feel. I wouldn't swear that color can take the place of mechanical air conditioning or fans.

At the other end of the thermal palette are the deep, warm, tweed-wool-and-fireplace colors that take the chill out of an environment. We have some friends in Seattle, Penn and John Curran, who found out what color can do when they bought a new home on Puget Sound. It was in pristine condition and the Currans were pleased with the wall colors the builder had used. They moved in, and a few months later began to have the feeling that something was awry. The library, where they had anticipated spending most of their family time, turned out to be an orphan instead; it sat there, unused and unloved. The room was nicely proportioned, with a serene northern exposure and calm blue walls. Penn and John had furnished it with large down-filled chairs, good reading light, sizable tables, and convenient storage cupboards. It should have been an inviting place to nestle in, to read or chat leisurely on the phone. Instead, the room still did not say, "Come in and stay for a while."

Finally, Penn realized what was wrong. The blue walls, plus the northern exposure, had a chilling effect. It was easy to correct, once she figured out the difficulty. Penn had the library repainted in a warm earthy brown, and overnight the Currans' library was transformed from a cellblock into a cordial, welcoming den. What is more, the furniture they had schemed for the blue room worked perfectly in its new setting. They had selected an upholstery fabric with a graceful blue pattern on an off-white ground, which relieved any smothering effect that all-brown walls can have, and neutralized the aura of masculinity as well.

I have noticed that in home decorating, fashions in color generally move in two-year spans. When we moved into our house, in 1969, it was painted refrigerator white throughout. We found that the color—or no color, technically—was cool and relaxing. And it felt right aesthetically. Our eyes had become accustomed to seeing white walls in all of the shelter magazines we follow. Then moods changed—ours and the world's around us. Economically and sociologically, people began to feel anxious about international affairs, and they worried especially about money.

The casual, even slapdash years were over. We had a need to return to more solid, graceful times. You saw it in clothes. Soft silk dresses and elegantly tailored suits replaced hippie clothes. We began to return to tradition in the way that we dined and entertained. And, of course, in the way we treated our homes. I think we all needed the security of things we were familiar with, and an ambiance that could comfort and smooth out the shocks of a hectic, difficult existence. All of which is to say, soft colors and a leaning toward graciousness have returned. The walls in our house, and in the homes of most of the people we know, are no longer stark white or lacquer red. They have been muted to soft beige, pale yellow, light apricot. It's a background that helps us regain some of the serenity we so desperately want in our lives.

I am not suggesting that you rush out and paint everything pastel. Soft colors may not be your style. They may not suit your home. You may be the kind of person who responds to opulence or dazzle. The point I want to underscore is that you must consult your individuality and your special circumstances, rather than what is "in." Fashion is only as good as it feels for you. Observe what is going on in the world, and then extract the ideas from what you see in a way that expresses your uniqueness. Originality is always in style, as long as it fits the boundaries of good taste.

Accent Your Best Features

People who have a feeling for what suits them best usually know how to highlight their best features, the way an attractive woman uses makeup to focus attention on, say, her beautiful eyes. The rest of her face may in fact be quite plain, but she gives the impression of being an attractive woman with exquisite eyes, and people don't notice her faults. The same technique works in decorating. If you accent the beautiful features in a room, the less attractive furnishings automatically recede. Haven't you ever walked into somebody's home and been so smitten by a lyrically carved Queen Anne chair or a lustrous antique sewing table that you never really noticed the other belongings? If you think back, you will probably realize that the chair or the sewing table was placed so that you couldn't help but see it immediately. The room made a good first impression because whoever decorated it had the good sense to spotlight its best feature.

We treated my piano that way for years. For a long time it was the only good piece of furniture we had in our living room. It dominated the room, just as it had when it was in my parents' home, and we let it. In fact, we learned to highlight the piano in order to minimize our other inexpensive things which were, to say the least, unprepossessing. This piano is a behemoth; it occupies seven feet of wall space and there is no use trying to pretend otherwise. So we decorated that living room around the piano by placing it so that it commanded your attention the moment you walked in. What we did, partly to accommodate the piano's size and partly to make it a focal point, was group all our chairs and the sofa on the side of the room opposite the piano. That way, when our guests were seated, what they saw besides each other was the majestic piano, and not the so-so furniture they were sitting on.

My friend Paul played up the one good piece of furniture in his first apartment in a different way. He had found a round mahogany side table with a piecrust top and pedestal stand at a secondhand store, did a little haggling, and took it home for $40. He put it next to his sofa, and the piecrust table faded right out of sight; not only that, the sofa seemed dimmer than before. He tried putting the table between a pair of upholstered chairs, but it was too tall. He abandoned that notion and took the table into his bedroom, where he tried to make it work as a night table. The height was all right, but again the table looked like nothing. And the rest of the room began to seem shoddy. Paul decided that the reason his table kept disappearing and exerting a bad influence on his rooms was that the mahogany was dulled by time and dirt, and bore the scars of drinks and cigarettes, besides. He didn't want to invest $100 or more in refinishing his $40 secondhand table, nor did he want to spend nights and weekends slaving to strip and refinish the wood himself. Paul asked if I knew any easy answers, and it happened that I did. I told him, "You have bought a very well designed table. It's a reproduction of an antique, but the lines are authentic and it is one of those pleasing, classic designs. Your table can be an important piece in this apartment, or wherever you move to from here. But you are absolutely right about the finish: it is in very bad repair. Furthermore, even though the finish is so dulled down, I can see by the sharp henna color that the manufacturer used a cheap stain in the first place. The piece is worth fixing up, Paul, and you don't have to invest a lot of hard work or money in it. All you need is patience and steel wool."

Refinishing Good Wood

Then I explained exactly how to go about refinishing the table. "Get yourself a boxful of the finest steel wool they make. It's called Number 00, and hardware stores carry it. Then rub the wood in the same direction as the grain, gently but firmly, until you get down past the stain that is on it now. It will be easier if you tackle about a foot at a time, and sort of overlap your rubbing from one area to the next, so you'll remove the stain evenly. Then, when the table is smooth and clean, take a tin of liquid furniture stain and apply it the same way you used the steel wool: evenly and smoothly, going over the surface again and again until the liquid is thoroughly absorbed and the color is all-of-a-piece. Incidentally, you don't have to stick with mahogany stain if you don't care to. I think a walnut tone would add distinction to this table. It would show off the carved rim, and give the table a softly luxurious look. There is one thing I urge you to do, however. Please stay away from those instant furniture-stain kits that promise 'Elegance in Just 15 Minutes.' All you will do is slap on another cheap coat of varnish. Use the steel wool and patience; it's the hand rubbing that makes all the difference."

I had two more pieces of advice for Paul that I recommend for all furniture. One has to do with protection, the other with prevention. I said, "When you have the table in good condition, protect all the surfaces—especially the top—with a finish that repels stains from spills and hot things. Bar wax is an old standby; use it as a rubdown every two or three months, depending on how much use your table gets. Besides bar wax, there is a constant stream of new products on the market you should keep your eye on. I don't recommend that you try them willy-nilly. Ask someone who has had experience: a friend or your decorator. Decorators are marvelous sources for information like that. They know everything that is going on and see the bad results as well as the good. For instance, I thought Scotch-Gard was the latest thing to protect fabric, until a decorator told me that there are several newer products on the market, to take care of the new fabrics that have come along."

The other thing I urged Paul to do was practice preventive care with his furniture. It is very important to keep what you have in good condition all the time, especially now that it is so expensive to replace things. And new workmanship is apt to be inferior to old. Oil your woods regularly so they won't dry out and crack. Glue parts that come unstuck right away, before one weakness leads to another and the whole piece collapses. Have your upholstery cleaned as soon as it shows the faintest soil, before it is so far gone you have to spend hundreds of dollars on reupholstering. I understand that it is tempting to postpone or ignore tasks of preventive maintenance. Whenever you are tempted, stop. Remind yourself of this basic budgetary fact of life: small repairs cost far less than major rehabilitation.

You might like to know that Paul's table turned out magnificently. Once it was properly stained, its pedigreed lines became apparent and when he placed it in the corner next to his sofa, the sofa itself seemed to take on more substance. The fact is, the table stood out as a work of excellence, and that gave Paul a brainstorm. Since it was the one distinguished piece of furniture in his living room, he moved the table out of the corner and over to the near side of the sofa, where you see it as soon as you come into the room. He placed it well forward, away from the wall, so its silhouette was played up. And then, to call further attention to his new classic, he put a few good things on top of it: a handsome brass box, a crystal match striker, a hefty ashtray with an Oriental design, and a framed original lithograph that, in fact, had been too small for the wall where it had hung.

Accessories as Accents

You can think in terms of spotlighting your good things to diminish the rest when it comes to accessories, too. We have a fine Korean bronze vase on our living room mantel, along with some less distinguished pieces of Eskimo sculpture. The bronze is set apart from the other objects, to lend it distinction. On the other hand, my mother has an accumulation of small vases that she keeps in a huddled mass on the bottom shelf of a two-tiered glass table. A few of the vases are the nondescript kind that florists send, some are fine Venetian glass that my father brought from Italy, and one is a fine Steuben crystal. I keep thinking, if this were my home I would cluster the Venetian vases and highlight the Steuben by placing it on a stand. But I don't tell my mother that because the arrangement she has is what pleases her. That, after all, is what is important.

❧ ❧ ❧

4

THE ART OF COLLECTING

Some people collect houses, art, jewels, others collect lifestyles. I like to think that Carolyn's and my enthusiasm for hoarding the touchstones of our lives combines the best of both. Between her unerring good taste and my unflagging appetite for people and places, we have created a very special ambiance, one that is distinctively ours. Our surroundings brim with beautiful things to look at, and with amusing and sentimental reminders as well, each a link with a particular place, a time, an event that has brought us happiness. It is as if the pages of a diary had become living theater, with a cast of characters that constantly grows and delights us.

People sometimes forget the intangible values that are attached to collecting. The pleasures they enjoyed as youngsters, saving baseball cards and bottle tops, are lost in later years. It is difficult then to call back the moments, the feelings of excitement, the triumphs and the small satisfactions. That is one of the reasons collecting is so rewarding a pursuit. Sometimes I look at dark-eyed, vivacious Sally, concentrating as only an eleven-year-old can on arranging her shelves of dolls, and I realize that she, too, is building a reservoir of memories. What is more, I feel sure that her native curiosity will provoke her to find out where her dolls came from and how they were made, and lead eventually to a chain of stimulating discoveries. Through her doll collection, Sally's world will surely expand for her as it has for every collector I have known.

Why People Collect

Collections are triggered by all sorts of impulses. Carolyn, for example, began to amass small picture frames for a very practical reason. Like most people, we have accumulated a mass of snapshots of our family and friends. The pictures were tucked away in albums that we used to thumb through once in awhile. Then, some years ago, it occurred to us that we could surround ourselves with pictures of the people we love, and look at them whenever we please. That is when Carolyn began to collect frames. Now when I look at the array of photographs that crowd our tabletops and sitting-room mantelpiece—so attractively showcased in their Lucite, silver, ceramic, and fabric frames—I am instantly immersed in happy times and places. In a corner of our sun-room, next to my old wicker chair, is a round table draped with flower-spattered linen that is host to a whole summer of good times. A glance recalls the morning we spent with our weekend guests, Sally and Barney Young, searching for shells to add to Sally's round-the-world collection. They had come up from Dallas to be with us, and the day before, we had given them a complete tour of our picturesque island: the historic whaling museum, the clapboard houses rimmed with generations of salt spray, the snug little village where you can buy scrimshaw or handcrafts, or just pass the time with your neighbors. It all floods back as I look at the picture of our eldest daughter, Regen. The snapshot shows her presenting Barney Young with a giant-size whalebone—his prize for finding what Regen proclaimed "the biggest shell on Nantucket Island."

Yet another photograph evokes the merriment of an outside-in picnic produced by our friends, Margaret and Larry McQuade. Larry is a handsome, outgoing man and a senior vice-president of the W. R. Grace Company. We have been good friends ever since we went to college together. On the afternoon captured in the photo, he was inspired. Refusing to let a three-day northeaster drench their plans for a beach party, Larry and

Margaret went to work and gathered armfuls of bright colored beach towels, spread them out on the floor of our sun-room, and garnished each with Styrofoam buckets of ice and drinks. For an authentic beach-party touch, they set out a bevy of citronella candles, so we would think we were outdoors amid the flies and mosquitoes. It turned out to be one of the best picnics of the season. The snapshot captures the crowd's exuberance and, I could swear, even the scent of citronella.

We have been fortunate in that our business forces us to continually sample the delights of the world's most dazzling cities. It is almost like living out the fantasy of being able to eat all the chocolates you like and not gain a pound. One of the photos that I am particularly fond of was taken right here in Dallas. It shows our good friends Laura and Bob Wilson, dressed in full Western rig, at a party in honor of the famous photographer, Richard Avedon. He was in Texas working on his book about the West, and Laura Wilson, who traveled with Avedon as an assistant, was our link to the renowned artist. Looking at the photo, I remember clearly how much we enjoyed the party, and what a pleasure it was to meet Avedon.

As I look around our serene, white-walled living room and the groupings of antiques and fine china that Carolyn has blended so amiably with the contemporary pieces we both like, it occurs to me that through her picture-frame collection—begun partly out of sentiment and partly through need—Carolyn has created a source of joy and continuing memories for all of us in the family.

Expanding Your Horizons

Some collections are selfish, but nonetheless worthwhile. A compilation of theater programs, restaurant matchbooks, or hotel ashtrays may mean nothing to anybody but yourself; they are prisms that refract strictly personal experiences. If, in addition, they heighten your curiosity and make you want to wade in and experiment on your own, so much the better. Curiosity has encouraged many an avid spectator to participate as thespian, chef, or gazeteer.

Perhaps you collect pure whimsy—frogs, pigs, eggs, top hats,

or comic books. Your horizons are limitless and you have the
fun of being on a perpetual scavenger hunt. Carolyn and I have
gone through any number of quirky phases, prompted by our
wish to find unusual items for our catalogs and by our own bent
for the offbeat. Last year we became fascinated by antique canes
and had a wonderful time rummaging in out-of-the-way shops
in cities from London to Bennington, Vermont. The next season
we concentrated on a quest for Scottish brooches, which took us
into village shops we had never seen before and introduced us to
whole clans of new friends. A person could spend years seeking
the one perfect Scottish brooch, and I suspect that our search
will open many more doors for us. On another tour, we put the
spotlight on jewelry made of old military medals, a notion we
had been smitten with after seeing a collection of medals at the
Hillwood home of Mrs. Marjorie Merriwether Post. Confirmed
collectors that we are, you can be sure we would have been
equally avid even if we were not in the catalog business.

Having a collector's focus gives you purpose, and opens doors
to all sorts of places and conversations. That is why collectors
travel well. My mother, for example, had been ill and unable to
leave her apartment for some time. Despite her confinement, she
is constantly busy shopping the magazines and getting ideas
from radio and TV for things that she thinks I might want to
collect for the catalogs. Although her world is not quite as broad
as it was when she was an active traveler and shopped the stores
in person, she still enjoys the collector's exhilaration of search
and discovery. It must be a family trait.

My own, ever-expanding collection of Bilston and Battersea
boxes got its start through search and discovery. I was on a buying trip in London a dozen or so years ago, and came upon a
shop on Brook Street called Halcyon Days. In talking with the
owner, a charming and enthusiastic designer named Susan Benjamin, I learned that she was a student of the century-old British
art of enamel-on-copper ware that once was expressed in gracefully designed, painstakingly crafted Battersea boxes. Appreciative of the need to preserve the art, Susan had single-handedly
undertaken to revive it. I was so enthralled with what she was
doing that I bought some of her boxes for our catalog. When I
came back home, I told everybody I knew how perfectly the

boxes were made, and advised them to start buying while the price was still low. Bert Honea, one of my friends in Fort Worth, really listened; when I went to visit him a few months later, I saw that he owned every Bilston and Battersea box we had ever offered. It dawned on me then that I would be wise to begin collecting Battersea boxes myself. Now what I do is save out the last of every lot we buy from Susan Benjamin and add it to my personal collection. And of course I shop for the old Batterseas wherever I travel.

My other collecting enthusiasms are handcrafts, musical comedy, and art. The handcrafts—circus animals, toys, and artifacts from all over the world—are very inexpensive to buy and most of the collection probably would not be worth very much if I wanted to sell it. Its value, to me, is in the preservation of a dying art. Each piece gives me a sense of history, of how the various cultures of the world developed. Just looking at an ancient Indian bird, feeling its texture, examining the workmanship, opens up avenues in my mind. I feel compelled to go to museums and read books and articles that will satisfy my curiosity about how Indians crafted these relics. What tools and materials did they use? Where did they get them? How did they manufacture the vivid colors that so closely simulate nature? One subject leads to another, and I want to know even more: whether the birds were used as toys or icons, what traditions were attached, when the art died out and why.

Getting a Free Education

One of the fringe benefits of collecting is that you can go into any shop, anywhere, and ask a lot of questions, even if you have no intention of buying. Carolyn and I learned this when we were first married, in 1960. We were typical newlyweds, living on a scrimpy budget with little more behind us than the modest checks we had received as wedding gifts. We held a conference and decided we would use the check from her grandfather for the best piece of art the money could buy. Since we had to be pretty careful, we also decided we had better take the trouble to find out what we were doing. We spent nearly a year educating ourselves, developing an eye for what is good. We would go into galleries that we knew were reputable and say to the dealer or manager, "We are interested in buying some art but we are new at it. If you have a few minutes to spare, we would appreciate it if you would give us some pointers on what to look for." You always want to make sure that you are not intruding when somebody is trying to conduct business, and that it really is convenient for him or her to talk with you. You will find that once that is cleared away, people love to talk about their area of expertise. I never have met anybody who didn't like to pass along learning—including myself.

One way to get your expert reeling out a free education is for you to say, very honestly, "I am just a beginner and my eye is not yet trained. Would you show me what you consider the finest piece you have, and explain what makes it excellent?" Ask them to tell you who are the best craftspeople in your field of interest: oil paintings, prints, art deco jewelry, Oriental porcelain, or whatever you have in mind. Tell them forthrightly, "I can't afford to buy a fine painting right now, but I want to be able to recognize good quality and be able to select the best my money will buy."

That is how Carolyn and I finally spent her grandfather's check. We were in a small gallery in Paris and the owner was one of those engaging octogenarians that Claude Rains used to portray, the sort of man you know is a canny trader but who gives off inviting twinkles of wisdom and kindness. We felt encouraged to ask his opinion: what did he think was the best value for our money? Straightaway, he led us to a lithographed landscape signed Johnny Friedlaender, a name we had never heard of. But we knew that if "Claude Rains" approved, so should we. What was more important, the lithograph pleased us both. We bought it, and still are stirred by its aesthetic qualities. The fact that our first piece of art is now appraised at twenty times what we spent for it is only incidental to the pleasure it has given us.

That was a real beginning for us as art collectors. We kept asking questions of knowledgeable people, learning as much as we could, and a year later we made our second purchase. It's a gouache by Milton Avery, and I don't even want to tell you how much it has gone up in value, just that we continue to love our

Avery seascape, and are still asking questions of the experts, developing our taste, and educating ourselves whenever we can.

Developing an Eye for Excellence

It was the eighty-year-old gallery owner in Paris who taught us how to recognize excellence in design. He quoted Coco Chanel, who once said, "Fashion changes, style remains," and then explained what she meant. He said, "Fads in fashion come and go, but a thing of excellence remains excellent forever. That is why the more you are grounded in the classics, the more benchmarks you will have to guide you in selecting quality that survives. After all, there really is nothing new under the sun; just new adaptations of centuries-old design, line, proportion, and use of color. It makes no difference if an object was created in the year 500 or yesterday; if its aesthetics are pure and harmonious, it will never look out of place or out of harmony with the times. It does not jar your sensibilities. Even when the look seems to be a sudden change from what your eye has grown accustomed to—simple minimal furniture after a period of baroque furbelows, or lines and colors in a startling new juxtaposition—if it is right, your senses will soon accept the change. Variations are always with us, but if you understand the foundations you will be able to recognize what is good and what is not."

There is a world of difference between variations and fads. Fads are often eccentric, sometimes vulgar; with no basis in real excellence, they slip in and out of favor rapidly. I think there is something rather sad about people who are so eager to seem up-to-the-minute that they rush after every fad that comes along. At the same time I can understand how they are swept along with the tides. The 1960s fervor for Tiffany lamps, Roseville pottery, Depression glass, and soup-can art may have sprung from nothing more consequential than the outpourings of enterprising publicists. But the publicity was difficult to ignore. Objects that for decades had been unloved and ignored suddenly acquired cachet. People began to doubt their initial aversion, or thought they were being stodgy and inflexible. They were not sure of their own opinions and succumbed to the tide. My advice when fads come along is to have a free mind and experiment, by all means. But be thoughtful. Edit out that which does not satisfy you personally. Remember that in collecting, as in everything else that you do, the most satisfactory life is when you express your own style. Beware the rush of the lemmings.

It has been my experience that people who follow their personal inclinations usually develop strong personal tastes. They are more sure of what they like and do not like, and are not afraid to let their confidence show. They understand that even though the Museum of Modern Art has exalted the design of Braun hairdryers, that does not mean everyone has to agree that Braun hairdryers are beautiful. Beauty is a matter of personal taste, and even the experts' judgments are subjective. If you learn to trust your preferences, in the end you will be your own best guide.

Education Is Free

As you develop your sense of individuality, you become more aware of the things around you. If you really look, you will find endless sources through which to develp your powers of discernment. I have found that you can get a free education almost anywhere. When I visit a well-appointed home or public place, I study the furniture and accessories, the same way I study photographs and captions in *Architectural Digest, House Beautiful,* and other shelter magazines. I examine museum exhibits, catalogs, and displays in fine-quality shops as if they were reference books in a library. I also enjoy reading books on the history of design, but I think this is something you should do only if you enjoy studying. Learning should be a pleasure trip, not a tour of duty.

Another good source for free education is acquaintances whose taste you admire. Among my "mentoring" acquaintances is Dorothy Rodgers. We were visiting with her one evening, and she told a story that sent me off on a collecting adventure. She told us about falling into a conversation with a taxi driver in New York who asked if she would mind if he stopped for a minute at a Madison Avenue gallery; he wanted to pick up one of his watercolors that was on exhibition there. Dorothy was curious, noted his name, A. D. Tobias, and a couple of days later went to the gallery to see what kind of artist her taxi driver was. She liked his work and wanted to encourage him, so she bought one of the pieces. I thought, Dorothy Rodgers has exquisite taste. If she considers Tobias's art good, I certainly ought to take a look at it. So on my next trip to New York I searched out the gallery and saw a Tobias that engaged my senses. It was a misty, ethereal cityscape of London right after a rain. The watercolor was quite inexpensive because Tobias was not yet a household name, and I bought it, making a note to call Dorothy and thank her for her guidance. After that, I began to watch for the artist's name. Just six months ago I noted that he was the centerpiece of a fairly large exhibition of American artists. So I had the satisfaction of sharing a "discovery"—there is always that tantalizing chance in the back of your mind—and of knowing that our choices had been good ones.

Collecting when You Can't Afford to Buy What You Want

Sometimes our tastes are bigger than our budgets. It can be a frustrating feeling, as I learned from Laura, a hard-working young dress buyer I know in New York. Laura, who has a great sense of design, admires Baccarat paperweights to the point where she craves them. She told me their gleam and purity all but break her heart. So does the fact that on her salary, she is unable to indulge her desire. When I realized how strong her need was, I suggested that she go into the Baccarat store on East 57th Street and explain her position. The person Laura spoke with there gave her as much technical information as he could, and suggested a book that would provide additional background. Laura got the book from the public library—you will notice that she still hadn't spent a penny for her schooling—and picked up facts that went far beyond what she imagined she would learn—how to authenticate a Baccarat piece by the "s" on its bottom side, what the "s" stands for, who Monsieur Baccarat was, his patrons, his lifestyle, his influence on other decorative arts. One snippet led to another and Laura found she was having all the pleasures of collecting, short of spending money and covering her tabletops with paperweights.

Laura has developed an area of expertise, drenched herself in the atmosphere of nineteenth-century France, and had a wonderful time feeling her enthusiasms grow. She says that now, whenever she browses for paperweights in curio shops, flea markets, auctions, or elsewhere, she feels as if she is holding history in the palm of her hand. Moreover, it has been just a short skip for Laura to transfer her zest for Baccarat to other nineteenth-century paperweights that she can afford to own, and from there to collecting related artifacts of the era: books on the subject, French artists' posters, writing-desk articles such as inkwells and seals. What happened to Laura is what happens to almost every collector you talk to—the more you explore, the greater your curiosity and the wider your horizons become.

I don't want to give the impression that the only things worth collecting are museum-worthy examples of art and design. Whimsy and sentiment are wonderful tastes to indulge, if that is what gives you pleasure. I know somebody whose hobby is collecting rainbows, of all things, just because they are pretty. She has drawings of rainbows, postcards, photographs she has taken in her travels, and a neon-art rainbow; and most important, a focus on something that brings her personal satisfaction. Another collector I know is constantly on the lookout for anything that reminds him of the kitchen in his grandparents' Indiana farmhouse, where he spent many pleasurable hours as a child. His collection of custard cups, colanders, tea towels, recipes, and other old-fashioned kitchen equipment is interesting because some of the things are antiques he has found at barn sales, and some are modern reproductions of old things. It doesn't matter, because antiquity is not the point of his collection. His idea is simply to have things around him that he enjoys. What I like best is that he uses the cups, colanders, towels, and recipes every day, truly linking his past with the present.

Collecting Abstracts

The recipes in my friend's farm-kitchen collection comprise ones handed down in his family, some he has clipped from magazines, and some he has developed himself. I once remarked to him that they are themselves a prize collection. My comment startled him. He never had thought of them as being of special value. I pointed out to him that it is not necessary to go out and spend money in a store for something to qualify as a collectible. My friend's repertoire of recipes is as distinctive a collection as somebody else's clocks or cameos.

One of my own collections of intangibles could be called Trivia: bits of lint that cling to the blue serge of my mind. I never know when I will have an occasion to pluck out a bit of trivia and weave it into the tapestry of life. Just recently I sat next to a woman at a dinner party who, it turned out, had been acquainted with Libby Holman, the late blues singer. It happens that for years I have been toting around snippets of trivia pertaining to Libby Holman. A cousin of hers had been my mother's best friend, and I grew up listening to their stories and conjectures about the mysterious death of Ms. Holman's first husband, a member of the R. J. Reynolds tobacco family. When my dinner partner mentioned that she was a Reynolds, the two of us were off on an exchange of stories that made us sound like lead singers at the magpies' reunion.

Trivia is the marrow of life for nostalgia buffs such as I. Our brains are crammed with collections of little-noted, long-forgotten data. We can tell you who played Ashley Wilkes in *Gone with the Wind*, the words to Cole Porter's rowdy parody of "You're the Tops," the names of all five Dionne quintuplets, and Alfred E. Landon's campaign slogan. To me, trivia breathes life into the past.

Curiosity, the eagerness to learn, is one of the most necessary and valuable qualities we can nurture. Whenever someone brings up the old parlor game of "If you could tell your children only five things before you die, what would you say?" One answer I always give is, "Be curious. Ask questions. Otherwise you will go through life misinformed and uninformed, clutching at false assumptions, never seeing the colorful threads that pattern the cloth of history."

The littlest threads can make the brightest cloth, often unexpectedly. One episode that took place years ago proved it to me once and for all. While I am certainly not the world's major authority on any of my hobby interests (even on Gershwin I register about six and a half on a scale of one to ten), by accident of having a relentless curiosity I once managed to turn up some valid and important information that the real experts did not know. In 1950, when I finished Yale, I took a trip through Scandinavia, France, and Italy. In Finland, where I visited a great many museums, I kept seeing paintings that looked to me like the works of the French Impressionists. I wasn't sure what I was seeing because I was still very green, but my curiosity was piqued and I wrote the names of the artists and the dates of their paintings in my travel diary.

When I reached France and visited museums where the acknowledged Impressionists were displayed, I noticed that some of the Scandinavian "French Impressionists" predated the French artists of that school. I took my diary notes and my questions to several art historians and asked if they could explain this chronological oddity to me. They couldn't, because at that time there was no published information on the subject. So there I was, with a fascinating and unique bit of scholarship to offer and several theretofore unrecognized painters to add to the historians' roster. What my story proves is that all knowledge has not been collected. It is always possible to stumble upon new and possibly important information if you are alert and receptive.

Sometimes it takes longer to put the pieces of trivia together so they mean something. Years ago I came across a Gershwin record that had been pressed in England. At the very end of the record there was some filler music—a few bars of an entirely different melody that had been added, to fill out the space on the record. I had no idea what the tune was, and I never heard it again until ten years later. By then I had garnered enough Gershwin lore so I could identify this small chunk of trivia that had engraved itself on my memory. It was a tune called "Walking the Dog," incidental music that underscored the ship's promenade scene in the Astaire-Rogers film, *Shall We Dance.* You have to be a true trivia buff to feel as elated as I did at having made the connection.

Tangible Collections that Don't Cost a Penny

People make connections out of all sorts of personal experiences, and sometimes build collections from them. One of our young friends, Jeff, evolved a significant collection out of some early adventures, and so far it hasn't cost a cent.

An advanced shell collector on his way to becoming a marine biologist, Jeff's hobby began when he was six years old, on his first trip to California with his parents. Jeff had been a clever baby; he selected a mother and father who not only travel a great deal, they take Jeff with them whenever possible. In the mere seventeen years of his life, Jeff has had the opportunity to scour the shores of California, Mexico, Hawaii, the Caribbean, France, and much of the terrain in between. He pursues his hobby on every trip, searching for the most unusual and perfectly formed shells he can find, preferably from marine life that is peculiar to the region he is visiting. At first he regarded his trove as memorabilia, souvenirs of the places he'd been. Gradually, he began to develop an interest in the shells' formations and historical backgrounds. He talked with local historians and with experts from universities and marine museums, eager to learn what he could. Back home, he did further research at the Dallas library and our natural history museum. By now, Jeff has become quite expert on the subject of mollusks and this year the science department at the high school where he is a senior showcased his collection in an exhibit. It was an honor he won't forget.

Jeff might have chosen to collect stones on his travels. Or native flowers that he could dry-press and learn to identify. None of these acquisitions would cost him a penny, and the chances are they would fertilize themselves and grow, the way Carolyn's ferns do. Raising plants is a hobby that literally grows on you. We started years ago with one fern plant that we bought for $2, after we were inspired by the exotic sight of Mrs. Marjorie Post's vast greenhouses. That first fern became the ancestor of the two dozen or so luxuriant plants that now hang indoors and outside of the house, and it will probably keep on proliferating for years.

Since I have a special interest in conservation, I have often thought what a fine thing it would be for somebody interested in nature to collect endangered species of plants, and help prevent their extinction. I have been leaning in that direction in the catalogs by offering lithographs of the endangered flowers that Fleur Cowles painted for us.

Making Friends Through Collecting

One of the pleasures of collecting is that one interest frequently leads to another, sometimes into spheres you cannot possibly predict. My musical comedy collection qualifies for that category. It began when I was in college and a devotee of Gershwin, Rodgers, Hammerstein, Porter, Youmans, and the other great composers of the 1920s and 1930s. I have been collecting ever since, foraging shops and flea markets from here to New York and Paris for sheet music, recordings, books, and photographs of my heroes. The accumulation has grown to considerable size, and shows no sign of stopping.

The Gershwin portion of my collection is quite special. In 1969, it swelled overnight from a modest collection to an impressive archive, and has expanded in all sorts of rewarding directions. Nineteen sixty-nine was the year that I saw a classified ad in the *Saturday Review* that read, "Complete Gershwin collection for sale. Write Frank Tuit II, Northampton, Mass." As you can imagine, I couldn't get my letter off fast enough. I haunted the mailbox for Tuit's reply, and when it arrived, I tore open the envelope in a fever of expectancy. I was disappointed. His letter explained that as a lifelong collector, he had amassed a Gershwin collection that was rare in its completeness and therefore very valuable. Then Tuit named the price he was asking, and my hopes crumbled. The figure was way beyond my means. But I had an idea. I wrote back and explained that much as I admired his collection and was eager to acquire it, I was still struggling to support a young family and couldn't afford to pay the price he had named. Then I told him about the Gershwin recordings in my own collection, and suggested that perhaps we could both benefit by exchanging recordings. He was interested, and we arranged to put our recordings on tape and exchange them, one at a time. Our arrangement continues to this day, and although I have never met Frank in person, we have developed a strong relationship.

Through our letters, we know each other's families; the children's schools, jobs, and travels; my business progress, his hobbies and friends. I have seen his son through college, marriage, and fatherhood. When Sally was born Frank sent us a baby gift, and when Richard Rodgers died, he wrote me his condolences. I told him about a Gershwin record that Libby Holman had sent me before she died. He answered with trivia about the singer's life that only a student of musical comedy could know. His letters are filled with fascinating inside information about the music and musicians we are both interested in, and in fact, his letters form a part of my collection.

Other connections have been equally rewarding. Back in 1949 when I was at Yale, my date for the junior prom weekend was a pretty Washingtonian named Phena Darner. She arrived in New Haven on Friday afternoon and told me that she had another friend in town, Dickenson Eastham. He was understudying Ezio Pinza in a new show called *South Pacific*, written by my composer-hero, Richard Rodgers. What an opportunity! They were staging a dress rehearsal for the tryout that very night at the Shubert Theater. All Phena and I had to do was find a way to get in. We did. We sneaked in through the back door and stood in a wing of the Shubert for two hours while we watched fabulous scene after scene unfold. We were absolutely dazzled; it was one of the most stirring experiences of my young life. When the play was over, we crossed the street to a restaurant and next thing we knew, sitting just two tables over, there were Richard Rodgers, Mary Martin, Ezio Pinza, and Juanita Hall. I don't know where I got the nerve, at age twenty, but I was so thrilled that I walked up to Mr. Rodgers and said, "Your music is simply beautiful. I would like you to know that you and Mr. Gershwin are my favorite composers." He was very gracious; that was his nature, even on this first awkward contact.

Over the years I kept close track of Richard Rodgers's career, collecting recordings and sheet music of all his songs and seeing as many of his shows as I could. Then the web of coincidence spun wider. Some fifteen years later, Carolyn and I were living in Dallas, where I worked as a merchandise director at the Neiman-Marcus store. The Marcuses, Edward and Betty, learned that their charming friend Dorothy Rodgers had a book coming

out called *My Favorite Things* and offered to have the store introduce it to Dallas. We set up tables in the china department, covered them with the books and Neiman-Marcus merchandise,
and advertised "Dorothy Rodgers's Favorite Things." It was a
great promotional idea and of course I was hip-deep working
on it.

Richard and Dorothy Rodgers both came to Dallas for the
event, and afterward the Marcuses gave a lovely dinner party for
them, and included Carolyn and me. That was one occasion
when I certainly didn't have to wonder for a moment what to say
to famous people; from soup through dessert I reminisced about
every step in Richard Rodgers's brilliant musical career.

After dinner, Mr. Marcus asked if I would play the piano.
With an energy born of thralldom, I lit into all of my favorite
Richard Rodgers songs, including one that had been cut from
South Pacific, "Philadelphia, P.A." He was astonished. "How on
earth do you know that song?" he asked me. I told him about
that night in New Haven, when I had heard the song in tryout
performance. I said it had been in my repertoire ever since, and
then swung into another Rodgers composition that few people
remember, "Nobody's Heart Belongs to Me." He was such a
modest retiring man, he couldn't believe that anybody my age
would know his work that well. The evening turned into a musical gala, and I picked up more Rodgers lore to add to my collection. One story that Dorothy Rodgers told concerned Dick's
show *Evergreen,* which opened in London in the early thirties and
came to New York bereft of one of its best songs. The American
producers had decided that "Dancing on the Ceiling" was much
too risqué to expose to New Yorkers. No wonder the Colonies
broke off from Britain.

After that night, I stayed in touch with Dick and Dorothy
Rodgers. To illustrate how thoughtful they always were of their
friends, one night they sent a note to our hotel asking us to go to
the theater with them. Not only did they send a car for us so we
wouldn't be delayed by the theater-hour taxi shortage, they
timed the evening so we could get back to our hotel early
enough so we would be fresh for our business appointments in
the morning. You can learn a lot from the way successful, gracious people manage their lives.

That circle widened still further, a couple of years later, to include fabulous Mary Martin. This time it was a dinner party at Stanley and Billie Marcus's home. Miss Martin was the guest of honor, and we were invited because Mr. Marcus knew of my interest in *South Pacific*, the show that had been a high spot in Mary Martin's career. After dinner, when Mr. Marcus hinted to her that I knew how to play the piano, she picked up the cue and sang all of her glorious songs from that show. Then she and another guest, a woman who had been a Texas schoolmate of Mary Martin, launched into a rollicking duet of down-home Texas songs. It was another spectacular evening, one that I could never have imagined back in 1949 when I was a student at Yale, with no idea that I would ever live in Texas, much less accompany a Texan named Mary Martin on the piano.

Gifts for Collectors

I find that when you have a special interest, as I do, people frequently relate to you through it. Your collection is their reason to stay in touch. I know that friends are forever calling to tell me they have seen this or that about Rodgers or Gershwin in the paper. Or they send me clippings, photos, or pieces of sheet music they have come across and know I will enjoy. Carolyn gets calls all the time from friends who tell her they have just spotted a pair of miniature shoes in such and such a shop, and thought she would like to know about it for her collection of antique bootmakers' symbols. Often, miniature shoes are her Christmas or birthday gifts.

People always know what to give a collector. It's like the old add-a-pearl concept. Once you know someone likes pearls, come Christmas, birthdays, anniversaries, or the Fourth of July, you know that a pearl will be the right gift. The best part is, it really is the thought that counts and not the price. A gift of sheet music that costs ten cents gives me as much pleasure as another person might receive from a yacht: it is personalization that makes a gift special. Like the needlepoint pillow our friend Sally Young made for my fiftieth birthday. It must have taken her months to stitch the motto she designed especially for me: "Gershwin died on July 11 but you don't have to believe it if you don't want to." The pillow is a genuine labor of love, and I cherish it.

Whenever Carolyn or I see something that we think a collector friend would like, we buy it then and there and store it away for the right moment. We have learned that if we don't, it will be gone from the store when we want it. Or we won't be able to remember where we saw it.

There is a theory behind shopping for gifts, clothing, and nearly everything else except groceries—buy what you like when you see it and never shop for anything specific. I think by and large it is true. I have never been able to find the exact ivory fan I have in mind for my friend Paul's collection of Japanese artifacts, but several times I have come across other Japanese objects for him by sheer chance. If I go to a store bent on buying a round-collared, long-sleeved yellow blouse for one of the girls or a pair of blue polka-dot pajamas for myself, I am sure to come away empty-handed. It is only when my mind is open to anything appealing that I am a successful shopper.

Too Much of a Good Thing

Being a known collector can backfire. Pauline Trigère, the fashion designer, named her home in Connecticut *La Tortue*, the turtle, which is a symbol of good luck. It is also a signal: everybody who visits Pauline brings a turtle for her collection. She has over 900 turtles now, and cannot stop people from bringing her more. The house is filled with turtle paintings, plates, chopsticks, hangings, scarves, stone trivets, iron trivets, cheese graters, chocolate turtles, and turtles in myriads of other forms. She once said to me, "It is a curse. I would rather have diamonds, but nobody believes me."

A writer friend of ours, Janet, is one of those creative people who always has to march to a different drum. When she first set up housekeeping, she began to collect coffee cups because, as she told everybody, she can't bear matching sets of anything. "It is monotonous to see everybody take their after-dinner coffee from identical cups." That remark made it easy for all her friends. For years, every time a hostess or birthday gift was in order, we presented Janet with a new cup and saucer for her collection. Last year she called a halt. Her china cupboard and every other available storage space was filled to the brim, and there seemed no way to stem the flow. She still thought the cups and saucers were beautiful and her friends generous and thoughtful, but enough was enough. Over lunch one day, Janet asked if I could help. She said, "I like beautiful things, but I like to *use* what I have. Roger, how can I convince people that I do not want any more cups and saucers?"

I told Janet, first of all, that I admired her wanting to use what she had. "That is real style," I said. "I know people who collect china and silver they never use, old books they never read, ashtrays and napkin rings that just sit lifeless in a glass case. It is so much more interesting when you make a collection a part of your life, instead of using it as a showcase for your economic perspicacity."

I told her about how we had handled the same problem with Carolyn's miniature shoes. A year ago we said, "Enough," packed them away in a carton, and hid them from ourselves. We forgot all about the collection until recently, when we happened to come across the box and opened it up. It was like rediscovering an old friend. We put some of the shoes back on the side table where they had been, and found a new home for others in our den. The new context gives them a fresh look, and we are enjoying Carolyn's curios all over again.

"Another thing you can do, Janet, if you are convinced that you never want to look at that china again and are short on storage space, is to start giving your cups and saucers away as special, treasured gifts to special, treasured friends. Whether your collection is valuable or an assemblage of inexpensive mementos makes no difference. What you are giving is something that has a great deal of personal meaning, that is sentimental as well as distinctively yours. It's a very caring kind of gift. Incidentally, if you happen to know somebody who has a particular interest in what you have collected and don't want any more, you could make a very grand personal gesture if you give them your entire collection. I guarantee, they will never forget your generosity or style."

Expanding on Themes

In the end, Janet took up a third alternative that I suggested. She expanded on her languishing interest in cups and saucers and began to collect unusual pieces of Wedgwood. You could do that with any collection you have tired of, or that your taste has outgrown. For instance, posters can lead to prints and prints can lead to original art. A hoard of Colonial candlesticks could become candlesticks of another era, candlesticks made only of china or brass, or a collection of candlesticks and other housewares of Colonial days. You might move on from collecting dollhouse furniture to handmade miniature costumes, or perhaps certain kinds of dolls.

In Janet's case, her cue came from one of her favorite cups and saucers, a contemporary Wedgwood design. She loved its shape and colors, and was curious about what made Wedgwood outstanding. Once her interest was aroused, it was easy for Janet to acquire information. Even if a welter of publications had not been readily available at the local china store and library, Janet could have dug up the information she wanted by getting in touch with the U.S. office of Wedgwood in New York, or headquarters in Britain. When she learned that Josiah Wedgwood was a technical virtuoso of the mid-1700s who had reached back into early Greek and Roman design for his ceramic creations, she understood immediately why his work has endured. It is classic art, impeccably executed: the top of the line in terms of culture and civilization.

Janet realized that many of the pieces are too rare for her financial reach. Aside from the legendary jasperware that is still produced in fairly large quantities, Wedgwood prizes have not been duplicated in great numbers. The ivory-colored Queen's Ware, so called because Wedgwood was the official potter to Queen Charlotte when he developed that line of earthenware, and the striking pieces fashioned of black basalt and marblelike material, are the province of museums and wealthy private collectors. But the information she gleaned gave her an idea that would satisfy her new found appetite: she could make a project of hunting down a few of Wedgwood's old ceramic designs, mix them with the later works, and create for herself a sort of historical encyclopedia. Mixing the new with the old would be the theme of her new collection. She would look for vases, teapots, plaques—anything but more cups and saucers—and fulfill her new sense of the continuity of history.

It is safe to conjecture that Janet's hobby will progress to other ceramics. She may branch out into Royal Worcester and have fun turning up historical oddities such as the pattern called Blind Earl, an early sort of ceramic braille that was invented for a blind earl so he could feel the raised design. She may decide to amass landmarks of her cultural heritage, as Austrian-born Estée Lauder has done through her collection of Gustav Klimpt, Egon Schele, and other Viennese artists. Mrs. Lauder's collection is very valuable in terms of money, but it is the aspect of historical continuum that I find most interesting.

Collecting for Love or for Money

You hear a lot of hyperbole about collection as an investment. Some of it is true, but to us inveterate collectors for whom desire is everything and monetary value is a minor point, the prime reason to acquire anything is because you like it. If the value of an article happens to increase, and you happen to want to sell it at that time, that is a bonus. In my opinion, the possibility of financial profit is not what motivates a true collector.

You can sort collectors into three categories:

1. The kind who buys a rare old Dorothy Doughty bird for $1,000, puts it away in the closet or vault, and five years later sells it for $2,000.

2. The person who buys the same Doughty bird, displays it in his or her home because its beauty gives pleasure, and then five years later sells it at a $1,000 profit.

3. The Doughty bird-lover who buys, enjoys, and keeps his or her treasure even when the price soars, because love of its beauty is more important to him or her than cashing in on an escalated market.

The truth is, most of us are a combination of the second and third types. We buy for personal pleasure, but in the backs of our minds is the titillating notion that someday this object will be worth a lot of money. Increased value is part of the allure of collecting and it is fine, as long as you don't get carried away and let the idea distort your collection. It is a lot more exhilarating to feel free to find something you like—maybe a silly-looking pig at a crafts show—and buy it just because you like it. I think people do themselves a disservice who say, "That pig is cute but I wouldn't touch it. The craftsman is unknown and will never amount to anything; I'll never make a dime on the pig."

Another psychological tug that gets to us fallible humans is being able to say, "Boy, did I get a terrific bargain! The dealer didn't even know the painting was a genuine Old Master. I practically stole it from him." I must confess that I have found myself in that position, although I am not especially proud of it. One time I was looking around in an antique shop on the Left Bank in Paris when I saw, way in the back, a dusty old lithograph that looked to me like a Léger. I asked the dealer about it and he said, yes, he thought it might be a Léger but he didn't really know. The lithograph was quite reasonably priced and I thought, "I like the work, so I'll buy it. If it turns out to be something wonderful, I'll have made a good deal. If it doesn't, I will still have a picture that I like." I took the lithograph back to Dallas and sent it to a restorer I know there. He cleaned it up and, amazingly, there was the signature, Fernand Léger, bright and clear. Now when I show my lithograph to people, I have a whole story to tell. Plus the fact that I have had my pleasure both ways.

Just the same, I am not in favor of investment collecting unless you are a professional. It is something that requires considerable skill and canniness. You need an encyclopedic knowledge if you are going into the business of speculating on the future value of art, jewelry, Oriental rugs, gold coins, French wines, or first editions. It's the same as speculating on the stock market. If speculating is your incentive, be sure you know what you are doing. I have seen too many people go into collecting because they were seduced by visions of sugarplums only to wind up with a fistful of raisins. You have to realize that when somebody tells you, "In two years this stamp/clock/cameo is going to be worth fifty times what you pay for it today," all that means is that you might have to pay fifty times more to buy the item two years from now. Whether you could sell it at that price depends on how shrewdly you could negotiate with the right buyer at the right time. And if the only buyer you can find is a dealer, you will probably only get half of what he could sell it for to another individual. What is more, you run the risk of discovering that your precious object is neither precious nor rare after all.

"Limited Editions"

Supply and demand is what makes the world go round: the rarer the supply the greater the demand. That is why you see those huge auction prices for certain objects that are in limited supply. And it is why you see ads aimed at collectors of limited edition plates, coins, prints, and so on. Some of the advertised items really are limited, and some are produced in the hundreds of thousands. The key is to be able to tell the real turtle soup from the mock.

First of all, a limited edition is always marked: something like 50/200, which means that this is the 50th out of a total production of 200. Or it will say "A.P.," meaning artist's proof. Occasionally you will find an item that is produced in limited quantity but is not marked. For authenticity, you should request a certificate from the seller, which puts him or her on the line. A genuine limited edition is also signed by the artist, further documentation that he or she has personally supervised and approved this reproduction of the original. People do not always understand that this is important. I have had letters from customers who see the signed lithographs by Fleur Cowles that we advertise in our catalogs at $175 apiece. They say, in effect, you have a nerve, charging that much for something that is just run off like a magazine. The explanation is that although the lithographed pieces do utilize the same basic technology as a magazine, they are not machine-produced in massive quantities. In fact, Mrs. Cowles allows only 150 each of her paintings to be reproduced, and she supervises and signs each one as it is pulled. That is what makes her limited editions special. The same holds true for other kinds of reproductions: prints, serigraphs, photographs, sculptures, books, clocks, coins, glassware, china, and so on.

There is a cloudy area about what quantity constitutes "limited." For example, in our own catalogs we have offered plates by Marc Chagall, Andrew Wyeth, and other fine artists. Obviously, enough plates have been produced so we can afford to offer them to our 30,000 customers without having to tell 29,998 people, "Sorry, we're all out." They are promotable collectibles, to be sure, limited only to a certain extent. Your reason for buying them should be purely because you like them, and not because you think they are going to increase in value—although sometimes they do. For instance, the Wyeth plate we sold in 1971 for $50 is now advertised elsewhere at $200. Not that this means anybody is paying $200 for it. Until money actually changes hands, the figure is fantasy and hope.

Sometimes you see ads for an entire "limited collection" of something that is not a "collection," in the sense that somebody has spent years scouring the earth for rare antiquities. An example would be the special edition of five Battersea boxes that Cartier and other fine stores have offered. Another would be the series of plates that portray endangered species of animals, with the proceeds from sales designated for the benefit of the World Wildlife Fund. These articles are undeniably expensive; the reason is that only a small, finite number of sets were made and then they threw away the mold, so to speak. That is all there will ever be. A hundred years from now, whoever owns the boxes or plates will know that only 150 sets ever existed in the entire world. Sheer rarity will enhance their emotional as well as their monetary value.

Promotable collectibles that are turned out in vast quantities are controversial, even among dedicated collectors. In my opinion, the key to whether they are desirable is whether or not they have classic beauty and are well made. That is the difference between junk or banality, and something of enduring excellence. The Wyeth and Chagall plates that I mentioned would bear the hallmarks of quality whether they were limited to small editions or not. It is when mediocre items produced in the thousands are fobbed off as "limited edition" and "collectors' items" that I worry. You have to educate your taste so you can apply the basic criterion: aesthetic value. Rarity comes next. The possibility of increased monetary value does not enter into the picture except incidentally. That does not mean that purity and commercialism cannot mix. Boehm birds, animals, and flowers, combine both and do it well. The Edward Marshall Boehm factories annually spew out $10 million worth of porcelain birds, beasts, and flowers that are beautifully crafted and extensively promoted. Even though Boehm limited editions are not really very limited, the distinctive quality of the porcelain statues makes them desirable.

Every time I see a Boehm bird I think of the wonderful story Tish Baldrige told me. A few years ago she went over to Rome with Helen Boehm, who had an audience with the Pope. Mrs. Boehm's plan was to use the occasion to present the Vatican with the large Boehm bird that President Nixon had taken on his first trip to China. The piece was valuable, intrinsically and historically, and part of its charm was the turtle that sat at the base of the composition—the turtle being a symbol of good luck. The night before the audience with His Holiness, Mrs. Boehm saw to it that the bird was securely locked up in a well-guarded apartment at the Vatican, as protection against possible theft. The next morning, when she took the piece from its cache, she was horrified to see that the turtle was missing. Some vandal had managed to penetrate what has to be the most secure fortress in the entire world, and sawed off the turtle so cleanly that Mrs. Boehm's only clue to the theft was her familiarity with the statue. When she made the presentation, every Italian eye focused on the planed-off empty space, looking for the good luck turtle they expected to see. To this day, the puzzle of the Vatican is: Who is the scoundrel who stole the Pope's turtle?

The Value of Provenance

Like the Boehm piece that traveled with Nixon on his historic trip to China, some collectibles increase in value when they have an important past: what the connoisseurs call *provenance*. The word refers to the derivation or heritage of an article, and its implications are in great measure psychological. Provenance is what lures tourists to overpriced beds placarded *George Washington Slept Here*. It is what imparts cachet to Clark Gable's socks, Grover Cleveland's fountain pen, and otherwise pedestrian articles. I admit that I have been tempted by provenance, and once came very close to bidding on a cigarette box whose claim to fame was that it had graced Cole Porter's coffee table. I must have felt that some of Porter's luster would rub off on me through the cigarette box. But then I realized what an expensive massage that would be. I thought, "This is silly, trying to burnish my ego by paying a premium for a sliver of nostalgia. I might as well buy an autograph that somebody else has collected, or one of those framed glossies they churn out signed, 'Best of luck from Roy Rogers.' "

On the other hand, past ownership has its uses. It is a way to establish authenticity and to verify the age of an object. You know that if the seller can give you legitimate guaranteed documentation—a letter, bill of sale, photograph, or reference in a reliable source book—that you are buying something of certifiable age and pedigree. I have to admit, an antique bed that once belonged to Marie Antoinette seems somehow more antique than a bed that nobody famous slept on.

Antiques

Antiquity is itself a collector's benchmark, providing you know what a genuine antique is. Most of us do not. "Antique" is one of those words that has developed a sliding meaning. The factual background is this: In the past, people were permitted to pass an article through United States customs without paying duty if they could show that it dated from 1830 or earlier; however, as time crept past the 1930 mark, the old ruling became burdensome. It meant that a great many imports that were well over 100 years old failed to qualify as official antiques and were taxed unduly. The 1830 rule had outlived itself, dealers complained. And they campaigned. They pointed out to Congress that the 1830—or before—stricture no longer made sense and was hindering the import of fine art to this country. They won their point. In the early 1970s a new regulation was created that would automatically keep up with the times: anything that is 100 years or more old is a certifiable antique and is not subject to import duty. The definition is easy to deal with and is now used as a general yardstick for everything, imported or not.

How do you know if something really is 100 years or more

old, and an authentic antique? One way is to get a certificate of authenticity or a written statement from the dealer who sells you the antique. Another is to check the hallmark on the object, a marking that signifies the date of manufacture. Some dates are in code, such as those on the Wedgwood china my mother owns, where the letters stand for "1926." Sometimes a hallmark reveals age because that particular marking was used only at a certain period of time, or by a certain craftsman whose productive years you can trace. Not that you have to become a secret decoder. There are several books on the market that list all of the known hallmarks. You just look up the hallmark on the article you are buying, and cross-check it against the listing. Or ask the dealer to show you his or her book of hallmarks.

Collecting Tomorrow's Antiques

The 100-year antiques rule enhances the value of old objects from another point of view. In just a few years an 1895 Victorian soap dish or a Rutherford B. Hayes campaign poster will become officially antique, and therefore may be worth more if you should want to sell it. Perhaps that is one reason why some people squirrel away artifacts of the day—stacks of *TV Guide* magazines, political campaign buttons, subway tokens, record album covers, programs from the World Series games, and other passing fancies of everyday life. They may be right. It could be that Lizzie's Snoopy collection and Sally's Barbie-dolls will become collectors' treasures fifty years from now, when they are no longer produced in mass quantity. So might the film cassettes I have begun to acquire for family entertainment. They represent the new technology today, but by the time we are deep into the twenty-first century, the cassettes will be just quaint enough to appeal to a collector's heart.

Occasionally the value of an antique decreases, due to current economics. Silver, for example. Whereas old silver pieces used to cost more than new because they were scarcer, when the per-ounce price of silver catapulted in 1979 and 1980, and the costs of labor and distribution soared as well, the situation was reversed. It became so costly to produce anything made of silver that a simple machine-made teaspoon cost more than most people were willing to spend. For that reason, silver that had been around awhile often represented a better value.

In addition to altering the trends in collecting, the economics of silver wreaked certain irreversible havoc. At the turn of the decade, when the price of silver bullion hit the Milky Way, people became crazed and began to melt down whatever silver they could get their hands on in return for immediate cash. The chairman of Towle Silver, Pat Mulligan, told me how appalled he was to see the hordes rushing into his factory, heirloom silver in hand, demanding that it be reduced to cash-by-the-blob. He says he had to step in personally one morning when a woman came into the plant carrying a perfectly magnificent 1930s tea set by Tiffany.

Pat, of course, has no need to buy more silver for himself: being in the business, he owns a mountain of it. But he simply could not let that fabulous Tiffany tea set be melted down to a puddle. So he made out a check to the woman and took the tea service home. He told me he felt like a conservationist who had saved one of the endangered species of civilization.

Collecting at Auctions

Auctions are wonderful resources for collectors. Besides offering antique and contemporary articles of special value that you could not find in an ordinary store, they are an ideal place to get a sense of the costs and availability of whatever it is you collect. Auction rooms are the real marketplace, where buy-and-sell activities provide instant information as to the prices certain items are selling for, what items are currently most sought after, and which ones are not in vogue this season.

If you know enough about your field of interest to be able to spot a find, you can sometimes pick up a tremendous bargain at auction, especially if you happen to show up on a day when competitive bidders stay home. That is how I acquired the handsome Jensen compote that Carolyn likes to heap with fresh fruits or candy and, at Christmas, with miniature Santa-red ornaments. Because nobody bid against me the day I was at the sale, I was able to buy the choice Jensen silver at the lowest price the auctioneer would accept. It was an eighth of the price I would have had to pay if I had found the compote in a store.

Two other factors were in my favor. One: I had made it my business to attend the auction preview three days earlier, a procedure I recommend whenever it is possible. At a preview you can decide which of the items you are interested in and inspect them at leisure for their perfection, the details of workmanship, and hallmarks that identify their origin or historical significance. Second: I made sure that before the sale I gleaned as much information as I could about what the compote's fair price should be. In this instance, I was ahead of the game. I once had served as chairman of the Georg Jensen company in the United States and knew that the piece was a rare prize and the estimate was on target. Ordinarily, I would follow other avenues of research.

• Look up the selling price of a similar item in a recent auction sale catalog.

• Look through library books on the subject to see if the item's design is authentic and to learn something about its approximate age. For example, if I were interested in a Picasso painting that was dominated by blue, I could learn from an art book that Picasso's blue period was the 1920s.

• Study auction catalogs. They are filled with all sorts of information and you can buy them for a few dollars in advance of almost every large auction. Auction catalogs list the items' previous owners, the preview exhibit dates, the conditions and terms of sale, and the anticipated price range of the final hammer sale. Usually the bottom and top estimated sale prices are listed: "Item #170: $1,000—$2,000," but you have to realize that the figures are no more than a guide. The actual sale price may turn out to be far lower or higher than what was published, depending on how tepid or heated the bidding becomes.

In the case of the Jensen compote, the bidding was not even tepid; it was nonexistent aside from my own. I am still thunderstruck by the bargain I walked off with. I happened to be in the right auction place at the right time, which is often a matter of luck. However, you don't have to trust entirely to luck. I have learned to try to attend London auctions in February, when there are few tourists to bid against and the natives are apt to stay home huddled by the fire. I find that January is a good time to shop Tokyo: the Japanese pay their taxes then, and are reluctant to spend money on nonessentials.

Good timing is just one of the secrets of smart shopping. Another of the ways to find bargains is to keep an eye on the antiques and specialty shops that carry things you like. Sometimes, when business is off, you can buy things at remarkably low prices because the owner needs cash, or sometimes the dealer is about to relocate and wants to sell out fast so he won't have to move all his inventory.

It also helps if you happen to know somebody who is an astute auction follower. Gerald Godfrey, the celebrated Hong Kong antiques dealer, is wonderful about keeping his friends and customers in mind when he shops. Just last winter I received a Telex from him offering me a fine, early-eighteenth century Afghanistan rug that he thought I would like. He noted that the rug was nicely proportioned for our new living room, and that it was ornamented with H's, besides. Gerald said he had bought it at auction well below the reserve, or floor price, set by the seller, and could sell it to me for an alluringly low figure. Although I passed up the offer, I appreciate Gerald's thoughtfulness. In spite of his kaleidoscopic life, perpetual travel, and myriad interests, he always takes the trouble to stay in touch, even though I am halfway around the world.

You don't need a Gerald Godfrey in your life to be a long-distance auction shopper. You can place bids by remote control. What you do is keep an eye on the auction ads in newspapers and magazines, and when you see a grouping you think might interest you, purchase the catalog by mail and then follow up on the details. Here's how it works. Sotheby Parke Bernet advertised an auction to be held in New York at a time when I could not be there. The ad listed the categories of items that would be put up for sale, and one fairly leaped off the page: "Composers' original manuscripts." I sent for the catalog, riffled through it, and screeched to a halt at Item #648. 'Porgy and Bess,' original manuscript notated by George Gershwin. Estimated: $1,000—$1,500." My collector's compulsion boiled to a froth: I simply had to have Item #648, notwithstanding the fact that I already owned a hand-noted Gershwin score from the same show. At least that previous purchase told me what a Gershwin score is worth, and that the auctioneer's estimate was fair. I mailed in my bid, which the auctioneer treated the same as bids made in person on the day of the auction, and waited for the results. I lost out. The music went for double the high estimate and I learned later on, from a friend who had been present, why the figure had zoomed. Four collectors had fallen to bidding against one another, and became so frenzied in their competition for the manuscript that they lost track of its real value. You have to watch for auction fever. It is a contagious disease that can reach absurd heights when two or more impassioned collectors begin to infect one another. The antidote is to use mind over money. Before the bidding begins, set a firm ceiling on how much you will spend. Cling to the thought. When the bidding becomes heated, remain cool. Stop and think. Is what you are bidding on really worth $5,000, or are you just paying an inflated sum for the sport of competing?

Storage and Display

Some things you add to your collection become an active part of your life—the English teacups and silver napkin rings you use every day, the period furniture with which you furnish your home. Other trophies, such as celluloid dolls, antique valentines, stamps, coins, or quilts, are for passive enjoyment—things to surround yourself with and look at. The question is, how to store or display your collection so it gives you the most pleasure and does not make your home a museum.

One display problem most of us face is that it is the nature of collections to keep growing, and it is the nature of modern living space to keep diminishing. However, as time has proven, necessity is the mother of invention and workable solutions can almost always be found. Sometimes the answers are in inventions that you see in your travels—imaginative store displays, shipboard storage, ideas in other people's homes that you can adapt for your own use. The rest of the time, you have to more or less invent the wheel for yourself.

I have found that the easiest, and frequently the most attractive way to conquer the space problem is to regard every surface as a possible storehouse for a collection. For example, the rear wall of our walk-in pantry closet blossoms from ceiling to base-board with dozens of baskets that are in temporary storage. We lined the wall with pegboard and hung the baskets from peg-board hooks. You could just as readily use picture hooks on a bare wall—those sleek-shaped, self-adhesive plastic hooks you find in hardware and novelty stores, or a rubberized plastic grid with S-shaped hooks on the horizontal bars.

You don't need closets to store things. Baskets and other col-lector's items are striking additions to otherwise kitcheny-look-ing walls, bathroom walls, or walls in any room where your col-lection would fit in ornamentally. I know a woman who collects hats. They are her trademark. Nobody has ever seen her without one, and all of her friends know where they can borrow a hat when they need one. Storing a hat collection could drive you out of closet space in an instant unless you had a flair for the non-traditional, as my friend the hat lady does. She wallpapered the long narrow entry hall of her apartment with hats, and the effect is stunning. The hats look wonderful, they are accessible, and they haven't robbed her of an iota of space that she needs.

I find that the best approach to solving many problems is to think fresh, think practical, think aesthetic. For instance, I like to keep some of my wooden handcrafts at home and some in the office, where I can see them during the day. You might think that finding display space in an office would be a problem, but it was simpler than I expected. Once I determined that "where there's a wall there's a way," all it took was a fresh look at space. What I did was move the conference table and chairs a foot or so toward the center of the room, which freed up one wall. Then I did the same with the furniture that hugged an adjacent wall. Next I had a series of metal strips mounted on the two walls, hung adjust-able shelves on the strips, and had the whole apparatus spray-painted white to blend in with the walls. Then I simply popped my trinkets and artifacts onto the shelves, and my problem was solved. The wall space in between the shelves gets used, too, for hanging up masks, pictures, and other whatnots. What I like is that the office is still functional, but it has acquired a personal distinction. And of course it is all very pleasing to my collector's eye.

Housing the handcrafts at home was a little more difficult. The place they fit best is in the poolhouse, but that structure has only one solid wall and it is made of brick. The office shelves idea would be a nuisance to implement here, and it would spoil the brick wall effect, besides. The problem percolated in the back of my mind for a week or two, then I remembered a trick I had seen at a museum. I tried it, and it worked.

First I played around with arrangements, laying out designs the way you do when you hang a group of pictures. The arrangement I settled on began with a random platoon of eight small shelves in one area. I added a four-step procession of medium-size shelves to the platoon, placed a larger shelf at the base to give a feeling of support, and then added a couple of larger shelves to one side for visual balance.

Next I cut a length of inch-thick wood into various shelf sizes, to accommodate the various handcrafts. I drilled a hole in each shelf on the edge that was to go against the wall. Then I drilled a matching hole in the mortar between the bricks where the shelf was to go. Finally, I connected the two holes with a metal rod and presto, there were my shelves. I painted them white, so they would blend in with the white brick wall and be unobtrusive holders for my display.

I have seen similar wall displays that use clear acrylic boxes instead of shelves. The bottoms of the boxes are fastened to the wall with toggle bolts, and the lidded tops of the boxes face the room. When you want to change a display, you just have to lift the lid or remove it.

If you want to hang something heavier than small shelves or acrylic boxes on a brick wall, a large picture perhaps, you can adapt the same basic technique. Take a strip of wood the same width as your picture frame and nail solidly into the mortar between bricks. Then drive a pair of picture hooks into the wooden strip, and hang the picture. Keep it from swinging in at the bottom by nailing a matching piece of wood under it there. It's simple to hang something heavy once you know the trick.

Ornamental baskets are a graceful way out of the collecting space pinch. Carolyn uses them as way stations for things we collect for which we haven't yet found a permanent place. One basket might hold family photographs, another will be piled with theater playbills, and a third with auction catalogs. The photos and playbills can stay in the baskets until we store or discard them; in the meantime, they add a decorative touch to the room. I keep about ten ornamental baskets in the poolhouse, which is where most of my collections are housed. The baskets are supposed to be presorting bins, but I find the assortments so attractive I often leave the baskets as is until they overflow, or I have spare time for sorting, or conscience prods me to clean up the poolhouse.

Placing collections in attractive baskets, boxes, and trays has a subtle effect, as well as practical. It sets your belongings apart and makes a statement about their specialness. A case in point—when we had an after-prom party for Regen and fifty of her guests, we were concerned about Carolyn's miniature shoe collection. The miniatures stood on the tabletop in the living room, and we were afraid that in the general arrangement, they might be knocked over and damaged. So we scooped them together and set them on a lacquered tray. It was like framing a picture. The setting immediately said, "This is a special collection," and warned the partygoers to treat the shoes with care. It was a simple solution, and as a matter of fact, Carolyn's shoe collection looked so attractive in its new arrangement that we have kept it displayed on the tray ever since.

You can often solve a display problem simply by rearranging what you have. For example, if you are laden with photographs or miniatures, as we are, try grouping a cluster of them together on a single tabletop, on a tray, or in a basket. The effect is amazing. Instantly, you achieve a visual cohesion that gives unity to all the parts. In effect, you create a single element out of many, and you have done nothing more than move things around. Another approach is to think in terms of function. This comes almost automatically when you are dealing with items such as books or phonograph records. You can imagine what a shambles my music collection would be if we hadn't invented a functional way to house it. The solution was to have a carpenter come in and build a series of storage cabinets along the wall at one end of the living room.

If you don't want built-ins, because you are in a rented place or because you don't want the expense of carpentry, you can use standing, waist-high, portable modular cabinet units instead.

Made of plastic or plywood, the units are clean-lined, good looking, and endlessly useful in every room of the house. A further advantage is that they can go with you when you move. You can achieve a built-in look if you line them up side by side and then lay a length of wood, painted the same color as the cabinets, along the waist-high top. That is what we did with our record cabinets, and the top not only unifies them, we find that we use it as a display for ornamental objects, as a serving table for trays of drinks and snacks, and as a catchall for keys, mail, and packages.

Each of the cabinets contains roll-out shelves and drawers. In my opinion, roll-outs are a life-saver in the kitchen, dining room, bathroom, or bedroom. Each of my music cabinet sections is earmarked for a particular set of items. Two drawers contain tapes and another is filled with sheet music. My songbooks occupy several of the shelves, and our stereo components rest on another. Several sections of drawers are filled with my records, filed in alphabetical order. The musical comedy scores are filed by the show titles. *Anything Goes, Bye Bye Birdie, Can Can,* and so on. All the other records are alphabetized according to the artist's name—the Ames Brothers, Harry Belafonte, Chris Connors. However, I am not hung up on the alphabet. I found that to make the arrangement truly practical, it has to be flexible. So I have separated the records that I play most often and store them on the top shelf. That way, I don't have to crouch down or bend over every time I want to hear Teddy Wilson, which happens to be nearly every night. I figure that just because one of my favorite pianist's name is near the end of the alphabet, there is no reason I can't have his music at my fingertips.

Some people like to categorize their record collections by the type of music, rather than by the artist—rock 'n' roll, the classics, Broadway shows, male vocalists, female vocalists. Other people arrange their records by the composer, the performer, or according to when the work was produced: Bach and Beethoven in their sections, Mozart in his period, all the way up through Gershwin in the 1920s and others through the 1980s. The best system for you is the one that meets your needs.

Books are very similar to records in the way you use and store them. Their bindings are far more decorative, however, and open bookcases are the obvious, simple, and effective place to keep them. How you sort them out relates to how you use them. We like to keep ours by subject matter—art, history, travel, biography, fiction. We subdivide within those subjects a bit, first of all by author, and second by usage. For some subjects we use a couple of separate shelf areas, sometimes in the same room, sometimes in the upstairs den or bedroom.

We have a neighbor, Jerrie, whose library system sprang from rather special needs. She is an immoderate culinary adventuress, unrestrained in her avarice for more and more cookbooks. It's a race between the intensity of her interest and the extent of her cookbook collection. You can imagine what a stew Jerrie would be in if she hadn't created a method for keeping her culinary library in usable, accessible order. What she has done makes good sense. Her books are grouped four ways.

1. By nationality: German, French, Chinese, American. And by regions within those nations: New England, Southwestern, and Southern Cuisine: Hunan, Canton, and Szechuan cookery.

2. By special subject: vegetables, seafood, desserts, barbecue, herbs, history.

3. By scope: books that defy categorizing are lumped together in what Jerrie calls her Everything section. She says that at least that way she is able to locate compendiums that contain a pinch of this and that but have no identifiable focus. "When I can't name the subject, I just look under Everything. It's not as confusing as it sounds, because all the Everything authors are stored alphabetically."

Jerrie's fourth cookbook section is the heart of her working kitchen. She explains, "When you get down to it, there are just seven books that I use all the time—two each by Craig Claiborne and James Beard, one by Elizabeth David, the latest Julia Child, and the notebook of recipes I have collected through the years."

Protecting Your Collection

There is a certain peril connected with collecting earthly possessions. If fire, flood, robbers, or hoodlums should come along you stand a chance of losing the treasures you have devoted so much time, care, and money collecting. People often ask me what they should do about insuring their collections against loss.

I tell them the answer depends strictly on the market value of their belongings. You would have to pay an exorbitant premium to insure articles whose value is sentimental. That is a hard truth, but it is a fact. However, there is an alternative way to protect the treasures you cannot replace—make copies. I have had all of our home movies converted to tape, so if anything happens to the originals, we will still have access to the Horchow family album. Our photo albums are something else that Carolyn and I care a lot about and could never replace. To make sure they are preserved, I am having copies made of the pictures, and for double insurance, I plan to store the copies in my office so they will be safe from whatever may damage the originals at home.

That reminds me of a story Kenneth Jay Lane used to tell on himself. He says he might never have gotten into the jewelry business at all if he weren't a good copyist and then been acquainted with some women who were afraid to wear their fine jewelry all the time. They asked him to make copies so they could leave their originals in the vault on occasion, and his craftsmanship was so exquisite that word got around, and soon more and more women began to ask him for copies. Gradually, Kenneth moved into producing his own creative designs, his clientele added KJL creations to their wardrobes, and in a few years his name became a national synonym for superior costume jewelry.

As for insuring intrinsically valuable articles, my recommendation is that you speak with your insurance representative and cover your cherished possessions for their highest retail value. Retail, not wholesale, because that is what you would have to pay for replacements. You will have to be able to prove the value of the items in order to collect on your insurance, so you should have photographs that show your inventory and a bill of sale or a recent appraisal in your files. If your things have considerable monetary value, it would be worth your while to pay a professional appraiser to give you a statement. If you don't know whom to call, I suggest that you get in touch with the Appraiser's Association of America, 60 East 42nd Street, New York 10017; or the American Society of Appraisers, Dulles International Airport, Box 17265, Washington, D.C. 20041. They will help you locate a qualified appraiser in your area.

Considering the way market prices seesaw, you should keep your insurance policy updated. A once-a-year reevaluation is usually sufficient. If you find that is too much bother, I suggest that you include a rider in your policy that automatically increases your coverage by ten percent each year. This will probably cover you adequately, if not munificently, if disaster should strike.

Now I must tell you about a collection that cannot be insured, has nothing to do with conservation or beauty, and in fact qualifies for none of the things that fascinate collectors. It is Carolyn Horchow's army of Chianti bottles. These bottles are not gorgeous, distinctive, rare, or even unusual. They are not amusing and they have neither sentimental nor monetary value. What they are is heavy. I personally have moved cartons of Carolyn's bottles several times in the past twenty years, from the basement of our first apartment to the attic of our fifth and present house. When I finally asked why she saved Chianti bottles, Carolyn sketched a little feather in the air and smiled, "Because you never know. What if we had a large spaghetti party sometime and needed a whole lot of candleholders?" I didn't say a word.

❦ ❦ ❦

5
WORKING
IN STYLE

Once in awhile when the sun streams into my office and dances over the bright colors of my easy chair and the small rug it sits on, or highlights the handcrafts and graphics I have brought in from home, I think back to the first private office I ever had. It was a 5-by-9-foot cubicle in the basement of Foley's Department Store in Houston: a spare little warren, but all mine. If I am still able to describe it in detail, it is not because I have a remarkable memory, but because the space was so tiny there were very few items to remember. There was no rug or easy chair, and no window for the sun to stream through. My cubicle was dominated by a steel desk entombed in coats of battleship gray enamel, a wooden chair of *Tobacco Road* vintage with a seat that listed rakishly to port, and a metal file cabinet, seriously scarred. The walls, of no definable color, were not so much painted as they were laden. Decades of nicotine, jagged bits of ripped-off Scotch tape, and assorted varieties of subterranean grime surrounded me. The cement ceiling was invisible most of the time; I think it was there chiefly to support the department-store light fixture that aimed its formidable glare at the uppermost reach of the walls, then hovered with a sort of ashen listlessness over the company-issue pencils and papers on my desk. This office was all business and no mistake, but for one cheerful exception: a Matisse postcard that I had taped onto the side of my To Do box. The card bore a reproduction of the artist's jubilant vision of gem-colored flowers bobbing against a vivid blue sky. It was my way of escaping the anonymity of my cell. The picture helped me recall the special afternoon in a museum when I had first seen the original. It was the one thing in that room that said anything about me, and it made me feel "at home" the way my easy chair, Oriental rug, and handcrafts do today.

Office Symbols of the Past

They used to say that you should fix up your office to convey a look of success. You were supposed to create a stage set that would flash intimidating messages. "I am the master—or mistress—of all I survey. I have power. I have arrived." It was a contrived theory, calculated to exploit people's uncertainty about who and what they were. I am glad that we have gone past all that, and that the stamped-out symbols that were supposed to notarize success have given way to expressions of personal style.

It has been interesting to watch the transition. A few years ago we used to let professional office planners dictate to us. We listened when they proclaimed with authority, "One should be conscious only of the person who occupies the office, the environment should be merely background." The office planners sold thousands of identical tables, desks, and chairs that way. They told us to keep accessories to a functional minimum. The round glass ashtray they recommended was *de rigueur*. An alabaster clock on the desk and unyielding drapes at the window marked every other office you walked into. A coffee table or a china picture frame that you might see in somebody's home was considered a daring departure; you could get written up in the papers for less.

Things reached an extreme during the phase when we were told that if we must have a desk it should be on a platform, and that the ultimate statement was to have no desk at all. If you had a desk that held stationery and files, and heaven forbid, a typewriter, that meant you would look like an underling, with no power or authority with which to impress the right people.

Emancipation Comes to the Office

Eventually it began to dawn on us that as long as we do our jobs well, it is all right to be comfortable, acceptable to surround ourselves with the things that bring us pleasure, desirable to show that we are individuals with interesting quirks of personality. Nowadays a Snoopy cup on the desk is not the symbol of a madcap at work in the office, it is simply the stamp of a person who thinks Snoopy is fun. And who is enough at ease to be willing to share that sense of fun with others.

I think that on the whole it was harder for women than it was for men to learn to relax about how their offices looked. Many were new to business, and afraid they might appear flighty if they didn't conform. It is true: we men were not accustomed to female executives, and we were just as uncertain as they about how the game should be played. I distinctly remember the first time I ever saw a woman president's office, and how pleasantly surprised I was by how comfortable her environment made me feel. It was in the early sixties, when "the corporate look" was still rampant, a woman president was rare as a bison, and I was the merchandise manager of the cosmetics department at Neiman-Marcus. The late Helen Van Slyke, who later became a best-selling author, was then head of a cosmetic firm whose products we sold, and I had been asked to a conference in her office. I walked in, expecting the usual impersonal, all but invisible, office decor. Miss Van Slyke rose to greet me, and my jaw dropped—a gesture I still hope she didn't notice. Instead of the vanishing institutional background I was accustomed to, I saw a workplace that was an extension of the woman who occupied it: gracious, hospitable, tasteful. There was a chintz-covered sofa with deep, soft cushions and lots of plump pillows for comfortable propping. She had boxes and organizers on her desk: traditional equipment, except that hers were upholstered in an exuberance of rose-printed linen. Other surfaces around the room were brightened by clusters of fresh-cut flowers in pretty china containers, and on the coffee table there was an old wooden tray that held Wedgwood cups and an antique silver pot for the coffee she promptly offered me. I thought, "Where is the round glass ashtray, the hard leather couch, the cardboard cups for instant coffee?" Then it dawned on me that I was in the presence of a woman who didn't need somebody else's style imposed on her. She had one of her own, and it was beautifully expressed.

Expressing Yourself

I am fascinated by the different ways people express themselves in their offices. Most of us spend a great many more hours in our workplaces than we do in our homes, so it is natural that our environments take on the traits of our personalities. In a way, it is analogous to how people grow to resemble their pets and vice versa. We have all known the imperious wolfhound tethered to the commanding *grande dame*, or the scruffy, playful terrier tripping alongside its friendly and casual owner. Sometimes pets and people even look alike. It's the same with a workplace. A neat, fastidious person almost always works in meticulously orderly surroundings. Somebody who is feminine, or motherly, very sophisticated, or extremely individualistic will inevitably spill those characteristics into the place where they spend most of their time.

I know one person whose office looks like her because she consciously planned it that way. I am thinking of Mme X, a well-known fashion designer who weighs in at a husky 225, when she has been on a diet. She is an absolute mountain of a woman, but she understands that it is important that she present a fashionable image. So she designed her office in scale with her personal proportions. Her chair, her desk, her tables, everything down to the lamps and ornaments in her office is as oversize as she is. You forget, when you are in there with her, that Mme X is so much larger than the rest of the world. All you see is a woman in scale with her surroundings. I suppose, unless there was a reason to want to seem fragile and vulnerable, a very small person might take the opposite route and deliberately scale down his or her furnishings. Otherwise he or she could appear overpowered. A Lilliputian in a world commanded by Gullivers.

Even people who have little choice about their office decor, because they work for a company that demands a certain look or because they have knuckled under to a dictatorial decorator, will show their colors, false or true. I am thinking of the time when I worked for the original Kenton Corporation, and the company hired decorators to do up its new headquarters office. The people ran around from office to office, hanging the pictures and arranging the accessories they decided should be on display. We were never consulted, even though we would have to live with the environment.

I guess you would say that I showed my true colors then and there, because I immediately went to my boss and explained that I couldn't work well in a dictated environment that had nothing to do with me. I said that I could understand the company's point of view—that they wouldn't want to present a garden salad of possibly tasteless furnishings to their public—but that I would appreciate a certain amount of choice in the matter. We agreed on a mutually pleasing compromise, and I learned a lesson that I have carried over to my own office in Dallas. I encourage the people who work there to decorate with things that they like, but I do some preediting to be sure that I will like their decor, too.

Whenever we get the feeling it is time to give our offices a face lift, I collect a carload of graphics from the house and bring it in to work. Then each person chooses what appeals to him or her, hangs it up, and we all carry on—happy as youngsters who got what they wanted for Christmas. I get an extra benefit: recycling artwork from our home gives me a chance to freshen up the look there, too.

Bringing Your Past to the Office

I like the idea of doing an office with furnishings from home. It gives a workplace genuine style, a personal signature. One of the most attractive and memorable offices I can think of to illustrate what I mean belongs to a corporate attorney in Florida. Margaret is a partner in a generations-old firm that works in a musty old building that also belongs to the family. Its offices and reception rooms wear the same faded green paint and the same uninspired oak furnishings they were born with, in the days when President Cleveland ruled the land. It is therefore doubly pleasing to be welcomed into Margaret's private office. She has chosen to ignore the monotonous "law office" look she grew up with, and make her quarters her own.

Her desk, placed at right angles to the single window at one end of the room, is the red Chinese dining table that she inherited from a world-traveling forebear, and the desk chair is a Chinese Chippendale that had been in Margaret's own dining room. A lovely Chinese rug covers the dark wooden floor, starting just under the desk and reaching almost to the daybed on the opposite wall. The walls themselves are painted stark white: a perfect foil for Margaret's antique Chinese furniture and for her collection of contemporary graphics as well. The total effect is one of agreeably compatible contrasts, arranged to provide the greatest comfort and pleasure. The room is definitely Margaret: unpretentious, tasteful, and natural.

We Lead Double Lives

It happens that Margaret's office looks just like her home. But people frequently furnish their workplaces quite differently from their homes. I think one reason is that most of us are two different people, perhaps with a chrome-sleek image of ourselves professionally, and a delicate rococo nature at home.

Dynamic C. J. "Jor" Kjorlien, the president of West Point Pepperell, expresses himself quite differently in his office and at home. With the exception of an antique English desk, his office on the 46th floor of a Manhattan skyscraper is a monochromatic sweep of contemporary furnishings. Everything is beige and simple: the texturey linen-covered walls, the straight-lined beige velvet sofa, the lacquered coffee table and no-color pewter ashtray. At the same time, Jor delights in the way his wife Ginny has flooded their 18th century traditional English apartment with color. Ginny loves flowers and, as she says, tulips in green, yellow, orange and white blossom on practically everything. Where Jor's pared-down office relies on a spectacular view and the vitality of its occupant for a feeling of activity, his and Ginny's home takes its cue from the elegance of its 1920s architecture enlivened by the vibrant shapes and colors of nature.

Personal Identification

Some people like to identify themselves with a trademark: a distinctive note they adopt as their theme. The Leo Burnett advertising agency, since the time it was founded, has been linked in people's minds with the bowl of apples that is always in its reception area. A rancher in Ft. Worth makes certain there is always a yellow rose of Texas on his desk. Tish Baldrige dotes on the joyous warmth of red, and splashes the color on her letterheads, her typewriters, her file cabinets. Estée Lauder's ornate, French blue, chandeliered office is shorthand for the message that she wants to get across to her public, just as a black cigarette holder identified President Franklin Roosevelt and a special blue box instantly says Tiffany's.

My own business trademark has been a white box tied with gold cord, as you may know, but years ago I had another, inadvertent identification. When I first came to Texas and went to work at Foley's, I didn't understand Houston weather. I clung to an Ohioan's belief that rain is likely to descend at any given moment, and therefore I always carried a precautionary umbrella. Around Foley's, I was known as Roger the Umbrella Man. I never was sure if they associated me and my umbrella with Mary Poppins or Neville Chamberlain. At least it provided conversation: people could always ask me if I thought it was going to rain.

Style and Work Habits

People express themselves at work in their procedural style as well as their decor, and I have found that you can learn a lot by observing the nuances. For example, the way Dean Witter Reynold's board chairman, Andrew Melton, keeps pace with the fast-moving brokerage business is by being systematic, unemotional, and pared to the absolute bone. He deals with each piece of paper instantly. Nothing is permitted to accumulate. Andy's desk top is barren except for his appointment book, a clock, an empty In box, and two paperweights with nothing to hold down. My office, on the other hand, is a constant clutter of people and things. Like Melton, my habit is to deal with papers and decisions immediately, and get them out of the way. But I go about it differently. The door to my office is always open, and people run in and out all the time, to show me something or make a suggestion. I say yes or I say no, and the matter is done with.

Beverly Sills claims she must work in a homey, overstuffed atmosphere to get through her long days as director of the New York City Opera. Indeed, there is not an officelike furnishing to be seen in her workplace. Meshulim Riklis, chairman of the multimillion conglomerate, Rapid American, operates his vast and complex empire with such taut efficiency that he could function with no paper or pens in his office. Riklis once said that he has no need for correspondence or phone calls; he has aides who are assigned those tasks, while he tends to the things he does best. Dallas executive Trammell Crow, who owns more warehouses than anybody else in the world, functions with no office at all. His is a shirt-sleeves approach and he works at a desk situated in the middle of the company bullpen, where he can communicate readily with his staff. To each his own, and the method that works is the right one.

Desk Power

Desks are a topic unto themselves. They have been used as pawns in the power game some people play in their offices, and as game pieces in books and articles about office power. I have a hunch that a lot of that material was written tongue-in-cheek, and should not be taken too seriously. Nevertheless, desks do play psychological as well as decorative and functional roles in an office.

We have all seen the setup where the desk is placed in front of a window so that when we sit on the visitor's side, we are forced to peer into blinding light while the person behind the desk watches us squirm. A desk can be used as a barrier between two people. It can loom as a symbol of authority. Its style can establish image. It can be noncommittal: a mere paper container in the background of a room's seating arrangement. In some offices, there is no reason for a desk to exist at all. When Alan Boyd was President Carter's Secretary of Transportation, it is said that he conducted government affairs via computer, and had no need for a desk in which to store papers and files. He would even call departmental meetings by simply punching up the appropriate data on his computer, which would immediately tell him who was available and then transmit the meeting times to other computers in the office. The scene may sound like something out of science fiction, but I assure you it is not. Computers have already taken their place in the work world, and it is my belief that before the 1980s are over, they will be as common for home use as hand-held calculators are today.

Accessories in Office Decor

I like the surroundings that reveal a person's individuality. Sometimes the accessories tell more than the furniture. Take my workplace, for example. I think that people who meet me outside of my office may assess me as a rather cool person; it's something about my reserve and tone of voice. But the minute they come in and see the hodgepodge in my office, with its shelves full of handcrafts, a Boy Scout mug jammed full of pencils, and a general air of cheerful informality, they know who the real me is.

Some offices are like pages from an album, and tell as much about the occupant's background as they do about his or her business, maybe more. I have heard that Brooke Astor, president of the Vincent Astor Foundation, likes to surround herself with vignettes of the past, her own and her late husband's. There are furnishings from his yacht, framed panels from a crate shipped from China to the Metropolitan Museum that related to her editorial job at *House & Garden*, and a thicket of photographs strewn along the window ledges and over her desk. You know that a woman who spends her time amid treasures such as these is a person of both taste and sentiment. She embraces the people who have been part of her past with as much warmth as she deals with the present. The mementos and photographs are a statement of the person she has become.

Photographs seem to crop up in offices in quantities ranging from one to one hundred and one. Sometimes they are links with home and family: pictures of laughing children, a moonstruck young couple, a triumphant angler dangling three startled fish before the camera. Sometimes pictures are in the nature of advertising: His Honor presenting an award for helping to boost economic development, an entire banquet table hanging on the speaker's eloquent phrases, dignitaries at a ground-breaking ceremony for the new plant. I am sure that you've seen them all. You would be fascinated by publicist Bobby Zarem's office. It is a forest of celebrity head-shots: pictures of the famous people he represents. A rising young store president I know has positively carpeted his office with photos of himself in exotic settings, letters from heads of state, and newspaper clippings of himself with important persons. Photos, degrees, and awards aren't just a way to blow your horn, they are the credentials that give people confidence in your expertise. And because the trophies are out there for anyone's inspection, they let you do away with the awkward business of having to drop names. "As my dear friend Princess Grace always says, when we meet for tea at the Paris Ritz before one of Truman's or Gore's parties . . ."

Somebody asked me if I think it is an imposition to foist family photos on people who come into your office. No, I do not. It is your privilege to surround yourself with things that you love. The only restriction I would place on family photographs is the same restriction that applies to everything in life: keep them in tasteful proportion. Style *is* proportion. It's the difference between understatement and overkill—the crystal chandelier in the tiny breakfast room, the one charm bracelet too many, the effusion of apologies after you have explained why you were late. Style is knowing when to stop.

The Importance of Details

The number of photographs you display or the freshness of the jonquils on the table may seem like minor considerations in an office, but it is attention to detail that makes or breaks an environment.

You may very well find, if you look around your home for things to recycle, that expenditures for nice accessories are unnecessary. The terra-cotta bowl that you picked up in Mexico may be just the touch your office needs. It could be a container for flowers or candy, or just something interesting to look at. Maybe the little Orrefors vase somebody gave you as an anniversary gift could be dislodged from the living room mantel and reincarnated as a holder for pencils. If you experiment, you may find some unexpected and pleasurable links between your home and your work lives.

If it's ideas you need, look around at other people's workplaces that you admire. I am forever inventing reasons to stop in and talk with the people who work with us in Dallas; they are such a creative lot that I like to see their ideas in action. You never know, from month to month, what imaginative new atmosphere they will have conjured out of blue sky—and for practically no money at all.

Fresh Thoughts on Walls

Right now, our Trifles buyer's office is painted an offbeat shade of mauve. Bess Duval is not a bit worried that mauve may be a mistake, or that she will tire of it in a few months. With a can or two of another color paint and an hour's worth of labor, she can roll on a different color that will suit her mood better.

Jacques, our display man, has gone beyond paint; he staples. I have seen him whip up magical effects out of the most mundane materials and a staple gun. One that impressed me particularly was his conversion of four six-foot rolls of corrugated paper into a dramatic backdrop for his work. All he did was staple the rolls to the wall, using the paper so the ribs run vertically. At one corner of the room, he left an end of the paper furled in a standing roll. The effect is both texturey and theatrical, and most effective when the corrugated ridges capture light and shadow in an undulating pattern.

The magic staple gun has taken our office through more attractive stages than I can number. Another of our buyers, Pat, once came across a giant bath towel strewn with abstract flowers. She ordered a quantity for our catalog, and some extras for herself. Within hours of the towels' arrival Pat's office became a fascinating garden of opulently soft velours. Pat says she had so much sight-seeing company during her toweled-wall phase, she was thinking of declaring visiting hours, as if she were a public institution.

Making Other People Comfortable

We are all of us public, in one way or another. We share our workplaces with colleagues in the next office, and with people from the outside who come in to see us. So it is not merely our own comfort we need to consider, but others as well. If you have ever had a colleague on the other side of the wall with a raucous telephone voice, or a radio that he or she plays at audible volume, you know how unnerving a thoughtless person can be. To tell you the truth, I even go a little crazy when somebody in the office opens up a lunch bag and the odors of salami and onion float out. That's why I like to keep some lemony air spray and scented candles around, the same as we do at home. It is not that I am out to sanitize the world; I just want to make it a more pleasant place to inhabit.

It requires very little effort or expense to maintain a hospitable atmosphere, just sensitivity to other people's needs and feelings. If you like to work with your favorite music in the background, as I do, it is easy to hook up a small cassette recorder to a single speaker close to your desk chair. You will have your private pleasure, and not disturb anyone else. If you find that visitors frequently have to wait while you answer phone calls, or sit in the reception area before their appointments, why not provide them with something pleasant to occupy their time—new magazines, an art book, crossword puzzles and pencil. I find that a bowl of mints or fruit is another small nicety that makes a big difference to visitors.

Hospitality is synonymous with food in the office as well as at home. The difference is, at work we usually call it a Coffee Break, or Lunching. But I see no reason to eat any less graciously at your workplace than you do at home or in a well-appointed restaurant. Like Helen Van Slyke, you can make coffee breaks pleasant occasions, and genuine breaks from work, just by using china cups on a pretty tray instead of paper containers. If lunching-in makes you feel like Cinderella left behind to sweep the hearth while everyone else is off at the ball, try using the linen and china all by yourself. It is amazing how much more flavorsome a solitary ham-on-rye tastes when you give it a little glamor.

I have a friend who is a business reporter for a national magazine. Karen says that in many of the cities where she travels for her stories, the best meals in town are inside of corporate headquarters. Karen reports, "The meals I have consumed in the line of duty have ranged from full-scale executive dining room presentations with four courses, two kinds of wine, and one waiter for every pair of guests, to a sandwich and coffee at an administrative assistant's desk. The good ones all had one thing in common—prettiness. And when someone shows that they care enough to make an effort to enchant me, they have won my heart."

Office Entertaining

When I asked Karen to describe one of the office lunches that qualified for her "pretty" list, she startled me by marching over to my supply closet. "You're looking at it," she announced. "Do you remember the first day I came in to interview you? We sat at your conference table and talked until our stomachs complained. Then you asked if I would like to lunch with you. I started to pack up my tape recorder, thinking we would move on to a restaurant, and you said, 'I've arranged for us to eat in, so we won't have to interrupt the interview. Is that all right with you?'

"While I asked more interview questions and you answered, you walked over to the supply closet. Always the snoopy journalist, I bounded after you, probably hoping to find the miracle file marked Corporate Secrets. What I saw instead was the secret of a well-organized, thoughtful man. There on a shelf were six Lucite trays, the kind with two-inch rims that stack on top of each other. Each tray was set with a lettuce-green, no-iron mat and napkin, stainless steel flatware, and a green-and-white china lunch plate. All you had to do was remove a couple of the trays and bring them to the conference table.

"When the lunch you had ordered earlier was delivered, I saw that you had them send salads as well as sandwiches. It made the

meal that much more appealing. I helped you shift the food from
the deli's cardboard cartons and sandwich wrap onto the pretty
china, and there we were, proper people enjoying a proper meal.
That fresh-brewed coffee afterward—that we sipped from china
cups, thank heaven—and the fruit and cookies perched on your
shell-shaped dishes, tasted like nectar and ambrosia. What
struck me was that it was little more trouble for you to produce a
nice lunch than if you had settled for what the deli sent over.
And it certainly didn't cost more. I figured out that if you had
initially spent $100 for the trays, the china, flatware, and no-iron
napkins, it was a one-time investment. Amortized over, let's say
five years' worth of office lunches a few times a week, that would
be . . ."

It Pays to Be Organized

Despite the clutter in my office, Karen described me as a well-
organized man and she was right. I couldn't function without a
system of files and baskets and gadgets to keep my projects and
papers from becoming jumbled with each other. Organizers do
for me what human memory cannot. I think this is true for most
other people, too. We need all the mechanical aids we can lay
our hands on, within the bounds of reality. There is such a thing
as getting so carried away by systems that your workplace is all
gadgets and no work.

In most businesses and professions that I know anything
about, the single most important organizing tool is a set of file
folders. The ABCs of filing are:

A. Decide whether you should file as you go along, once a
day, weekly, monthly, or sporadically. Then do it.
B. File each day's papers and clippings in the folder where
they belong, or else in a folder marked To File.
C. Never have a file marked Miscellaneous. Miscellaneous
is a monster that swallows whatever you feed it. Once
swallowed, the material will never resurface.

Those are the basics. The spinoffs and furbelows are up to you
and your particular needs. One way to tailor a workable system

is to ask yourself what it is that bothers you, then figure out how to get rid of the problem. For example, I found that I was annoyed every time I wanted to get at the files I use daily. They were squeezed in so tightly with the rest of my files, it was hard to get papers in or out of the folders. As soon as I defined the problem, a light bulb went on over my head. The solution was obvious. Remove the files that I need only once a month or so and put them in a drawer in the supply closet. Now my daily-use files have plenty of breathing space, and my life is much simpler.

Another solution came out of the fact that I found I was hunting for the same things over and over. For instance, I kept all references to lamps and lighting—Lamps/Home, Lighting/Residential, Light Fixtures/Business, and so on—in one folder labeled Lighting. I spent a lot of needless time and effort every time I wanted information about any of these subjects, because I had to paw through all of the other material. It was almost as bad as having a Miscellaneous file. Then I hit upon subheads with color-coding. Now each category has its own different-colored folder, separately labeled. Color-coding makes it easy to see things at a glance, especially if you are like me and sometimes forget your glasses when you go to the file. Incidentally, I have learned to write "Lamps/Home," or whatever designation applies, at the top of papers to be filed, so I can slip them speedily into their appropriate slots.

The editor-in-chief of *Town & Country* magazine, Frank Zachary, has devised a filing system that keeps changing its shape, depending on whether he is in the middle of getting out an issue or has just put one to bed. Actually, it should be called a piling system. There are days when Frank's office is an ocean of piled-up books, photographs, clippings, manuscripts, and layouts. They swirl in large, amorphous masses over every available surface. The floor is carpeted, the windowsills, desk, and tables are piled high, shopping bags overflow, and even the chairs are up to their armrests in paper. Other days, Frank's office is neat as a barracks, with just a few orderly stacks of magazine material lined up on the windowsills. I once asked Frank how he makes these overnight miracles come to pass. He laughed at the image I had ascribed to him, and explained that what looks like wild disorder to me is a rational filing system to him.

"I'm a clipper and a note jotter," he said. "I come in here every morning and empty my pockets of the accumulation from the night before. A clipping about India lands on one pile, a note about a beautiful home in California goes on another, and so on. The piles are not labeled, but I know exactly what is in each one. It happens that I have total retention of irrelevant facts, and remember everything that is in each pile. At some point, a fact in the pile on the left-hand windowsill combines in my mind with a fact that is in a pile on the right-hand windowsill, and becomes the idea for a story. At that point, I pull the material together from the different piles and work with it, adding more stuff and pushing it around until the story is done. Multiply this performance by the number of stories in each issue and you can see why my office becomes periodically engulfed in paper. To answer your question about the 'miraculous' transformation: in the lull between issues I simply reassemble all of the papers, put them back into order, and file them away."

I was curious about Frank's nighttime clipping and jotting sessions, and asked if he had an office at home. "There are five of them, if you want to call my work areas office," he answered. "They really are just convenient parts of the house. You see, I am visually oriented and can lay out a whole magazine in my head, so I don't need a formal office setup. Just someplace where I can make sketches and notes that will be reminders to me when I come to the office in the morning. I work in bed. I usually wake at one-thirty or three in the morning, and dream up stories and layouts in my mind. Then I get out of bed and go to my sketch pad at the bedroom desk. Sometimes I use the desk in the den, where I have reference books. And sometimes I sketch in the living room or the kitchen. It may sound scattered to you, working all over the house that way, but you have to remember that my notes and sketches are only reminders—the complete stories are engraved in my mind."

Carving Out a Workplace at Home

The idea of working at home appeals to many people I know. They like the fact that they can cut down on rent, do away with commuting, and work at their own hours and pace.

But with the way living space has diminished lately, some rather inventive juggling may be called for, in order to create a work area that functions efficiently and at the same time harmonizes with the rest of the household. It can be done. I have seen complete, comfortable offices squeezed into what seems to be no space at all. John, a product developer who needed an area for his bookkeeping and research, staked out a 4-by-5-foot alcove of his bedroom for work needs. He installed a deep writing-level shelf all around the three walls, with drawers and a pair of white file cabinets tucked under the shelf. A series of bookshelves climbs two of the walls to the ceiling, and the window wall is hung with luxuriant green plants. The walls, like the files, are white so they will blend in with the rest of John's bedroom. The finishing touch is a pair of louvered doors, which he closes whenever he wants to conceal the work area. It's a home office that has all of the virtues. It is neat, inviting, unobtrusive, and it works.

I have seen people separate their offices from their living quarters by fencing off the work area of the room with folding screens, bookcases, or trellises. The dividers have several advantages. They stake out the work space physically, and psychologically as well. Screens provide flexibility, too. You can move them around, and you can change their appearance with a fast coat of paint, or by stapling on some good-looking fabric or wallpaper. Trellises, too, can be painted any color, and they certainly have an airy, pretty look. But the look is not compatible with every type of decor.

Investing in Home Office Equipment

The more pleasant your working conditions, the more you enjoy what you do. The corollary to that truth is that a makeshift setup can wear you out. You can spend killing amounts of time and energy if you have to chase to a different area every time

you want a reference book or file material. And it is definitely
misguided economy to try to use a wobbly little table for a desk,
crumple your spine in the wrong chair, or make do with lighting
that is so bad you have to squint or hunch over. Proper equipment is a necessary outlay: a one-time investment in years of
comfort and efficiency.

Basic necessities aside, it makes sense to be a bit stingy with
yourself when you first launch a business and have no guarantee
of success. But it is possible to have a great-looking workplace
anyway, if you look around and see which of your home furnishings you can recycle for office use.

Sondra Gilman is an expert at making her furniture and even
her rooms lead a double life. She is the co-producer of several
motion pictures and Broadway musicals. However, when she
first went into business in 1976, she had no idea how long it
would take to succeed and made a conscious decision to keep
her overhead down. The setups she contrived have worked out
so well, she hasn't needed to change or add anything.

Sondra's principal work center is her bed. "I have never been
able to bear sitting at a desk," says the petite, dark-haired producer. "It's a carry-over from college days. I work best where I
am most comfortable." Sondra describes her "bed-quarters" in
her New York townhouse: "I have things arranged so that
everything is at fingertips' reach while I work, and out of sight
when office hours are over. The bed is massed all day long with
books and papers. But when my husband, Charles, comes home
at night, all the paraphernalia disappears. Books and papers get
piled onto the windowsills, I close the louvered blinds over the
stacks, and you would never know the bedroom was used for
anything but sleeping.

"Next to the bed I have a table with two drawers. I keep recy-
cled candy and jewelry boxes inside them, so pencils, business
cards, and whatnot are categorized. The top of the table holds
the TV recorder, telephone, phone book, and so on. My phone
book is covered in a coral suede, to match the color of the room.
Underneath the bed there's a big metal drawer that holds all my
ongoing files and reference materials. I just pull out the drawer
in the morning, then slide it back into hiding at night. I also have
one of those decorative hanging pockets that tucks between the

mattress and box spring. This holds the pencils and colored pens I work with during the day. I use lots of pillows to lean against; they are covered with shams that match the headboard. At our other house I have a headboard that is like the back of a limousine. It's thickly upholstered and has an armrest that flips down, for leaning on. As for lighting, I use wall brackets so as not to use up worktable space. I have on-off switches on the cords attached at hand level so I can just reach out and control the light from where I sit."

I wondered what happens when visitors call on a bedroom office. Sondra must have read my mind. She smiled and said, "You probably have visions of me conducting a meeting while I sit straight up in bed, hiding a wrinkled skirt under the covers. No. I never get dressed until I have to go out to a rehearsal or lunch appointment. I wear robes in bed, and have a wardrobe of them, the way other people have closets full of blouses and skirts. Anyway, I use a different room for meetings. Would you like to see it?"

We went up to the top floor of the Gilman townhouse and Sondra showed me her conference room, formerly the children's playroom. The space still serves as their party room, and as a guestroom as well. The guest beds are lined up under the front windows, with tailored red-and-blue covers and matching bolsters to unify them; the twin beds look as if they are a single, extra long and deep couch. Facing the couch is a pair of wicker chairs that used to be on the Gilmans' country house porch. The seat cushions are covered in the red-and-blue fabric of the couch, and the blue is repeated in a pair of painted chests that once were pale wood. The white drop-leaf conference table, a buffet table when there is a party, was a dark wood dining table in Charles's bachelor days. There isn't a piece of furniture in the conference room that has not led another life in its youth, but Sondra's color-combination makes the room look all-of-a-piece.

I noticed that two corner walls are filled with dozens of black-and-white photographs of Sondra's husband and two children. She told me it is important to her to have her family around her when she is working: in Lucite frames if not in the flesh, as they are apt to be when she works in bed.

Carolyn likes to work in the bedroom, too, but she prefers to sit at a desk. Hers is surely one of the most compact and efficient workplaces I have ever seen. It consists of a Queen Anne cabinet, an antique three-cornered chair, and that's all. Carolyn had casters put on the chair so she can move it back and forth easily, and added a cushion to the cane seat for comfort. The Queen Anne cabinet already had a pull-down writing shelf, with shelves above it where Carolyn keeps her stationery and files in wallpaper-covered boxes. Her pencils and pens rest in a cylindrical china vase, and random notes are pinned under a Baccarat paperweight that I gave her when we were engaged. Actually, the paperweight does more than keep Carolyn's notes tidy. It is on her desk because she likes to look at it, and because it is a personal touch that relates to our lives. To me, that has always been one of the most charming things about Carolyn: she knows how to blend beauty with efficiency without sacrificing one to the other. She has a style that could only be hers.

Carolyn's style, her identifying hallmark, is as evident at her workplace as it is in the rest of our home. The effect is cheerful, pleasant and productive. If you stop to think about it, you will probably notice that the same is true of most of the successful business and professional people you know. Almost always, their workplaces have a distinctively personal atmosphere. I think one reason is they have learned that surroundings affect mood and mood affects achievement. The other reason is a workplace without individuality is like a bottle of fine wine with no corkscrew. You can look at the container, but you cannot savor the qualities that make it unique.

❦ ❦ ❦

6
PERFECT WEEKENDS

Weekends, to me, are like little vacations: bonus time when I can step back and enjoy my family and home, indulge in my hobbies, and see the friends that workdays crowd out. If a weekend should bring guests to our home, too, then I feel that I have been given an extra bonus—two or three whole days in which to learn more about people I like, and add new memories to our store of reminiscences. A weekend together is a chance to expand the reference points that friendships are made of, and strengthen common bonds.

My idea of a perfect weekend with houseguests starts with four basic elements—comfortable surroundings, good talk, a pleasant program of activities, and people who know what it means to be responsive to one another. It seems to me that it is more important than ever, nowadays, that we nurture our personal relationships with care. Living in tight quarters as we do, without household help or stylized ritual to lean on, we are forced into an intimacy that can upset delicate balances.

Guests can either fit in with your routine or intrude, take responsibility for their own entertainment or demand all your attention, make your life more pleasant while they are with you or prove the wisdom of the old adage about guests and fish that linger more than three days.

Thinking Things Through

Accustomed as Carolyn and I are to welcoming guests to our home, we still go through the same exercise of start-to-finish planning before every visit. It is our experience that the better prepared you are, the more your guests will enjoy their stay. You have to combine your enthusiastic anticipation of their visit with the hour-to-hour realities it will bring, and sketch an agenda so nobody will feel bored or left out. What we do is mentally walk through the entire time span in advance, from the minute our guests will arrive until we wave them off with promises to meet again soon. We try to think through all of the details, such as who will pick them up at the airport and whether they will need a rest if it has been a long trip. It really pays. A little trouble ahead of time can eliminate last-minute oversights and confusion.

We like to outline each day's and evening's meals, parties, and excursions, so there will be a variety of things to interest our guests. But we also like to leave loopholes, in case they are not in the mood for a gallery tour after all, or in case the weather sours our plans for a picnic or drive. I think that if you truly want to please people, you have to give them options, and keep your plans for their visit flexible. Otherwise you might as well invite them to a weekend in a hard-labor camp.

Give Guests a Choice

Usually when somebody arrives for a visit, we take a few minutes as soon as it is reasonable to do so—while we help them get settled, or over a cup of coffee—and explain what we have thought they might enjoy. Unless it is something we are firmly committed to, such as a party in the guest's honor, we always ask them to tell us if they would really like to do what we have suggested. We might say, "We thought it would be interesting to go see the Ft. Worth stockyards Saturday afternoon, or else we can see the Southwestern art exhibit at the museum. If you would rather just stay around the house and relax, that's fine with us. Or perhaps there is something else that you have in mind that you would like to do while you're in Dallas. Please, let us know and we'll help make the arrangements for you." Now we have given them our ideas of things to do on Saturday afternoon, and left the door open for them to choose something that they may like better.

My friend, Bill Windle, the investment broker from Boston, has an unprosaic but efficient way of letting guests know what activities and options he has set up. Carolyn and I learned about it last fall when he and his wife Fabia invited us and two other couples to a country home near Bordeaux, France. When we went to our bedroom, we each found a list on our night table, an almost moment-by-moment scenario of the things Bill had planned for us to do. Nonetheless, it gave us our outs. It read:

SATURDAY

8:00–9:00	Breakfast in the dining room.
10:00–1:00	Trip to LaTour vineyard and cellar. We would love to have you come along, but if you don't care to join us, please feel free to stay here at our chateau, or let us know where we can drop you off.
1:00–3:00	Lunch at Le Perigord in Bordeaux. Le Perigord is an auberge, very informal. Local sausage and omelet kind of menu. If you do not plan to join us, let us know in the morning so our cook can prepare lunch for you here.
3:00–6:00	You're on your own. You can shop in town, or do as we usually do in the late afternoon—nap, read, write letters, or just stroll around in the fall sunshine.
7:00—	Cocktails and dinner chez Windle. Wear comfortable clothes. Slacks and a sweater is best, as there is an evening chill here now.

Notice that Bill allowed plenty of time for us to get from place to place, so we wouldn't feel pressed and harried. It's a point worth taking into account, whatever kind of schedule you are setting up. You can work it out easily if you think your timetable through, and then plan backward. If you have tickets for a concert in town at 8:30, for instance, you will probably want to call cocktails and dinner for 5:45 so there will be ample time for conversation and catching cabs or parking the car. It takes a lot of the enjoyment out of an evening if people have to keep checking their watches through dinner, and then race to their seats at the very last minute.

Bill's thorough planning was well suited to the kind of weekend it was, with three couples who had traveled to strange territory and were completely dependent on him and Fabia for instruction. But I have seen the list idea work just as charmingly on more familiar grounds. I am reminded of the light-handed way Carolyn's friend Ann-Elizabeth choreographs her guests' weekends at the farm where she lives. She'll leave a series of notes on your night table or bureau that give provocative hints, such as, "Have you been down by the barn to see Howie's apple orchard yet?" "You'll hate yourself if you don't go over to West Street and visit Uncle Ned in his workshop." "If you want to know what a 300-year-old mill looks like, go pay a call on Joe Brown's farm." What Ann-Elizabeth does with her scavenger-hunt notes is set you up so you have to ask "Who is Howie? What is so special about his orchard? How do we get there?" She makes you curious, gets you involved, and succeeds in creating things that you can't wait to do—in a countryside that is not exactly famous for its tourist attractions.

Expressing Your Needs

I think a good guest should always be honest about whether he or she would like to go along with a host's suggestions. If you hate museums or walks in the country, say so. You will do everybody a favor because when you suffer, so do they. Besides, think how you would feel, as a host, if you had gone to a lot of trouble to get tickets for a ballgame or a performance of *Swan Lake,* and you learned after your guests left that they had dragged themselves along for your sake, loathing every minute. Wouldn't you have been delighted if they had told you up front what they like and don't like? They could have said, "Thank you so much for getting the tickets; it must have been a lot of trouble. The truth is, watching football is not something we enjoy very much. Wouldn't you like to take somebody who will appreciate the game? You don't have to worry about us. We'd like to go antiquing and Sunday will be a perfect day for it. Just tell us what time you think you'll be through, and where we should meet you after the game."

Usually, when tickets are not involved and the situation is more loose, you can come up with an alternative activity that everybody will enjoy. A movie instead of the church fair, a day at the beach instead of tennis and bridge at the club, a Chinese instead of a Mexican restaurant. Bob Boor, a friend of ours, gave us an excellent idea that he says has saved the day for him more than once. He keeps lists on hand to remind him of what he calls "contingency maneuvers." Bob says, "If you are anything like me, your mind has a habit of getting stuck just when you need it to move fast. Somebody will ask me something easy, like name some of the new restaurants in town, and I'm a blank. Can't think of a single one, because they have caught me off guard. Or I'll have houseguests who say they would like me to show them the interesting parts of Los Angeles. Here I am in my own home-town, and I have to think and think about where to take them. Half the time I grasp at the first straw that comes to mind, and we wind up doing something dumb. I finally decided this had happened too many times, so I sat down and made lists that I keep in file folders. One is headed *Restaurants.* Places that I know are good, interesting, affordable, offbeat, or famous. Another says *Recreation,* and it lists quiet beaches, picnic spots, nearby golf and tennis facilities, places where the walking is good. There is one headed *Culture,* for museums, symphony halls, little theaters, things like that. And another for sight-seeing."

Sight-Seeing

I was interested in Bob's idea of sight-seeing in Los Angeles. The city is so varied and so vast, nobody could absorb it in one gulp. He has to have made an effort to focus on small digestible portions.

Bob told me, "My idea of sight-seeing is that it should always be very specific. I think just general driving-around is a big groan. What's intriguing is a destination that has a point to it. Here is what is on my current list of places to show off to visitors. The Hancock section that is being rehabilitated with the help of the neighborhood historic preservation society. The old movie lot that has been converted into an art gallery. The new produce market, the botanical gardens, the film stars' cocktail lounge where you can see souvenirs of the film stars who used to congregate there in the 1930s. The thing about my list is that it's like a connoisseur's menu; I can pick out the kind of thing that suits my guests' special tastes. If I offer to take Bob, the horticulture fan, to the gardens or Susan, the architectural history buff, to the rehab district, they will feel that I am giving them an individually tailored, personalized trip that I have designed just for them. And I know that they'll be genuinely interested in what they see."

Ordinary Pleasures

A weekend doesn't need to include sight-seeing in order to be pleasurable. We have spent many a Saturday and Sunday with friends who are happy to tag along with what we ordinarily do. We might all go and watch Sally play soccer, or we might ask if they would like to come with us while we drive around on our errands. I grant you, there is nothing exceptional about going to the hardware store or the shirt laundry, but it's a nice way to show visitors how the natives live at the same time you take care of Saturday chores. After all, the point of visiting is to be together; *where* the experience takes place is secondary.

Conquering Previsit Anxiety

I have known people who go into a tailspin when they learn that visitors are coming. They become overwrought, and kill themselves trying to get all of their errands and housekeeping out of the way beforehand. I wish I could tell them to relax. My advice would be: get as many chores out of the way as you can, let some of the dirty work wait, and don't worry about the rest. You'll find a way to weave important errands into the time you spend with your company, and with just a bit of forethought, you can cut down on nerves and flurry while your friends are visiting. For example, I would say to an anxious host, you can plan your menus and do the marketing before people arrive. You can cook ahead, too, or else figure out meals that are fast and simple to prepare, so you won't be chained to the kitchen for hours while everybody else is itching for you to join them. As for housekeeping, why worry about polishing every piece of silver in the drawer or tackling your messy closets? It is your guests' comfort, not your conscience that counts. All you really have to do is tidy up enough so they will walk into a pleasant atmosphere, and run through their sleeping arrangements to make sure they will have everything they want.

The Guestroom

In fact, it's a good idea to pretend you are a weekend guest in your own home every once in awhile. Really sleep in your guestroom, or on the sofa, or wherever else your visitors stay. Be a critic, test how it works. Check out whether all the amenities are in place, and add whatever will make your guest quarters more hospitable. Here is a list of the things we have learned to look for over the years:

> Mattress or sofa: comfortably firm. If it flunks the test, replace it if you can, or else buy a bedboard.
> Pillows: plump and firm. Extra pillows for reading in bed.
> Blankets, quilt: clean and in good condition. An extra blanket for chilly nights. Electric blankets that work.
> Bedside and room lamps, light bulbs bright enough for reading, makeup, dressing for evening.
> Window shades to keep out morning light
> Alarm clock
> Radio
> Books, new magazines
> Paper and sharpened pencils
> Ashtrays
> Coaster
> Water glass

Kleenex
Luggage rack
Wastebasket
Mirror, full length
Closet and drawer space
Hangers for dresses, skirts, pants
Heat and air-conditioning controls in working order. Show
    guests how to use them.
Last-minute niceties: fresh flowers. Room freshener. Fruit,
    crackers, nightcap. Clear away clutter and stored items.

For the Guest Bath:
Towels: face, hand, and bath sizes. Towel bar space.
Toilet paper in place, plus extra roll
Kleenex
Soaps
Shower cap
Shelves for cosmetics and toiletries
Disposable razors, toothbrush, toothpaste
Aspirin, digestive aids
Drains in working order
Cleaning tools: sponge, toilet bowl brush, cleaning liquid.

When You Are the Guest

The ideal guest, like the perfect host, knows that preliminary
planning is essential, and responds to invitations quickly and
clearly. It is not fair to leave your host dangling while you bog
down in indecision about whether you will visit them or not.
They have other people to invite and plans to make that depend
on your reply. People who can't make up their minds should be
taught the eleventh commandment: Thou shalt respond to all
invitations within twenty-four hours of receipt.

You also owe it to your host to say what time you expect to
arrive, and when you plan to leave. I can tell you from our own
experience how maddening it is to have slated a sensational
Sunday lunch for your guests, only to have them pop from their
rooms that morning, baggage in hand, with the news that they
are going to drive off right after church. If only they'd had the

courtesy to let us know at the outset. I suppose that incident was our own fault. When a guest accepts an invitation but fails to say, "We can stay until about four o'clock Sunday afternoon," or, "When would you like us to leave?" it is up to the host to ask, "Can you tell me what time you will be leaving?" Or to say, "We would love to have you come on Friday and stay with us until five or six on Sunday." If you want to be more subtle, you could say something like, "The new schedule lists the last plane at six o'clock." The point is, it is courteous to be clear about the length of the stay in the beginning, so your host can make plans accordingly.

Mixed Company

Another courtesy is to let guests know if anybody else will be along on the weekend, and to make it easy for them to back off if the company is not to their liking. Naturally, as a good guest you would never bring anybody with you unannounced, even if an emergency comes up and you suddenly have an unexpected friend or child on your hands. The thing to do if that happens is to call your host and say, "You were very kind to invite us but I am afraid we can't come. Jim's college roommate is staying with us that weekend." Or, in another situation, "Our sitter has backed out so we will have to stay home and look after young Jimmy." A statement like that leaves the door open for your host. He then can answer, "Oh, that's too bad. Let's plan another weekend instead." Or else he can say, "We would love to meet Jim's roommate, and we have plenty of room. Please do bring him along." Either way, you have made it easy for the other person to let you know what he or she prefers, and no hard feelings have been incurred.

You have the same kind of obligation when you are the host. If you have invited more than one guest to stay with you for the weekend, it's a kindness to tell your invitees about each other. Guest A may be a person who likes to have quiet, intimate talks with nobody else around. Or guests A and B may happen to dislike one another. It's not fair to throw them together without warning. Give them a chance to say to you, "Thank you for inviting us. I am sorry we won't be able to come." No explanation is necessary; just let it go at that. Most people do altogether too much apologizing, in my opinion, and it makes everyone uneasy. The adage, "Never complain, never explain," was invented to remind us not to go on and on, shuffling our feet and babbling excuses that nobody wants to hear. Good form is knowing when to stop.

Situations that involve mixed company can crop up during the course of a weekend, too. Your neighbors invite you to a terrific party, and you have to tell them that you can't come because you have a houseguest. If you are lucky, they will ask you to come anyway, and bring your guest along. Or they may say, simply, "We're disappointed that you won't be able to join us." At least you have given them the option, and you can be pretty sure that they will invite you again the next time they have a wonderful party.

Sometimes you can have your cake and eat it too. Carolyn and I did, literally, during one of our Nantucket summers. Pebble and Dun Gifford, the Boston lawyer and her enterprising husband, called and said, "You must come for dinner Friday night. There will be several people here I know you will want to meet: Russell Baker, the columnist; Russell Morash, producer of Julia Child's show . . ." She listed a pantheon of fascinating celebrities we'd have loved to meet, but we had to be honest. We told them it was Regen's last night at home before she went off to college, and we wanted to be with her. We were terribly sorry, but we just couldn't come to the dinner party. But we said we would like very much to be with them for a little while; would it be all right if we three came over later for coffee and dessert? The Giffords said they would love to have us join them then, and the evening worked out perfectly for everybody. We had our time with Regen, and we got to meet Russell Baker and the others, as well. Furthermore, Pebble's dinner table wasn't upset by our bringing Regen as an extra guest at the last minute.

Nantucket is like that—open house on certain occasions and by-invitation-only on others. Everybody knows that their friends are more likely than not to have houseguests. So when an invitation for a cocktail or beach party is sent, it almost always says, "Please bring your houseguests with you." When the invitation is for dinner, we all understand that our houseguests are not included unless they are specifically asked.

Weekend Wardrobes

One more item a wise guest will cover before taking off for a weekend is wardrobe. It is perfectly appropriate to ask what your host's plans are, so you will know whether to bring a long skirt, a coat and tie, sweaters and pants, walking shoes, or what-have-you. Ask for specifics. If your host lets you know that there is to be a house party on Saturday night, take the next step and ask exactly how you should dress—in floor-length dinner wear, silk pants and blouse, a dressy dress, or something casual. Assume nothing. You have to bear in mind that what they wear in Greenwich, Connecticut, bears no resemblance at all to what looks right in Los Angeles, and that even perfect hosts occasionally slip up and forget to tell you everything you should know.

When we were invited to go with the Windles to the chateau in Bordeaux, friends who had made a similar trip told us we would be called upon to dress for a formal evening. We could see ourselves in regal garb, dining in their stately banquet hall with a white-gloved footman behind every chair. We imagined me in my tuxedo and best cuff links, and Carolyn in her most elegant floor-length silk. But before we packed, Carolyn, in her wisdom, phoned ahead to make sure. Our vision of life in the chateau could not have been more off center. Bill told us that we would be weekending in a small country house, not the castle we had dreamed, and to bring only sweaters, pants or skirts, and good sturdy shoes. Good host that he is, he added, "If you're wondering about the weather, I can tell you that it will be sixty to sixty-five degrees, and that it will probably rain while you are here. But don't burden yourselves with rain gear. We have plenty of extra ponchos and raincoats right here. It's all so informal, everybody always just grabs what they need and tramps around in it."

The same advice goes for sports gear. Ask what you should bring, if anything, for tennis, golf, scuba diving. It's a great pity to miss out on a chance to play at your favorite sport simply because you are not prepared, and needless to load up with equipment that your host already has on hand. It also makes you feel rather foolish to trudge up to somebody's front door bearing rod, reel, and wading boots when there isn't a fishing stream within 200 miles.

Bringing House Gifts

People sometimes wonder whether they should shop ahead and bring house gifts with them when they visit, or wait until later and send something as a thank-you. The answer is, you can do either or both, although in most cases I would feel rather uncomfortable if I arrived empty-handed. Even if it's a small token, like a jar of preserves or a pack of cocktail napkins, I feel better when I acknowledge somebody's offer of hospitality. As a host, though, I never give it a thought when a guest comes to our home without a proffering. I guess that's because what is uppermost in my mind is the reason we extended the invitation in the first place—to spend time and share experiences with somebody we like.

As I say, preserves, cocktail napkins, candy, cheeseboards, any of the usual house gifts fills the bill perfectly well. They are useful, pretty, and neutral enough to fit into any home. But with a touch of imagination, you can choose an especially thoughtful gift that your host will remember long afterward. A professor friend of ours, knowing that Nantucket weekends inevitably mean cocktail parties, once brought us two pounds of smoked salmon for our hors d'oeuvres table. Smoked salmon is a delicacy that is hard to come by on the island, so it was a special treat. What made the gift even nicer was that our thoughtful guest had had the salmon presliced, so we wouldn't have to go to any extra trouble when we served it. Another guest always brings games for the girls and puzzles for the grownups, surefire antidotes for the gloomy days that are always possible at a summer place. As a matter of fact, it is Carolyn's habit to keep a partly done jigsaw puzzle on a table in the sun-room, so anyone can sit down and work on it when the mood strikes.

Wine and spirits are always welcome house gifts. They vanish in large quantities when there are weekend guests, and no matter how well-heeled your host is, it is nice to help replenish the supply. I also believe that it is perfectly acceptable to bring a bottle of whatever it is that you like to drink in addition to the gift that caters to your host's taste. For me, a bottle of white wine tucked in with a quart of my host's favorite bourbon can be a lifesaver. When the highballs are passed and everybody is relaxed, I am assured that there will be a glass of wine for me, too.

Thank-You Gifts

There isn't a great deal of difference between the type of thank-you present you send after a weekend visit and the one you bring with you, except that the post-visit gift may be something that you have learned your host will especially appreciate. You might have noticed, during your stay, that your hosts really could use a portable grill for picnics, a certain serving dish to go with their china, or a two-dollar gadget for squeezing wedges of lemon. The best thank-you gift you can choose is not necessarily lavish or costly; it is something that shows your personal concern. I assure you that if you gave an inexpensive begonia plant to a begonia hobbyist, it would mean more to him or her than $50 worth of impersonally chosen caviar. In my opinion, the more personal your gift, the more truly it expresses your appreciation.

The thank-you we sent to Fabia and Bill Windle is an idea you might like to adapt sometime. It was personal, not terribly expensive, and something that will be a long-lasting reminder of our weekend together. I'll tell you exactly how it evolved.

That weekend when six of us, including the Windles, went to the country house in France, I had brought my camera along and clicked away at every conceivable moment. At the time, I thought I was taking pictures for my own pleasure, but when the prints came back from the photo shop, I saw that I had a complete graphic diary of our three days together. There were photos that showed Fabia and Bill alone and in various assortments with the others in the party as we cocktailed on the terrace or chatted in the living room, watched the grape harvest, shopped in Bordeaux, laughed and posed and did all the convivial things you do on a weekend like that. I knew that this was a collection that simply couldn't be duplicated, and that Fabia and Bill would enjoy having a set. So I edited the mound of photos down to the two or three dozen that told the story best and put them in chronological order along with the menus, matchbooks, cocktail napkins, and postcards we had picked up along the way. Then I inserted all the pieces in a good leather-bound album, and wrote the running saga of our weekend alongside each photo or souvenir.

The book began with a photo of the Windles that I had shot as we arrived. The first caption read:

"Friday, October 2. The six of us—Carolyn and Roger Horchow, Ann and Monte Wallace, Fabia and Bill Windle—rendezvous at Chateau Mont Lambert for the start of the Great Weekend. After much confusion, with mixups about who should sleep where, we unpack, have a drink, and hatch inspired plots for our tour."

That page also displayed an airline baggage ticket, and a small map of the area as mementos of the day. The album continued almost hour by hour, with photos, souvenirs, and notes like:

"We drive south of Bordeaux and see the historic Chateau Haut Brion, now owned by the children of Douglas Dillon. Fabulous lunch at La Reserve in near by Pessac, where we meet M. Flourens, owner and manager, and an old friend of Bill's. Shopping in the afternoon. Carolyn buys out the town's supply of almond-paste candy, to tuck away for Christmas gifts.

"Cocktails and dinner 'at home.' Much good talk and laughter. Roger at the piano, as usual, conducting a late-night songfest. Brandy and bed by eleven, ready for another stupendous tomorrow."

Incidentally, Carolyn did not hoard all of the Bordeaux candy she had bought for Christmas giving. She had overheard Fabia confess that she had a raving sweet tooth and could never get enough of the almond-paste delicacies that are a local specialty. That evening after dinner, Carolyn got one of the five-pound boxes from our room and presented it to Fabia, saying, "That was such a delicious dinner and we have had such a glorious day, it's been like Christmas in October. Thank you, Fabia. Here's a present that we found under the tree for you." Carolyn's genuine appreciation was obvious, and the light note she added to her little speech removed the possibility that others in the room might feel they had been remiss because they hadn't given Fabia a gift, too.

You can pick up a lot of clues about things your host would enjoy just by listening and being observant. One weekend Pat and Sam Beard came from New York to stay with us in Nantucket. He is president of the American Institute for Public Service, of which I am a board member. One day when we all went into town and walked through the Nantucket Looms shop, Pat noticed that Carolyn was especially fond of a soft blue wool throw that was on the weaver's loom. While the rest of us were occupied in the front room of the shop, Pat took the weaver aside, gave him a check, and arranged to have the throw delivered to Carolyn, with Pat's card enclosed, as soon as it was finished. You can imagine Carolyn's delight and surprise when the gift arrived. "How in the world could Pat have known?" she asked. When I told her what Pat had done that afternoon when the four of us were in town, she was deeply touched.

Nonreciprocal Trade

In my book, if you are not going to reciprocate in some way, you shouldn't accept an invitation. Still, we all know people who are perennial nonreciprocating guests; the curious thing is, they get away with it. I am thinking of one couple in particular whose description probably matches somebody you know. They are exceedingly good looking and beautifully dressed, charming to everybody, and adroit at bringing people together. They are bright and well informed, and you can count on them to leap into any conversational lull and save the day. Their very presence ensures a successful party. And that is how they figure they pay their way. They are professional guests, and have even trained their ten-year-old daughter to be an enchanting addition to other people's homes. Not once have they entertained any of the people whose guests they have been, yet they keep being invited back by the same people again and again. The only moral I can draw from all this is that scales do not always balance the way we expect them to.

Household Disruptions

Unpleasant houseguests are a rarity. Most people whom you invite know enough to practice the good advice of Lady Mendl, Elsie de Wolfe, who cautioned, "Be handsome if you can. Be witty if you must. Be agreeable if it kills you." Still, even the most gloriously agreeable houseguests imaginable cannot alter the fact that certain of your schedules and rituals will be altered when they come to stay. The most noticeable disruptions seem to be in our morning routines. I think that most of us are quite rigid about our habits then, and are not used to having outsiders around while we try to get our day into gear. Furthermore, you never know for sure, unless they are thoughtful enough to tell you, which of your guests will turn out to be early risers and which ones like to sleep late. That is why the first thing that is apt to cross a host's mind, when a guest's morning habits are different from the rest of the household's, is "What will we do about breakfast?" The solutions are simple.

Weekend Breakfasts

First, clarify everything the night before. Explain what time you will be serving breakfast, and what the menu will be. Show your guests where the coffee maker is and how it works, in case they get up before you do. Ask if they have any special requests so you can respond to their needs. When the tables are turned and you are the guest, it is up to you to make your needs known if the host doesn't ask you first. It is just not fair to ring last-minute surprises such as, "My doctor has me on a salt-free diet," or, "I cannot start the day without yogurt." It's not necessary to suffer because you are a guest in somebody's home, either. You may be accustomed to a full-scale breakfast, while your hosts start each day with nothing but coffee and toast. There is nothing wrong with your saying, "I don't want you to go to any trouble, so if you have eggs in the refrigerator, I'll make my own in the morning." You can offer to scramble a batch for everyone in the house, as a treat. They might take you up on it, or they might just say, "No, thank you. But you go ahead and help yourself to whatever you'd like."

Forethought and preparation make breakfast times easier.

Some hosts like to set the table the night before. Others set trays and leave them on the kitchen counter so guests can pick them up at will. Either method accomplishes three things: (1) it provides guests with what they need; (2) it eliminates early-morning clatter and fumbling in drawers and cabinets; and (3) it lets you show off your prettiest china and place mats, and underscores your wish to make your friend's visit a festive, special occasion. In short, it shows that you care. I think it is rude when people don't bother to trot out their best for you. And I really dislike it when they say, "Come take potluck with us; we won't go to any trouble. You're just one of the family. It'll be real old-shoe." I *want* them to make a little effort for me. If they are going to treat me like an old shoe I would rather stay home where I'll be more comfortable. A little garnish can go a long way, and it's the small extras that make the big difference. Think of how much nicer weekend breakfasts would be if you thought ahead and ordered extra newspapers delivered for each of your guests to read. For only a few pennies, the touch would tell people you care, and it would be remembered for years.

Weekend Lunches

Lunch is another meal that most of us are not used to serving to guests. If you are not geared to constant entertaining, you may wonder how on earth people prepare and serve a midday meal gracefully, without letting the effort show. The trick is to keep it simple. No elaborate dishes that keep you slaving at the chopping block and stove. No multicourse menus that are intricate to serve and a bother to clean up. Most people find that one-dish lunches work best—casseroles, pasta, anything that keeps the work load and costs to a minimum. Carolyn's favorite company lunch is quiche, salad, and fruit. Or she might arrange a platter of cold fried chicken or cold sliced meat from the night before. If she serves dessert, it is something light and easy, such as fresh fruit, ice cream, or bakery-bought pastry. What matters is that the food tastes good, looks good, and that nobody feels there is altogether too much time and labor attached to the occasion. A relaxed host means relaxed guests.

Guests in the Kitchen

Guests are bound to ask if they can help in the kitchen. Let me rephrase that—guests ought to ask if they can help, before they bound into the kitchen. That gives their host leeway to say either, "Sure, come on in; I can use all the help I can get," or, "Thank you, but no. I turn into an idiot when anybody is around. What I would like, though, is if you'd bring the glasses in from the sun deck and then chat with our other guests while I'm busy in the kitchen." That makes your guest feel that he or she is being helpful, and keeps him or her out of your hair at the same time.

Nan Birmingham, the magazine journalist, author of *Store*, and lecturer on such homey topics as "How To Entertain and Enjoy It Anyway the Night the Turkey Falls on the Floor," says that her days of commanding guests, "Out of my kitchen!" ended when she became a working woman. Nan is as open and straightforward in expressing herself as she is talented a writer and hostess. Along with her fast wit, rollicking smile, and miles of anecdotes, she is a superb cook and has the ability to put everybody at ease immediately. You wouldn't mind being stranded on a desert island with her, especially if the island had a kitchen.

Nan lives in a comfortable house outside New York City, and has two kitchens, one indoors and another in her poolhouse. She says, "I have learned that guests like to be in on the act. It's the new kind of entertaining. It's different from years ago, when I was a housewife and entertaining was my ego trip. Then, I wanted to do everything myself. These days I don't have the time. Or the money. And I don't need the ego-stroking anymore. So when people say, as they always do, what can I do to help, I *tell* them. They especially like to putter in the little poolhouse kitchen; it's like a playhouse to them and it's a catalyst because they can help and be close to the poolside action all at once. I think if you get people involved in the routine, they have a better time. That's why I had everybody come inside to the big kitchen and write their names on the cake I made for my friend Joan's birthday party, so they would feel they were doing something and were in on things. Of course, you have to feel out who wants to be a guest at the party, and who wants to play the role of Insider. Some people, when they can say to the room at large, 'I'll do it, Nan, I know where you keep the sugar,' enjoy the implication that they are your close personal friend and in the know. Anyway, I have found that the more input people have the better they like it. That's probably why you see fads for what I call participation foods—fondue, hibachi grills, ice cream sundae bars. Participation gives people something in common to talk about."

Nan's houseguests are as apt to be Ava Gardner and Hedy Lamarr as they are relatives from California or the assorted cosmopolites she meets in her journalistic travels. I asked her what happens when celebrities come to stay. "If you mean, is it difficult or demanding, the answer is no," Nan replied. "However, although most of my guests are the kind who pitch in, my celebrity guests are the kind who—how shall I put it?—are not very adept around the house. I suppose it's because they have plenty of help in their own homes. Anyway, you somehow don't feel you can say to Hedy Lamarr, 'Would you run downstairs and throw in the laundry while I fix the cake.' It's just fine with me if they sleep late and stay out of the way, while I get the house to look as if it is tended to by a vast staff that has taken the day off.

"The funniest part about entertaining celebrities is your friends' reactions. Even the nicest people you know can be quite rude, because they don't want you to think they are impressed. For instance, I had a big garden party for Ava Gardner and nobody would talk to her. I'd go over to a group that was chattering away among themselves and say, 'Did you meet my guest of honor?' They would answer, 'Well, she seems to be getting enough attention without me.' Or they'd demur, 'But what would I say to her?' I longed for the nice, old-fashioned, innocent type who would go up to Ava and say, 'I adored your last picture.' All you have to say to any celebrity is, 'I loved your last . . .' and whether it was a film, a book, a television show, the star will fill in the rest, believe me. The phrase is an opener guaranteed to turn them on.

"Ava wound up talking a lot with the kids in the jazz band at that party, and the same thing has happened to Hedy. Actually,

they are both charming women, and Hedy is particularly entertaining at a party. She rises to the occasion—tells fortunes, does
card tricks, and is utterly enchanting."

Whether you do it by telling fortunes or radiating a cheerful
spirit, when you are a houseguest you have an obligation to be
entertaining. One of my pet peeves is people who sit in a lump
waiting for the host to bring on the dog-and-pony show. It helps
if you have a specialty—an ability to tell fortunes, play the
piano, make duck and cow noises for the youngsters, perform as
an ace tennis partner or a sparkling raconteur. Lacking a specialty, you can do your part in other ways: keep the conversational ball in play, offer your expertise as a carrot scraper and
pot scrubber, and behave as if meeting fifty strangers at a cocktail party is your all-time favorite diversion. When you get down
to it, what a good houseguest does is fit in socially and agreeably
with everyone else's rhythm.

When Guests Invite Guests

Actually, I have never seen a guest who stayed out of step. But
I have heard stories. There's the one about the woman, whom
we'll call Clara, who went to visit her old school friend in Min-
neapolis. Without a by-your-leave, Clara got on the phone and
proceeded to invite everybody she had ever known in Minneap-
olis to come over and say hello to the returned warrior. She set
up the visits in relays, and Clara's poor host found herself
checking coats, producing trays of hors d'oeuvres and drinks,
clearing away glasses and crumpled napkins in between waves
of men, women, and children who came to kiss Clara's ring. I
think that what she should have done at the outset was tell Clara
that if there were anybody in town she would like to see, the best
time to ask them over would be on Saturday between two and
five o'clock. Period. Or else she could have offered to drop Clara
off at somebody's house Saturday afternoon, and pick her up at
five if she couldn't get a ride back home. With a takeover person
like Clara, it probably would not be wise to donate the use of
your car. You would either wind up chauffeuring the woman all
over town or Clara would commandeer the car and drive off into
the sunset—on your gas.

The Horchows' living room has become a very special gathering place and reflects the family's interests. The grand piano is the focal point for entertaining, and there are separate areas for conversation and games.

The Horchows' living room is multi-faceted. Although it is quite large, it never overwhelms. The space is cleverly divided into smaller areas with furniture and rugs.

The Horchows' dining room is a reflection of the Horchow style. It presents an inviting air, and the mirrored table top allows a more contemporary approach to table setting.

Collecting is a way of expressing one's personal style. Right, English enameled copper boxes can be favorite collectibles. Today's contemporary re-creations will be as treasured in the future as the charming 18th century antique ones are today.

Below, friends always know what to give a collector. A labor of love stitched by a friend for Gershwin aficionado Roger Horchow's fiftieth birthday.

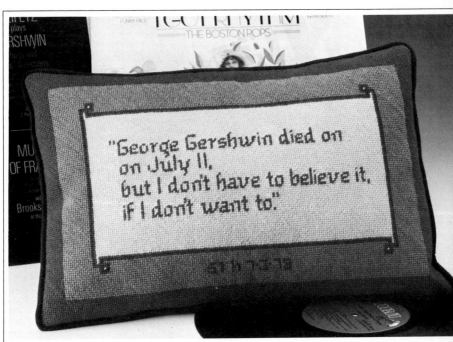

Top, hostesses today create imaginative arrangements with a single prized stem in each vase, for a dramatic dining table centerpiece or coffee table accent.

Bottom, the Horchows' sunporch is a relaxed, casual and comfortable family living area, mixing antique wicker furniture with contemporary table and chairs.

Folk art is one of Roger Horchow's collecting enthusiasms. His ingenious solution to displaying his ever expanding collection is a wall of staggered shelves which shows off each piece and creates a gallery at the same time.

Left, today's offices have become expressions of personal style. One senses Roger Horchow's interest in folk art and an engaging side of his personality upon entering.

Below, the art of showcasing a collection. Miniature shoes are placed on a lacquered tray which sets them apart and makes a statement of their specialness.

The personal touch in table setting.
Right, bandanas used as napkins present a creative approach to buffets.
Below, three different approaches to entertaining, by dressing the same table with three different dining personalities.

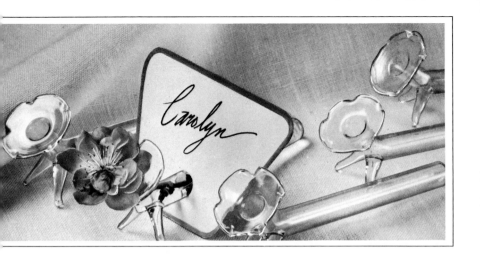

Place cards and fresh flowers add style to even the smallest dinner.

Above, mirrored place mats replace traditional mats or table cloth, adding drama to the table and accenting china and flatware.

Left, the hostess book, a must for any dedicated host or hostess. Carolyn Horchow finds hers invaluable in avoiding repetition and recording successes.

Above, a monogram makes a gift unique and personal.

Above right, the Horchows put their special stamp on New Year's Eve with personalized plastic glasses.

Right, imaginative gift wrapping can become part of the gift itself and enhance the pleasure of receiving.

Below, the elements of a most memorable fiftieth birthday gala, the three-day Roger Horchow Film Festival.

Gift wrapping is another expression of style. A special closet or storage space in your home filled with anything and everything, including bubble pack, ribbons, paper; allows you to be creative and to style the gift wrap for the gift.

Above, traveling with the Horchow girls was never a problem, thanks to their mother's thoughtfully prepared "busy kits," filled with diversions, and even snacks.

Right, "brown bagging" with a difference, using a status label bag. It's an elegant way to enjoy air travel with a meal of your own choosing.

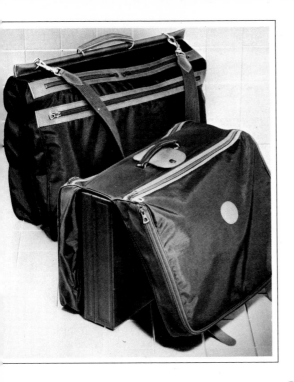

Left, knowledgeable travelers always pack an under-the-seat bag. It avoids standing in baggage claim lines on shorter trips and is a survival kit in case of lost luggage on longer ones.

Below, a thermal coffee pot brings the distinction and graciousness of the home to the office coffee break.

Below right, foldable luggage solves the storage problem in apartments and small homes. It also serves as an extra bag for travel purchases.

Desks now express their owners' style. Clear acrylic organizers give a well ordered look, even to contemporary drawerless desks.

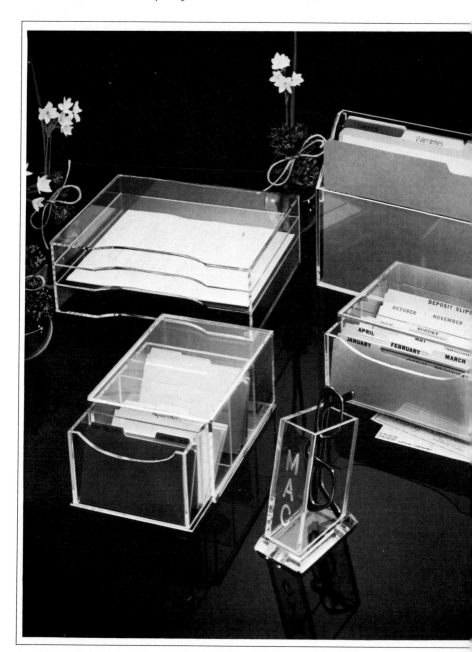

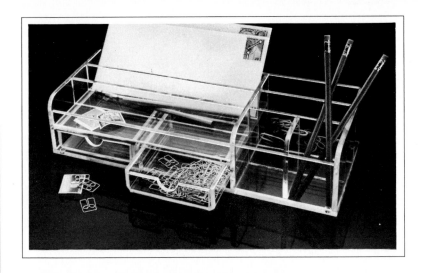

Top, organization is essential in this busy world. Keep all those little essentials right at hand in the kitchen or on a desk.

Above, file folders are the single most important organizing tool. Who says they have to be plain Manila? A flap and a tie assure you you'll never lose anything.

In our mobile society, stacking units can replace built-ins in the kitchen, bedroom, office or bath. When you move, so can they.

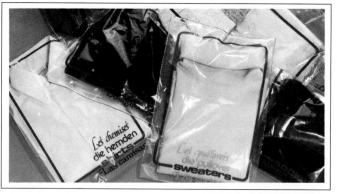

Plastic travel bags prevent wrinkles better than tissue, hold assorted loose items, separate laundry and wet bathing suits in a suitcase.

Today, with smaller living areas, adding storage where you can becomes a must.

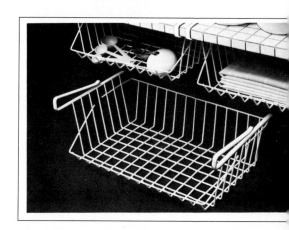

Guest-of-Honor Parties

I would not like to have a Clara around who expected me to wait on her covey of admirers, but I do like to invite our friends to come and meet our weekend guests. It's a way of sharing a dimension of our life: we get to show off our out-of-towners to the people we see every day, and our visitor gets to see how we live. Carolyn always says our friends come to see us, not our neighbors, but it is hard for me to resist. So, what we do when we have a cocktail or dinner party for a visiting fireman is make it one big affair, then spend the rest of our weekend more intimately.

There are some visiting firemen, though, for whom we make a purposeful effort to arrange whole series of parties. I am thinking of friends who are considering a move to Dallas and want to know some prospective neighbors, singles who would like to meet a new man or woman, activists who want to exchange ideas with people involved in our museum or symphony. And just plain gregarious folks who love a weekend of partying.

Getting Offstage

All weekends come to an end, and all good guests have been trained from the cradle to ask their hosts if they would like the bed stripped, and where to put the used towels. Nan Birmingham tells a story about how good manners backfired on her. "I had been the houseguest of a lady who maintained an impeccable menage at a resort on the East Coast. Although she had a man and woman who lived in and kept the house sorted out, I tried to be tidy while I was part of the household. The day I left, I managed to locate the linen closet, stripped and changed my bed, and folded my towels neatly on the hamper. I went downstairs and said good-bye, thanking my hostess for everything including her irreproachable friends and the series of four-star meals she had presented. I also gave her the housekeeping information about my bed and towels. That's when she let me have it. She said icily, 'What do you think I pay help hundreds of dollars a week to do? What do you *mean* meddling like that! I should have known it would come to this from the way you went around all weekend offering to bring plates into the kitchen, introducing my guests to one another.' By the time I got myself offstage, she had scolded me for every move I made during the entire weekend, and any foolish notion I might have had that I'd played my part well or had a good time was erased. Need I tell you, I never visited there again."

⚜ ⚜ ⚜

7
GIFTS PEOPLE
NEVER FORGET

I think we all have received gifts as a children that we remember all the rest of our life. For Carolyn, it was a gold charm that her father gave her when she was eight years old. She recalls, "Dad had returned from one of his trips for the lumber yard our family owns in Little Rock and I was watching him unpack, as I always did when he came home. This time I saw him rummage around under a layer of shirts, and then hold up a mysterious package wrapped in shiny red paper, tied with gold cord. I can still see it in my mind's eye. Dad held the package out to me and said, 'I brought this from Chicago for you, Carolyn. It's something I thought you might like.' I was thrilled, as any child is with a present, and tore away the ribbon and paper to find a beautiful, gold charm. It was the first time I remember that Dad brought me something from one of his trips and the unexpectedness took me aback. It showed me that he really did pay attention to me, and that he cared. I have never forgotten that day, and the charm will always be one of my favorites.

The Philosophy of Gift Giving

Carolyn's story sums up our feelings about gift giving. It is personal thought and effort, not lavishness, that distinguishes memorable gifts from mere obligatory offerings. There was no mistaking the intent behind Carolyn's charm. The gift said, "I want to please you, and it has pleased me to take the trouble to find something that I believe you will like." It makes no difference whether the something is a book, a tin of brownies, or a cloud of black sable; if the object is to give someone pleasure, then the gift is right.

We sometimes worry too much about *what* to give, and forget that it is the why and how that counts. Kenneth Jay Lane has a wonderful recollection that underscores the point. Although he has traveled the world, counts the most celebrated members of society among his friends, and is as urbane a man as you will find, Kenneth says the most unforgettable gift he ever received didn't even have a card enclosed. "It had all the elements of surprise," he muses. "I think that is what made it so thrilling. When I was a young boy we lived in the northern part of Michigan. The woods there were full of Indian arrowheads, which I collected. I had quite a trove and was always on the lookout for more. An uncle who took a special interest in me knew of my collection and decided he would buy me a bagful of arrowheads as a gift. But he went a step further. Instead of wrapping the arrowheads and handing them to me for Christmas or a birthday, he scattered them on the grounds all around where we lived. He never said a word about what he had done, but let me come across the arrowheads by myself, so I would believe that I was an explorer discovering Indian artifacts on my own. I was beside myself for weeks. Each time I went for a walk I 'discovered' another Indian arrowhead. My uncle made his gift to me so much more exciting that way. It wasn't until much later when my cousin, his daughter, told me the story that I learned how he had planted the arrowheads. I have always adored unexpected gifts, especially when they are things that the other person knows I will treasure."

The Personal Touch

It is interesting to learn the different kinds of things that trigger people's responses. I was in New York one day, sitting in the executive office at Cartier having a chat with the fabled jewelry company's president, Ralph Destino. We were talking about current trends in gift giving, and I posed the question to Ralph, "What was the most memorable gift you ever received?" Ralph has a mind that can turn on a dime, and his answer was hair-trigger quick. "You can see it from where you sit, right over there on the shelf," he said, pointing to a large leather folder stamped *R.D. April 7, 1936.* He brought the folder over to my chair and opened it to show me the contents while he explained. "I received this just three months ago as a birthday gift from a dear friend. It's the complete, original, slightly yellowed issue of *The New York Times* that was published on the day I was born. I find it absolutely fascinating, and moving as well. The birthday newspaper represents nostalgia, which is always moving, but more than that, I am touched by the fact that my friend took the trouble to present me with memorabilia that is directly related to my own personal experience."

Ralph put the bound *Times* back on its shelf and continued, "I know it's a cliché to say, 'You have to think about the other person,' but it bears repeating. All anyone has to do is open up his or her mind and be adventuresome, to tap into that personal connection. If you use your creative juice, which everybody has, you will come up with gifts that are exactly right. I'll give you another good example of a personally targeted gift. It's one that I gave to a friend last Christmas. It didn't come from our store, it was not at all expensive, and I know that it was appreciated.

"This friend is inordinately peripatetic. She is always on the move. One month she sent me a postcard from Italy, the next month from France, the next from someplace else. I hardly saw her all year, and when Christmas came I decided to send her a gift that reflected her globe-trotting life. I took an old book and cut out the center of the pages to form a well, leaving just an inch and a half all around as a frame. Inside the back cover I pasted a sheet of heavy white paper which I had marked off in twelve sections, each headed by a month and the name of the city she had been in then. Under *January, Pisa* I attached a small, inexpensive charm of the Tower of Pisa. *February, Paris* was marked by a charm depicting the Eiffel Tower. *March, Nassau* had a charm that was a yacht. And so on. I had the cover of the book hot-stamped *1979 Diary*, with her name in gold just below the title. I understand that she shows it off to everyone, the way I showed you my 1936 *New York Times*. It was a gift that could not conceivably belong to anyone but her, and that is what made it so special."

People cherish things that you have obviously given thought to, particularly gifts that you have made with your own hands. Several of our friends who are known for culinary specialties make it a practice to give their creations to people they especially want to please. We always hope that we will be on the list when Carolyn's friend Jane Jenevein bakes her renowned lemon dobish cakes. Another person, Esther Romero, who keeps house for Carolyn's friend Janet Kutner, supplies us with delicious Mexican and American cookies at Christmastime. Carolyn herself has a reputation for the zesty pesto sauce she creates when fresh basil is available. She always makes extra quantities to keep in the freezer, and give to friends at Christmas or when we go visiting. It costs little, but it is the personal touch that lends importance and makes the gift impressive.

Shopping for Gifts

You can be creative at home, and you can find gift ideas when you shop. It seems to me that ought to be fun, but too often I hear people groan over their gift lists, as if shopping were like having an impacted molar extracted. There should be a joy involved. Timing has a lot to do with it. One of the simplest ways to remove the chore aspect from shopping is to do it when the stores are not jammed, and while there is a broad selection of merchandise. I can see why high noon in a department store two days before Christmas is no fun. But if you have done your buying when the shopping is easy, you could be sitting in a cozy cafe at high noon, sipping something cheerful while visions of sugarplums dance in your head.

Carolyn and I shop all year around—for Christmas, for birthdays, for no occasions at all. Anytime we see something that we know one of our friends will enjoy, we buy it on the spot and tuck it away in our gift storage space. We keep a whole closet just to store the gifts we pick up as we go along. It is a warehouse of things we have garnered on our travels because we know somebody is going to want them, sometime. For instance, my attorney, Gene Emery, is an exuberant and devoted runner. To him, running is a full-time hobby. Wherever he is in the world, he runs. I think he can cite every trail and tree from here to Baden-Baden. One day I was pawing through a flea market in Connecticut and came across a bronze plaque dated 1912 that depicted a runner in his shorts. It cost two dollars. I bought it, had it framed for ten dollars, and tucked it away in the gift closet. When Christmas rolled around, I presented the plaque to Gene with much to-do and flourish. He loved it. In fact, he has been showing off that two dollar runner's plaque to everybody he can collar for the past eight years, and tells the story again and again.

Even if we don't have anyone special in mind, we are apt to buy things that capture our interest, Carolyn will see an unusual strand of beads, for example, and get one for herself and a duplicate to give to a friend sometime later. We especially like to buy things that are peculiar to the places where we travel, things we know people can't get where they live. That's why we do much of our Christmas shopping in August, when we're in Nantucket. You can get folk art, handwoven throws and shawls, cotton fisherman sweaters, even foods that the people back in Dallas have never seen. If we are in New Orleans we'll pick up a regional cookbook or a gumbo file that only a New Orleanean would find familiar. We like things that are symbolic of an area. Our friends in Chicago are delighted to receive a nachos kit from Dallas or a box of Texas chewy pralines.

Perennial Gifts

Not that every gift has to be offbeat or hard to find. Anything that is a classic and in good taste will always be in good taste. A simple silver key ring or a well-designed tray never goes out of fashion, and some people have adopted items like these as their signature gifts. Whenever they need to give a graduation, Christmas, or wedding gift, they simply phone their favorite store and order "the usual" to be sent to the recipient of the moment. Danny Zarem found a repeat that also has the bonus of being unusual. On a trip one time he discovered an exceptional recording of a well-known Gershwin score. Gershwin himself was at the piano, which made the recording extremely rare. When Danny discovered that everyone he played the record for was enchanted, he got in touch with the music store and ordered a dozen and a half of the records. For over a year he had the joy of passing along his very special Gershwin recording to friends who enjoyed it.

The Gift Closet: Keeping Track

If we have put away a gift for a certain person or a particular occasion, we mark the package as protection against our own unreliable memories. I am sure we are no different from other people when it comes to identifying objects in storage. Haven't you ever come across something that you bought months ago and scratched your head, wondering why on earth you bought it? I think we all need reminders, as we scramble through this high-voltage life, to help us keep the important things sorted out. We not only use a marking system, we add a little insurance to it by cross-referencing the gifts that have known destinations in our gift diary. On the page March 12, where we have written "Charlie Sanders's birthday," we add, "Nantucket fisherman's sweater (in closet)." Then on a page ten days before March 12, or however long it is going to take to get the package delivered in time for Charlie's birthday, we write in, "Mail gift to Charlie Sanders, see March 12."

Different people evolve different systems of record keeping, and I think that whatever comes naturally to you is the best system to use. A floral designer we know is accustomed to working in tight space and is therefore in the habit of consolidating everything possible. Her gift reminder system is the same as ours, on her diary pages, and she also jots down everyone's birthday and anniversary on her telephone/address wheel. It gives her an additional cross-check, and she never has to stop and hunt up addresses.

What I plan to do next is program my card file and diary listings in a home computer and let it do the annual entry work for me. The entries are not etched in stone, and I can always make additions and changes to the latest input.

Gift Wrappings

Next to the hoard of gifts on the closet shelf, we keep wrapping materials that we accumulate as we go along. This can mean wallpaper leftovers, fabric remnants, the gold or silver paper that comes inside other people's gifts to us, stylish boxes with discreet logos that we can mask with a card or picture if we wish, and the plastic bubble filler that comes with breakables. We keep yarn, cord, ribbon, strips of velvet, dress trimming like rickrack in whatever colors we happen to get our hands on. It is not much exaggeration to say that practically everything that comes into our house passes through the recycling machine that we call a gift closet.

Actually, the wrapping materials in the closet are only the tip of our packaging iceberg. We like to present gifts in a way that sets up the recipients' expectancy, the way an overture in the orchestra pit whets your appetite for the show about to be unveiled. Like an overture, the wrapping usually gives a clue to what is inside. It is the signal that something special is waiting to be unfurled.

Carolyn has a knack for creating gifts within gifts. She'll put homemade jellies and cookies, together with the recipes and a pretty plate, in an interesting basket or beach bag, or wrap them up in a colorful napkin or bandanna. Bottles of fine olive oil and seasoned vinegar will nest in a salad bowl, then the bowl will go into a bag or box stuffed with lettuce-green tissue, its green wrapping paper topped off with a pair of salad tongs. When she decided to give a friend some dried homemade pasta, she tied the sheaf with a red checkered ribbon, lined a colander with a matching napkin, and wrapped the whole thing in a red checkered towel with solid yarn cord. When she gives somebody stationery, she often ties a decorative pencil or felt-tip pen onto the ribbon. Books are popped into a tote bag, with a bookmark tied into the bow that seals the tote's handles. A bottle of wine goes into a colored cloth or paper sack, with a corkscrew tied on around its neck. And she has been known to give someone an anniversary gift of a jug of wine in a picnic basket that also contains a pair of wineglasses, a loaf of bread, and a serrated knife.

Chinese-Box Packaging

Gifts within gifts within gifts are fun to receive. They are like reading a suspense novel: just when you think you know who dunnit, another layer of the mystery comes to light and you have to keep digging to reach the denouement. One of Regen's high school graduation gifts was like that; we thought the discoveries would go on forever.

A friend of ours who has known Regen since she was a baby understands what tickles her sense of humor, as well as what she needed to go off to college. So our friend, Sally, gave Regen a straw, ribbon-banded handbag that could double as a picnic tote bag. Regen took out the crumpled blue tissue paper, looked inside the tote and found another handbag. It was a tailored clutch, suitable for everyday use, but the great thing was that it was made of bold blue leather, a color that she probably would not have bought for herself because it's not "basic." Regen opened the blue handbag and found that it held another of Sally's surprises: a third bag. This one was an evening purse that Regen could use for dress-up occasions. We thought that must be the last of the Chinese-box mystery, until Regen unsnapped the clasp and, you're right, nested inside was yet another gift: a paisley-covered date book in which the freshman-to-be could record her engagements for the year. I think Regen had as good a time opening the packages as she had using the gifts Sally had chosen for her. And although I must admit that the purses and datebook added up to a fair amount of money, basically it was the fact that Sally had Regen's pleasure in mind that made the gift so right. That and the extra kick in the way she presented the gifts . . . like a kangaroo with a pouchful of surprises.

Sometimes it is incongruity that sets off a gift and makes it amusing. Or unexpected. Or dramatic. The first time I proposed to Carolyn, in the Palm Court of the Plaza Hotel, I handed her a matchbox: the small ordinary kind you keep in the kitchen. Carolyn was baffled. She asked, "What on earth is this for, Roger? You know I don't smoke." I suggested to her that I was trying to light another kind of fire, and asked her to open the box. She did, and there, glinting like a tiny sunbeam, was the best engagement ring I could afford at the time. Carolyn was truly stunned, and couldn't say a word until I took her hand and asked her to marry me. I guess I overdid the unexpectedness part, because she turned me down.

A month later, Carolyn was home in Little Rock with her parents and I flew down to visit, with another box rattling like chattering teeth in my pocket. This time the engagement ring was encased in a Band-Aid box, and when I finally presented it to her at what I deemed the right moment, Carolyn asked with a smile if I thought she looked wounded. I answered that the Band-Aid was for me: I was trying to heal my broken heart. She knew instantly what was in the box and when at last she said yes, she made me promise her a simple wedding band and no more crazy gift wraps at the wedding. I never was happier to make a promise in my life. We kissed, told her parents that we were engaged, and set the date for the following December. To complete the story: my best man, Gene Pfeifer, did remember to bring the ring to the ceremony and it was not in a matchbox or Band-Aid tin. The rattling sound that I heard was the sound of my own knees knocking.

The simplest wrap can be the most sensational, if you use your imagination. Ralph Destino told me about one that he received. He had given a huge, dressy party with a number of social and theatrical luminaries as his guests, an event which *Women's Wear Daily* reported in its next edition. One of the guests thereupon sent Ralph a thank-you gift wrapped in that issue of *Women's Wear.* The first thing he saw when the package arrived was his own name, and photographs of his guests. He says he has forgotten what the gift was, but will always remember the wrapping paper. And the person who had the wit to send the president of Cartier a gift wrapped in yesterday's newspaper.

It was the personal touch that made a lasting impression. Another corporate chieftain I know mentioned to his secretary that he was taking cooking lessons. That Christmas his staff gave him a ricer, with a gift tag bearing all of their signatures on one side and a recipe on the other. He told me he still treasures that two dollar ricer and fifty cent tag, because the gift symbolized a million dollars worth of thoughtfulness.

The Guilt-edged Gift that Backfired

The story reminds me of the expensive peace-offering gift that was absolutely worthless because the donor didn't think about the other person. The donor was a husband with a wandering eye, who usually covered his tracks pretty well. But one night he made the error of staying out too late. When he returned he and his wife quarreled, and he wanted to make up with her. So he spent a fortune on a gift that he was certain would make her run back to his arms. He chartered a seventy-six-foot yacht to cruise from Fort Lauderdale to the Bahamas, and manned the yacht with a French chef whose specialty was opulent sauces. Then he chartered a Lear jet, and flew his wife down from North Carolina to Florida and the great surprise. The trip lasted three days and was a complete fiasco. He had ignored the fact that his wife did not like the Bahamas, and besides that, she was on a rice diet that ruled out rich sauces. He spent thousands of dollars but not five minutes' worth of thought, and the peace offering led to anything but. As his wife remarked, "He never stopped to think what would please *me*."

Abstract Gifts

A gift is not always something that you wrap in a box. Some of the nicest presents are things that cannot be bought in a store. The gift of time. The gift of luxury. The gift of service. You just have to ask yourself what it is the other person would dearly love to have: what it is that he or she covets or that would make

life just a bit more pleasant. You'd be surprised at how many answers will come to you with very little effort, and often for very
little or no money at all. Friends of ours from Fort Worth, Bert
and Patricia Honea, have a summer house in Truro, on Cape
Cod, and every year Patricia has to face the annual beach wife's
lament, marketing for groceries while everybody else lolls on the
sand. Patricia says that for years she felt like Sisyphus with his
endless task of pushing boulders uphill; as soon as she filled the
larder to the top, it emptied itself, like rocks rolling back downhill. Two summers ago, as they were packing up for their annual
sojourn, Bert gave Patricia a gift that has made her the envy of all
Cape Cod. He had just retired from various boarding school po-
sitions and was appreciative of the fact that for the past twenty
years Patricia had been his constant hostess. It didn't seem fair
that she had to keep on with all the hostess duties while he was
retired and they were on vacation. So he presented her with the
Patricia Honea Retirement Plan. Each week while they were in
Truro, he would do all of the supermarket shopping while she
lolled on the beach, read, or did anything else she liked. Patricia
says Bert's gift has made her summers pure heaven, and that she
never would have thought to ask for such a service herself.

Last Christmas Bert extended Patricia's Retirement Plan with
another gift of personal service. Every Sunday he trots off to the
kitchen, prepares breakfast, and brings it in to the bedroom
where Patricia luxuriates over her tray of toast and honey as if
she were the king's favorite, most pampered princess.

I can think of other similar gifts where the intent was to take a
tedious job off somebody's hands. Regen once bestowed a Valentine's Day gift on Carolyn that has never been forgotten: she
cleaned her perpetually cyclone-struck closet from top to bottom. And kept it clean for a solid month. If you know teenagers,
you will understand why Carolyn regards that deed as a real act
of love. A friend of Regen's, eighteen-year-old Jim, took Regen's
gift as a cue and donated himself to a favorite aunt. He made her
a birthday present of coming to her house one day a week for
the entire birthday month, to run whatever errands needed to be
run: the hardware store, the cleaners, the car wash, and so on. I
know another teenager who gave her mother a season's worth of
car washing, a woman whose gift to a best friend was to act as her

stand-in in the Wednesday afternoon car pool, a third person who gave his niece the services of a housekeeper for a half-day every week for a year.

Get-Well Presents

Gifts of service are particularly apt for people who are ill. When Tish Baldrige was recuperating from an operation, five of her friends got together and arranged for a catering service to send in a complete meal each of the ten days she was housebound. You could do something similar for people who are in the hospital and not on a special diet. Think of the glee you would feel if you were confined with a broken leg and somebody brought a lunch or dinner tray that did not feature institutional custard. Never underestimate the power of food as a gift. Besides the fact that colors and sizes don't matter, you can count on the fact that everybody eats.

You don't have to go as far as paying a catering service to cheer up a sickroom. You can treat a friend who is flat on his or her back with a dish of fresh, hulled berries. Or rent a TV set with remote controls for them, or a hospital table, if they are at home. Give them extra-long tongs to pick up things off the floor. Do their errands. Bring them notepaper, stamps, a bundle of completely frivolous magazines guaranteed not to improve their minds. Treat them to bubble bath, lotions, perfume, a single fresh croissant with a jar of wonderful French preserves. And phone them at least once a day, whether you go to visit or not. It can be lonely lying there disconnected from the world outside.

A friend of ours, Judy, came very close to having that experience. She was scheduled for a relatively simple operation, and checked in early one January for a week's stay at one of the hospitals at the top of Parker Hill in Boston. Judy says that she would have gone out of her mind during that week if it hadn't been for the telephone, and the thoughtfulness of her friends. She recalls, "I woke up the day after surgery, feeling groggy but fine, looked out the window, and saw nothing at all. The entire landscape had been replaced by a giant, impenetrable blanket of thick white snow. As I learned later, I had awakened to the first day of the great storm of '77, the one that coated the Northeast with a layer of ice so solid it never melted until May. The city was immobilized. Nobody could walk, drive, or even ski the streets, and only heavy-duty emergency vehicles were able to maneuver the steep climb up Parker Hill. The friends who might have come to see me were as isolated in their homes as I was in my hospital room. It was an eerie sensation, and not at all pleasant. There wasn't even anybody who could smuggle in a bottle of wine, or come and tell me the latest gossip. I could foresee a week of total abandonment.

"Then the phone started to ring. It rang in relays. I received at least four calls each afternoon, and four more every night. It was wonderful; I felt so cared for, knowing that somebody out there was thinking of me all week long. As a matter of fact, I even felt rather like a belle—so popular that a cabal had been formed just to cheer me up.

"As it turned out, that's more or less what had happened. A couple of my more enterprising friends, Ellen and Robert, having made sure I was up to talking on the phone, took it upon themselves to form a kind of telephone chain letter. Each of them suggested to another of my friends that a call a day would help me keep gloom away. It certainly did, and since then whenever anybody I know is hospitalized, I remember what the phone calls did for me and I start a telephone chain for them. It's the nicest medicine I know."

You could apply Judy's get-well calls to people who are not on a hospital sick list at all. It costs next to nothing, in time or money, to connect with somebody who happens to be going through a rough patch or who has moved away and needs the warmth of familiar voices. Long distance calls are an inexpensive form of indulgence, now that night rates have been shaved to small sums. Judy says that she often calls her cousins in California after 11:00 P.M. Boston time, when it's 8:00 or so on the Coast. For a couple of dollars they can have wonderful long chats, and she feels she has given them a gift they couldn't possibly go out and buy for themselves.

There are so many delightful and inexpensive gifts of thoughtfulness you can give to people who are not really sick, but are feeling off-center. It's a well-known fact that a quart of sinfully rich chocolate-chip ice cream will do wonders to cure the common sniffles. And a bunch of sunny white daisies, with a card that says, "Feel better," will do as much for someone who happens to have the blues that day as a session in a psychiatrist's office. I think that friendship is the sweetest balm you can apply to any affliction.

Long-Playing Gifts

It is pleasant to give what I call extended gifts, too, especially if they fill a need or satisfy a yearning. With one stroke you can keep a series of gifts coming for as long as a year, even longer. You could give somebody a course of lessons, if you know they are dying to learn how to cook, dance, ski, play bridge, or speak Spanish. You could make them a member of the Horticultural Society, a museum, or other organization devoted to activities that you know would engage them. Or you could appeal to some other interest. For instance, Carolyn knows how much I like hyacinths and how little I am apt to run out and buy fresh ones for my office. Her anniversary gift to me in 1980 was a half-dozen fresh hyacinths, to be delivered to my office every Monday morning for a year. My mother, who doesn't get out as much as she used to, is somebody who really enjoys extended gifts. One year we gave her a birthday present of fifteen days of a rental limousine, to be used whenever she liked during the next twelve months. A gift of a book of taxi coupons would have been equally welcome. The Christmas before, we had a package of frozen steaks sent to her house once a month. We knew that she likes to have friends in for dinner, but that it is difficult for her to run out and shop. Another time, to save her trips to the post office, we gave her a box of personalized notepaper with a stamp already stuck on each envelope.

Duty Gifts

All of the people you give gifts to are not personal friends or relations. Some are business associates, others are the people who help you around the house, and sometimes you are called upon to give a gift to somebody you don't even know. These situations are common, and not as much of a dilemma as some people think they are. I'll tell you how we usually handle our obligatory gifts, without being completely impersonal about them.

One answer is money or a gift certificate, which gives the recipient the freedom to choose what he or she likes, and eliminates the nuisance of having to exchange something they don't want. I should add that our own children adore it when their grandparents give them one of those bank envelopes stuffed with a nice check for Christmas or a birthday. Also, in many communities it is a common practice for friends to pool their resources and give a check to a husband and wife on their anniversary. Personally, I would prefer something that had been thoughtfully selected for our house, or a donation to charity. Still, a gift of money does have its merits; it permits the couple to go out and get what they really want.

Another time we give cash is at Christmas, usually in the form of grocery-store certificates, to the people who help take care of the house and my office. What we like to do is give them the gift before the holiday so they can spend it when it is needed most. Then, at Christmas, we usually add a small personal gift—a scarf or a wallet, just to say that we appreciate what they have done for us through the year. Sometimes we skip the scarf or wallet and give our helpers something for their children instead—a warm sweater or a durable toy that they wouldn't be apt to buy themselves, such as a cloth kite or a scooter. Last year Carolyn gave our housekeeper's children a kitten for their very own. Realizing that the gift could have created expense and inconvenience for our housekeeper, Carolyn made sure the cat had already had its shots, and was delivered with a generous supply of food and kitty litter as well.

Toys and Other House Gifts

Toys and games are good gifts to bring when you visit people whose tastes you don't know. We try to choose things that are fairly substantial and that will appeal to all ages, such as a beach ball and bats or a new board game. Or we bring a house gift that can be used during our stay. Food, usually, for where there are houseguests there are always drop-ins to provide for. As summertime hosts, Carolyn and I know how much we welcome any help in taking care of such contingencies. Last summer when we had our Cambridge Street Gang Reunion, for instance, one of our fourteen houseguests phoned before she left for Nantucket and asked if a cooked round of beef would upset Carolyn's plans. Carolyn said a roast would be most welcome, and indeed it was. We sliced and served it all weekend long, and Carolyn was spared some of the shopping and cooking for a crowd. Another of the Cambridge gang brought an enormous tin of brownies and cookies, something you never have to call ahead and ask about.

We have had main-course food arrive with guests without warning, but it has been the nonperishable kind so we didn't have to shuffle our plans. I remember once when one of Sally's chums from Dallas came to visit us in Nantucket. Her mother put her aboard the plane with a housegift package containing a smoked turkey. She knew that it would keep if we didn't want to use it right away, and that it was a special treat because we couldn't buy smoked turkey in Nantucket.

Carolyn says she wished she had thought of smoked turkey when she was choosing a thank-you gift for Lizzie to send to a friend in Sun Valley. Lizzie had spent a week there and came back so excited about the skiing and the scenery that she hadn't a clue as to what her friend's parents would like for the house. Carolyn had never seen the house and didn't know the parents, so she had to play Ellery Queen:

> CAROLYN: How is the house decorated, Lizzie?
> LIZZIE: Gosh, Mom, I don't know. It's very pretty and sort of, um, quiet.
> CAROLYN: "Quiet." Do you mean it's dark plums and browns, or cool green? Or is there a lot of pale white? What's the sofa covered in?
> LIZZIE: It's sort of big roses with blue things running through.
> CAROLYN: Like Grandma's sofa? It sounds as if their taste is on the traditional side. Can you remember what kind of music they like to play?
> LIZZIE: Oh yes. A lot of Beethoven and Mozart. And when

we kids were around they'd put on a stack of disco records for us.

CAROLYN: I think we are on the right track with traditional, but I'm not sure. Maybe we should think about something for the kitchen. Did you happen to notice anything that they need, like a waffle iron or some good carbon-blade knives?

LIZZIE: I'm sorry, Mom. I was too busy eating to notice the cooking. Oh wait! I just remembered that the grownups like to take their breakfast rolls and coffee out on the sun deck. I used to think how much easier it would be for them if they used mugs for their coffee, instead of juggling cups and saucers.

CAROLYN: Good, Lizzie! I think you have solved the mystery. Let's send them a set of six china coffee mugs in that nice rose-flowered pattern that reminds you of Grandma's sofa.

As Carolyn says, no matter how stuck you are, you can almost always come up with a gift that will really please a person if you just take a few minutes to think it through.

What to Give the Man Who Has Everything

Carolyn and I went through the mental exercise of thinking it through when we were invited to a fiftieth birthday party for one of my oldest friends, Jere Mitchell, Director of the Cardiopulmonary Laboratory at Southwestern University Medical School. Jere and I have been in close touch with one another for nearly twenty years, and I think it is fair to say that I know his possessions and his likes and dislikes as well as anybody. If anyone should know what would be the right gift for Jere, it would be me. But I was stumped. So was his wife Pam, when we called to ask her for ideas. She said, "Roger, you've heard about the man who has everything? Jere is different; he has twelve of everything. The best suggestion I can give you is to come to the party and let it go at that. He enjoys your and Carolyn's company so much, your presence would be the best gift you could give him." That was sweet of Pam and I thanked her, but I wasn't satisfied. I wanted to mark Jere's fiftieth birthday in a special, memorable way.

Then I remembered a gift that a friend of Lizzie's, Suzanne, had given to a group of her schoolmates. She had collected snapshots that she had taken of them through the school year—dancing at the prom, visiting the zoo, posing on their skis and bicycles. Suzanne selected the best of the photographs, pasted them up in an artful montage, captioned each photo, and then had the montage reproduced at a copy center. At graduation, she gave each of her friends a copy and I guarantee you that those gifts will be treasured long after the silver pens and leather travel kits have worn out.

With a slight adaptation, the idea was perfect for my friend Jere Mitchell. The night of his birthday party, I took along my camera and flashbulbs, and clicked away all evening long. Jere thought I was just having my own private fun. But two weeks later, when he and Pam came to a cocktail party at our house, he realized what I had really been up to. We had invited the inner circle of close friends who had been at the birthday party, and at the right moment I asked them all to gather around while I gave Jere his "unavoidably detained" birthday present. He didn't guess what it was until he unwrapped the package. My gift to Jere was a photo album containing snapshots of all his best friends disporting themselves at his fiftieth. It is a personal record of a significant milestone in Jere's life, and something nobody could have bought in any store. He confided in Pam, later on, that as generous as his other friends had been, the photo album was his favorite fiftieth birthday present.

Personal Gifts for Men

A photograph immediately personalizes any object and makes it unique. So does a monogram, inscription, and anything else you can think of to add a personal touch. It is a fact that people love to see their own names or images preserved in some way, something to remember if you want to transform a mundane item into an outstanding gift, or if you have a Jere Mitchell in your life. Men, especially, seem hard to buy gifts for. At least, that is what people keep telling me. I don't agree. Neither does

Ralph Destino. He is positively vehement on the subject. "It's a myth that I defy," he exclaims. "All it takes to make the difference between a ho-hum, plain vanilla gift and a *great* gift is a small personal touch." His outburst unleashed a spate of ideas for "the man who has everything."

• Give him an attaché case with a blazer patch representing his school or club attached to one side. Even if he already owns three other attaché cases, this one will be unlike any other in the world.

• Have a pair of cuff links designed especially for him, or make a pair yourself if jewelry-making is your hobby. It won't matter that he already has a mountain of cuff links in his bureau drawer. Yours will be the ones that stand out.

• Give him a subscription to *Time* or another magazine, and make your point in the presentation. Create a gift notification out of a sample copy, onto which you have pasted his photograph: "Cover man of the year."

• Find a nice picture frame and then make it remarkable by fitting it with a high school yearbook photo of the astonished and flattered recipient.

• Give him a book on a subject you know he is interested in, inscribe the flyleaf with a personal message, and then deck a page with a bookmark bearing his initials, the date, and a message in your own handwriting.

• Please an amateur chef with a good copper saucepan or butter warmer, and exalt the gift by having it engraved with his initials. It will be the pride and joy of his kitchen, and you can be sure he will never forget who gave it to him.

You can personalize practically anything with a monogram or inscription: disposable plastic glasses and mugs, ordinary #2 pencils, hand-crafted pottery, a poem you have written yourself. The list is as long as your imagination will take it. And the effect, I promise you, is dramatic. Personalizing is one of the best ways I know to give a Rolls Royce gift on a skateboard budget.

Exchanges

Some people worry about having a gift marked because they think the recipient might want to exchange it. My answer to that is, if you believe that the person is likely to want to exchange your gift, you have probably not made the right choice and had better rethink your idea to find something he or she will enjoy.

As with nearly every rule of thumb, this one has an exception. When you give something to a close friend or relative, it is perfectly reasonable to do as Carolyn's family does. On their gift cards, they add the initials U.P., Usual Proviso. Meaning, no feelings will be hurt if you wish to exchange this present. I should add that U.P. gifts are never engraved.

Gifts for Specific Occasions

Certain occasions demand gifts that are specifically geared to the event. Going-away presents for people who are off on a long or important trip, for instance. We have found that our friends really appreciate it when we take the trouble to write up lists for them of restaurants, museums, and shops that we have visited and recommend. It is useful to include price ranges wherever you can, if not in specific figures, then Inexpensive, Medium, and Expensive. If they are going to another country, we give them a written list with phonetic pronunciations of the words and phrases we found most useful, in addition to a standard pocket-size translator. On occasion we have made up a whole travel packet that includes a logbook with the names and addresses of our contacts written in, a passport/currency case, small local guidebooks, foot warmers for the air flight, and lightweight paperbacks in case they run out of reading material on the plane.

Kenneth Lane prefers to surprise his friends by arranging to have an indulgence waiting for them at the other end. As he points out, it is so easy to do now, through credit cards. You can hire a limousine to meet your friends at the airport, have books or a basket of fancy foods in their hotel room, give them dinner at a famous restaurant, or reserve seats at the theater or opera.

Once I was on a buying trip and happened to land in Birmingham, England, on my birthday. Now, Birmingham is strictly an industrial city, and not the place I would choose to celebrate my birthday alone. I was in my hotel room feeling a bit forlorn, when there was a knock on the door. I opened it, and there stood a man dressed in black livery complete with visored cap. He recited, "Good morning. I am your birthday present. Mr. Bob Alpert in Dallas has asked that I drive you wherever you would like to go today, or this evening if that is more convenient. You will find a picnic basket in the car, and Mr. Alpert suggests that you might like to share the occasion with your local friends, whom I will be happy to pick up at their homes or offices. I am at your service for any five hours of the day that you choose."

Bob's thoughtful gift sent from hundreds of miles away certainly restored the sunshine to my birthday. It was a wonderful indulgence and in fact not nearly as extravagant as the driver's speech made it sound. You can hire a car and driver by the hour in a great many cities for less than the price of a modest birthday party. In my opinion, the pleasure you bring is worth every nickel.

Housewarming Gifts

Another occasion that calls for a special gift is when people move into a new home. It seems obvious that a housewarming gift should have something to do with the house; the hitch is, often as not you are not in a position where you can know what people want, or need. They may not have completed their decorating. They may be bringing everything with them from a former home that you've never seen. And if you ask what they would like, they may be unable to tell you. We found ourselves in that kind of a spot when we went to visit Pat and Jack Schutts' new house on Nantucket. They had invited us for a fall weekend, when all the summer renters have gone home and Nantucket is at its peaceful loveliest. The Schutts' had looked forward for years to having their own year-round house near the sea, and we wanted to give them something very special. We had no idea what that could be.

We solved the quandary by spending the weekend snooping around the house, spotting holes in their inventory. By the time the weekend was over, we knew what to do. On the plane flight back home, Carolyn and I put our heads together and wrote out a list of ten things the Schutts did not have.

A good paring knife
Tea strainer
An efficient corkscrew
Cocktail napkins
Gardening shears
Cheese slicer
Pencil and pad for the telephone
Ashtray for the upstairs bathroom
Kleenex box for the guestroom
Jigsaw puzzle for fun on a rainy day

When we got home we put together a CARE package of all ten things, none of which cost more than three dollars apiece, and sent the box off to Nantucket. The Schutts really loved it. We were glad that we had waited to see what the house truly needed, and I am sure that Pat and Jack were, too.

Margaret, a friend of ours in Boston, told me she has invented a housewarming trick that never fails. When someone she knows is moving, she goes to their decorator and says, "I would like to give your clients a house gift, and I would like to spend X dollars. Since you are on intimate terms with their new home and know what would fit best with my friends' decorating plans, I would like you to buy the gift in my name. Or else tell me what I should go out and shop for." This saves a lot of wrong guesses about the right ashtray or lamp, or whatever Margaret's budget will bear at the moment. She says that the decorator she has spoken with most often, a wonderfully thoughtful as well as tasteful woman named Marguerite Greene, invariably adds a house gift of her own to her clients's homes. Each time Marguerite completes an installation, she orders a charming arrangement of flowers, in a pretty basket or cachepot, to be delivered to the new living room with her card. Sometimes she brings her clients a casserole, too, for the first meal in the new home. It's a nice touch, I think, and it goes a long way to personalize her business relationships.

Besides furniture and accessories, you can outfit a new homeowner or renter with something to mark the new address. If the people are moving to a new city, they will probably want a fresh address book. A restaurant guide, a transit map, and a year's subscription to the local magazine makes a thoughtful welcome package. What we like best is to have postals or stationery imprinted with people's names and their new address when they move away. It helps set them up with the trivia of housekeeping, and reminds them, subtly, that we want them to stay in touch.

Gifts of Friendship

It has been my experience that good friends don't wait for special occasions to give gifts to one another. They send spur-of-the-moment, un-birthday things—"just because it's April." Or just because they are thinking of you. It is a habit I dote on for a number of reasons. Unexpected gifts let people know that you care about them. They are a way of staying in touch. And they give you a chance to have fun. Some of my favorite nonoccasion gifts have been downright silly and even outrageous. Like the tee shirts we received for no reason at all from an old schoolmate of mine, Larry McQuade. He had seen an ad by some company that said, "T Shirts Silk Screened. Custom Orders." Larry couldn't resist. He sent for five electric-blue tee shirts, had the fronts stamped with each of our names, and on the backs he had them print, "An Original from the Horchow Collection."

When you travel as often as we do, you see a lot of weird things that are just too funny not to pass along to your friends, or pick up as reminders of the good times you have had. I was in Canton, China, with Charles Sanders, a Boston friend and the head of Massachusetts General Hospital. We stayed at a hotel called Tung Fang, an odd place full of wild colors and strange services—like room waiters who never knocked; they *scratched.* And a very Oriental cocktail lounge that specialized in Elvis Presley music. We had such a good time and so many laughs that when we got back to the States I had a half-dozen water tumblers imprinted Tung Fang in bright red and blue, and sent them to Charles with a note, "Just because we were there."

Many years ago Carolyn and I traveled to Japan with Stanley and the late Billie Marcus. After we had gone through customs and were settled in our hotel, Stanley asked us to give him our extra passport photos. You know how awful passport photos are; we couldn't imagine what he wanted them for. Six months later back in Dallas, when we had forgotten the incident, we were at a dinner party at the Marcuses' home, eating our way through an elegant five-course feast. Dessert was a glorious sorbet served in exquisite Steuben bowls set on white service plates. As we spooned away the sorbet, there peering up at us from the service plates were our own faces. Stanley had taken our dreadful passport photos to one of those quickie places in Tokyo and had them transferred onto china dinnerware, which could be done in Tokyo overnight. It was one of the most hilarious finales to a meal that I can recall.

The story has a second punch line. Years later, when the Marcuses thought the timing was right, they served dessert on the very same photo-plates at another dinner party in their home. This time they gave us the plates to keep, along with another memory of a delightfully entertaining evening with a surprise ending.

If you like the Marcuses' idea, you could use it without having to travel to Tokyo. All you would have to do is get some inexpensive plastic plates at the five-and-ten or hardware store, and either paste your friends' photos onto the plates, or send away and have them transferred, as Stanley did. They would be a great house gift, and I think it would be funny just to send the plates to somebody for no reason at all. Or to invite them for dinner or a picnic and give them their photo-plates the same way Stanley Marcus gave us ours.

For the Fun of It

Some gifts are strictly for fun. The former head of the public television station in Dallas, Bob Wilson, and I have spent years trying to outdo each other with outrageous birthday gifts. The rule was, the gifts had to be in the worst possible taste, exceptionally hideous, and trite. I think we have finally hit our stride. For the past twelve years we have given each other a birthday necktie printed with a picture of Mt. Fujiyama. We can't get much worse than that, or maybe we can. Now that each of us has a full set of a dozen Mt. Fujiyama neckties, I am thinking of having them made into place mats.

Off-the-wall, nonoccasion gifts don't have to be outrageous, of course. My friend Ted Nierenberg, who is the president of both the American Crafts Council and Dansk Designs, is one of the hordes of people who know that I have an avarice for the hot pretzels they sell in the streets of New York. It is a fetish that stems from my having grown up in Cincinnati, where hot pretzels were sold at my school during recess by an old German baker. Ted was passing one of the New York vendors' carts one day and was suddenly reminded of me and my pretzelmania. On impulse, he bought four dozen pretzels, had them packaged and shipped to me in Dallas, and even sent me the recipe that he wheedled out of the bewildered vendor. We froze the pretzels right away, and for weeks whenever I had a yen, all I had to do was defrost one of Ted's gifts . . . and think of what a good friend he has been through the years.

✿ ✿ ✿

8
CONQUERING
THE SPACE SQUEEZE

When our eldest daughter, Regen, went off to Yale in the fall of 1980, Carolyn and I reacted the way I suppose every other mother and father reacts to that event: with sadness and joy. We had been on a wave of elation all spring, ever since we learned of her acceptance to my alma mater. We were proud to know that our beautiful and ebullient first-born had proven her intellectual capacity and willingness to work hard, in one of the toughest tests in the nation. The summer whizzed by in an eddy of preparations as we helped Regen shop for a New England wardrobe, and for furnishings for the suite she was to share with three roommates. Suddenly, it seemed, the day of departure arrived. D-Day. Carolyn and I were not prepared for the strong ambivalent tugs of parental emotion. We felt both forlorn and happy. As delighted as we were for Regen's sake, we had to admit that we also felt bereft. We contemplated the overnight change our entire household was about to undergo. No more messy room at the end of the hall upstairs, with lipsticks, hairbrushes, sweaters, textbooks, and assorted whatnot in a chaotic jumble only Regen could make sense of. No more boys coming to call, chatter about last night's party, hours spent agonizing over the results of midterm exams. Worst of all we knew that we would have to face all our breakfasts and dinners with only four at the table—and an empty chair to remind us that Regen was no longer a day-to-day family presence. I tell you, it's not easy to have your first fledgling leave the nest. I hope we behave ourselves more coolly when the time comes for Lizzie and then Sally to depart.

After the drama of seeing Regen off was over and we had settled into accepting the facts of our new Regenless life, Carolyn and I realized that we had gained something from the experience. In addition to learning that it really is all right for a young woman to be independent of her parents, providing you have armed her with good training and sound values, we had come to understand the world of the 1980s a little better than we had before. Particularly the practical part of how to live in it. Furnishing Regen's room is what really opened our eyes to the fact that most people today must make do with physical environments that are entirely different from what they were when we started out. What struck us as the greatest difference is *space*. It is shrinking to smaller and smaller proportions by the year. I have this wild mental vision that if housing space keeps on diminishing, our grandchildren will have to learn how to set up housekeeping in a phone booth.

Regen's two-bedroom suite was originally intended for two occupants, but housing is a problem at Yale the same as it is everyplace else. So four students must share the suite. That means that two occupants instead of one have to study, sleep, dress, and store their personal belongings in each bedroom. And four roommates, plus their guests, must do their relaxing cheek-by-jowl in a living room designed for two.

Space-Saving Beds

Some of the solutions Regen and her roommates came up with are worth taking a close look at, because the principles apply to everybody who is pinched for space. Their first move was to create more floor space in the bedrooms by using double-decker beds. An attractive alternative, which I have seen used in guestrooms, dens, and children's rooms, is the trundle bed. It's a device that looks like an armless sofa by day. At night you slide out the lower portion which becomes a separate cot, a sort of kangaroo-in-the-pocket. A third alternative is a convertible bed, which you can find now in many new styles. Some look like upholstered sofas, others like chairs, and there is one that Regen bought for her college living room that is a hassock. Unfold one part and the hassock becomes a chaise. Open the hassock all the way and you have a bed. It is one of those pieces destined for a long and varied life.

Regen and the friend with whom she shares the bedroom decided that making up a double-decker bed was enough of a nuisance without having to fuss with fitted bedspreads. Still, they wanted the room to have a finished look so they bought matching quilts that they can just throw on top of their blankets. They were rewarded with a bonus: the quilts take the place of extra blankets, which they would have trouble finding a place to store.

Solving the Storage Squeeze

They kept the remaining furniture in their bedroom to a functional minimum. Two desks, crammed in, desk chairs, and swing-arm lamps mounted on the walls to save surface space; indoor-outdoor carpeting spread wall to wall so the room would appear larger and so they wouldn't be plagued by dust balls; and simple vertical blinds on the windows. When it came to eking out space for their clothing and miscellaneous whatnots, the gauntlet was thrown down. There was only one closet for the two of them, and drawer space simply did not exist. Carolyn came to the rescue. She told the girls, "The fact that your closet is a cubicle with a pole and a shelf does not mean that's all you have to work with. You can squeeze a great deal of use out of the closet if you approach it in terms of what you want it to do for you, not merely what facilities exist. Make the closet flex to your needs. Remember, it has both linear and square-foot space, with three walls, a ceiling, and ledges that can be fixed up inexpensively and give you a lot more mileage than you imagine. You could remove the pole and install custom-cut brackets with swing-arm hangers on the wall of the closet. You can place one bracket above the other for skirts, pants, and tops, and hang a single bracket for dresses and long things. That would triple your closet's hanging capabilities, but I'm afraid it's rather expensive for your budget. But you could still gain more hanging space than you have now, if you get rid of the single pole and put up a series of either tension or screw-in rods, in much the same way as the expensive installation: a high and low rod for tops and bottoms, and a single rod for long things.

"You have a shelf above the pole that you can make into several shelves, to take care of your handbags, shoes, linens: things that you don't need to use every day. You know those rubberized slide-out and stacking gadgets people have in their kitchens? There is no rule that says you can't use them in a closet. You can stack the slide-outs, as well as the stackable units, you know, and have the advantage of being able to get at things in the back easily. Another thing you can use your shelves for is your suitcases, flat or standing up. Fill them with your out-of-season or travel articles, so that interior spaces will work for you, too."

The great thing about Carolyn's approach to organization is that she always thinks of the prettiest ways to be practical. She continued her closet inventory: "Why don't you hang some good-looking, stick-on plastic hooks near the front of the closet for your belts and necklaces. The jewelry will be like Christmas-tree decorations every time you open the door. And put a couple of those hooks in the corner, at the back of the closet, for your belts. The rear wall has possibilities, too, that you shouldn't overlook. You can hang a rubberized grid or a pegboard there, and attach hooks and bins for your gloves, tennis balls, scarves, that kind of thing. The floor is another surface that shouldn't go to waste. Use it for your boots and shoes and labeled cartons of all kinds of little things. I like to save shoe and gift boxes because they are neat and attractive, and use them for my sewing things, paper files, light bulbs: things that in a traditional house would have a traditional niche someplace else.

"There is one more area we haven't tackled: the closet door. You're lucky that this one is a standard door and not the folding or sliding kind. It eats up a little room space when you open it, but look at all the things you can store on a door. Belts, boots, brushes; a mirror with a basket below it for jewelry, scarves, or whatever you want to put in it. Supports for your tennis racquets, ski things, skates, rods to fold pants over."

Carolyn was nearly as amazed as the girls by all the ideas she had come up with so readily. I think we all store more information in our heads than we realize; we just have to be prodded by some need and out it will flow, for as far as your imagination will stretch.

You can make a closet yield a torrent of usefulness, but you can't make it take care of everything you own. You still need drawers for fold-up clothing, and surfaces for books, record players, and all the other necessities and pleasures of day-to-day living. I suggested to Regen that she and her roommates consider the merits of the sleek new, wonderfully designed, molded plastic tables that you see in the stores nowadays. The originals are Italian imports, but I have seen copies of the designs that are cheaper and work almost as well. I love the sharp, bold colors and the clean unrumpled lines as much as I admire their very sensible arrangements of drawer and shelf space. And they are good buys because they are multifunctional: useful and decorative accents that fit happily into any space where they are needed, including hallways, kitchens, bathrooms, and the garage. The girls chose wisely, I think. A pair of 15-inch square tables with two shelves that they can tuck next to beds and chairs, or into corners. They also chose a coffee table for the living room that has two tiers, so they'll have added storage space for books, records, and magazines. Next to the sofa on one side they have a low, paint-it-yourself bookcase for yet more storage, and on the other side they made a hideaway for their floor cushions and phonograph records by draping a Dior sheet over the round pedestal table that one of their families donated.

Chairs that Lead Double Lives

You realize, I am sure, that Regen's freshman adventures in decorating represent just one small slice of life in small quarters. Hundreds of people face the same sort of challenges she did, every day of the week, and solve them in hundreds of different ways that are as refreshing and practical as they are artistic. Among the more attractive options I have seen is an inexpensive, workable solution to the seating problem. You can make ordinary wooden, cane seat, or director's chairs perform double duty, as living or bedroom seating and at the dining table. They look particularly effective when they are laquered the color of children's balloons, or sleeked up with glossy black, chocolate, or white paint. You could do four or six chairs all in the same color, or mix the hues, like a sparkling tossed salad. These kinds of chairs almost always need seat cushions—for comfort, for height, and for an extra dollop of color. It's not at all difficult to cover the pillows or cushions yourself. Choose a washable, durable fabric such as denim or sailcloth, and cut it in two pieces, each a few inches larger than the cushion. Working on the wrong side of the fabric, stitch or staple the seams together on three sides, then turn the seat cover inside out. Attach the snaps to each edge of the open side, slip the cover over the cushion, snap the open end closed, and there you are: custom slip covers, in a mere whiff of time and labor, at rock bottom cost.

Another way to beat the seating squeeze is with sectional furniture. It has come back from a period of disfavor, and there is good reason why. It has the flexibility and scale that people who live in small spaces require. You will notice that sectional furniture has always been used in hotel lobbies and other public areas. Institutional decorators, whose job it is to cram the most seating possible into limited space, understand that traditional armchairs and sofas are often too bulky and rigid for their purpose. Sectional furniture provides options. You can take two, three, or four armless chairs, and one-armed chairs for end pieces if you wish, slide them around, and create all sorts of comfortable, good-looking seating arrangements.

It seems to me that the less space we have to work with, the more flexible we need to be: in our thinking as well as in our furniture arrangements.

Making Plain Spaces More Ornamental

A friend of my mother's, Frances, is like that. She is what I call a thirties person. Although Frances is very chic and up-to-date in her clothes and her politics, she is absolutely frozen in time in the way she decorates her home. What you see when you walk into her bedroom, for instance, you would swear is right out of a Norma Shearer movie: peach lampshades, mirrored vanity table, blue satin spread, and an honest-to-goodness chaise longue. I think the effect is charming; it suits her style and it is what she truly loves.

Frances is nearing seventy-nine now, and a couple of years ago she moved from her 1930s house into a new high-rise apartment, where she would have fewer rooms to take care of, and service people to help. She had a hard time adjusting. She missed the ornate moldings and carved doors that she was accustomed to. I agree with Frances that slab-straight walls are not particularly graceful or interesting, and told her that she didn't have to be stuck with them. I explained, "Do you know that you can buy molding in almost any style you like, and have it nailed to the walls at ceiling heights? The stores sell it by the running foot. Or you can use it as a chair rail, around a doorway, or as a baseboard. Another thing you can do with molding is change the appearance of the slab doors that came with the apartment. You can also apply decorative panels to the doors. Just look around in the stores, or see what you can pick up at an auction sale."

Frances's eyes gleamed. She could envision her new thoroughly-thirties room as I spoke, and it was just what she had been searching for. I had another idea: "The wallpaper you have chosen for your bedroom is a lovely, soft print. Why don't you get a complementary border pattern, perhaps a similar design in stronger colors, and have it applied all around at ceiling heights? The border will create the ornamental definition that you like. Then for a finished look, you can add a plain half-round of molding where the wall joins the ceiling." I reminded Frances that she had seen something like that in our downstairs powder room. It's a small room, and we wanted to make it interesting. Our decorator, Maggie Green, suggested that we choose a floral fabric and have it printed in three complementary colors: dusty rose, teal, and reddish aster. The top two-thirds of the walls, the area you see when you walk in, are covered with the lightest of the three flower prints, and the bottom third is covered with the darkest color. Where the two patterns meet, a little lower than chair-rail height, we used a four-inch strip of wood covered in the third color, aster. The effect of the subtly varied detail is engaging. It keeps our space from looking like every other downstairs powder room we have seen.

Furnished Rentals

Rented apartments like Frances's are perfectly pleasant places to live, once you add your own touch or style. It's furnished rentals that can give you the blues. Usually the furniture and accessories that come with them are things the owner considers expendable; if the tenant causes damage, the loss will be small. As a tenant, that means you are likely to move into a place featuring Salvation Army decor—rump-sprung chairs embedded with generations of soil, chipped kitchen counters and appliances, poisonously colored landscapes in frames from the five-and-ten, yellowed Venetian blinds, and spaghetti-limp curtains the color of grime. Oh yes, and the lamp on the inevitable three-legged gate table—a plaster statuette of either a ballet dancer or a Gloucester fisherman, with a green, cone-shaped shade that has a dent in one side. Most of us have lived in such rentals at one time or another in our careers. Fortunately, there are a hundred ways to make them less dismal.

If you want to spend a thousand dollars or so, you can replace the furniture that displeases you with inexpensive pieces you can use when you move to another home. To be practical, look for fairly sturdy material and construction that won't fall apart in a few months, like the molded plastic tables Regen uses at school, or the "temporary" unpainted bookcase that we bought years ago, that now serves as storage shelves in Sally's closet.

If you don't want to go out and buy anything major, you can improve the appearance of the things you have inherited with your rental. Instead of replacing the chairs and sofa, you can rejuvenate them with slipcovers: either ready-mades from a department store or covers that you make yourself. Designer sheets lend themselves well to slipcovering. They are good looking, come in a wealth of designs, and are quite inexpensive. They won't wear for a long time, but durability is not the main thing you are after. You want to create an environment that will make you feel good about where you live.

You can remove the Woolworth prints from the walls and put up your own graphics—photographs, prints, a good reproduction from a museum gift shop, or a page carefully sliced from a high-quality art book. To showcase the picture at little cost and with no effort, you can put it in one of those Lucite cube frames. They are wonderfully simple to handle: you don't even need to mount the picture or attach screws and wire on back. You just pop the picture into the box and locate the hole in the back over a hanger. Do-it-yourself frames are one of the best inventions to come out of the 1970s.

If your landlord permits, a coat of paint or paper will revive your tired-looking kitchen quickly. Otherwise, try using plants to mask the dismal condition of a wall. Or hang one of those plastic-covered wire grids, fitted with shelves and hooks, and cover the wall with neatly organized cooking equipment. If you are leery about leaving holes in the wall, you can hang the grid from the ceiling molding. If there is no molding, choose a grid that folds like a screen and stands by itself.

If your landlord's blinds or curtains are not appealing, remove them. If the window is located where other people cannot look in at you, or where bright sun will not bother you, as it would in a bedroom, you may want to leave it completely bare. I have seen many rooms where an untreated, uncluttered window actually makes the room look fresher. Inexpensive alternatives to shabby, "furnished" window treatments are: spring-roller shades, matchstick blinds that roll up or draw aside, louvered aluminum vertical blinds, and thin-slatted horizontal blinds. Instead of shades or blinds, you might want to place portable shelves in a window, and garnish the shelves with plants or colorful fruits and vegetables such as eggplant and squash. Then you can keep changing the decor as you eat your way through it.

Accessorizing

Whether you live in a furnished rental or a custom-built mansion, the way you accessorize your home says a lot about you. You might say that accessories are to decorating what herbs are to an omelet; they can change its basic nature. Hypothetically, you could visit two identical homes, each furnished with the exact same tables, chairs, fabrics, floor, wall, and window treatments. One would be utterly charming, hospitable, interesting; the other mediocre, vapid, and in some way off-balance. What separates the two is a matter of style. One owner has a

flair for pulling a room together with the small touches that reflect his or her individuality and thoughtfulness. The other just
lets things happen, and settles for the first thing that comes to
hand.

I'll give you an example. Let's say these two identical rooms
are both contemporary in style and done in crisp white with
touches of salmon and blue. In each room there is a small table
for the telephone. The table in the dull, aesthetically impover-
ished room bears the following articles:

Black phone
Yellow 8½ × 11 ruled pad
Two worn-down yellow pencils

The table in the room that nourishes your senses looks like
this:

White phone
Address book covered with salmon-and-white patterned
paper
Notepaper stacked in a Lucite container
Bouquet of sharp-pointed white pencils sprouting from an
antique white vase.
Salmon-colored ashtray
Salmon-colored matchbook
Magnifying glass with ornamental handle

Here is a person after my own heart. This is someone with an
eye for color, scale, design, and comfort. Not one accessory was
chosen haphazardly. Each was purposefully selected to enhance
the mood of the room and provide convenience for anyone who
uses the telephone. The accessories here are a part of the whole:
grace notes in a carefully composed symphony.

Some people seem to have been born with a flair for composing symphonies. The fact is, they are just like you and me. What
we call flair is a cultivated ability born of years of observation,
learning, and a sense of the magic that is possible. It has been my
experience that most people have more flair and good taste than
they think they have, they just need to nurture it and assert their
own feelings. All good decorating, in the end, is choosing beau-

tiful things and arranging them for people's comfort and pleasure. Good sense leads naturally to good composition.

Scale

One of the vital elements in composing a room is scale: the relationship of one group of objects to another. Do you remember what our decorator Tonny Foy said about our new living room? It needed large-size furniture, in keeping with the large size of the room, otherwise the room would look as if it had malnutrition. The idea of scale is equally important in the accessories you choose to harmonize with your furniture. However, that does not mean that in a large room every ashtray and pencil holder must be gargantuan. Accessories relate to the other objects they are with, not necessarily to the entire room. In our living room there are two large slate tables. One has a small, 5-inch crystal ashtray on it, and the other bears a 12-inch Imari ashtray. They both look right. It is the juxtaposition of the ashtrays with the other objects on each table that told us one should be small and the other large. The trick to deciding which accessories look right and which look wrong is to look at the particular group of objects you are arranging, not the whole room. We made our choice by playing around with different objects in each grouping until we hit on the most pleasing look.

Imagination frees you from decorating clichés. The imaginative home is not decorated by formula, with matching hobnail lamps on the bureau in the Early American bedroom and a patchwork quilt on the bed. It bears the owner's signature. The lighting in its Early American bedroom spills from standing bedside lamps, and the patchwork quilt hangs framed on the wall, displayed as the art that it is. The accessories are in scale and underscore the mood of the room, and it is the unexpected ways they are used that make the room personal.

Small Touches for Big Effect

Accessories can also help to create illusions. You can make a small room appear larger than it is if the things in it are simple in line and color. For example, our friends Mary and Tim Baldwin have a cracker-box kitchen in Nantucket that seems quite open and comfortable, due to the fact that they have painted and accessorized it in a calm buff that is almost no color at all. The phone, the tissue box, the wall organizer, and even the can opener are buff. The accessories give the room continuity without visual potholes to stumble over. But the Baldwins know when to stop short of an antiseptic look. To animate the room, they have hung two lollipop-colored prints on the wall, bought equally bright-colored potholders that they keep in a straw basket, and called on nature for other irregular touches—a row of blooming cacti on a ledge over the sink, and a colander filled with bright peppers. There is just enough variety mixed into their monochromatic kitchen to express the Baldwins' personalities and give an overall impression of graceful good taste.

On Being Orderly

Mary and Tim Baldwin not only have a flair for composition, they are orderly people, too. They are a lot like Carolyn and me; they find orderliness essential to pleasure. Chaos disquiets them, intrudes, makes them edgy and distracted. How you feel about it is a matter of personality. For some people, clutter is a cheerful companion, evidence of a busy life that encompasses a spectrum of interests. They feel that bothering to keep things tidy is nit-picking detail. I don't think there is any right or wrong about orderliness except when there is too much or too little of it. An obsessively austere monk's cell bothers me, and so does tumultuous mess. As with most things, someplace between the extremes is the medium that makes me happy.

In our lives, Carolyn and I cover a fairly broad range of order and disorder. On weekdays our bedroom and sitting room look as if they had been in the path of a hurricane. We keep adding to the piles of books, clippings, and samples of things we are interested in, and as the days tumble after one another, the piles burgeon and sprawl. Invariably, by Saturday we feel that we are up to here in welter, and file everything where it belongs so we can enjoy a peaceful weekend. Of course, on Monday mornings the pile-up begins all over again, but at least we know we have a method for coping with it that will satisfy our basic need for serenity. And we have developed a number of devices that cover our needs for beauty and comfort, as well.

Tricks for Keeping Order

The draped-table trick is a well-known device. That's the one where you shove your accumulation of newspapers and whatnot under the floor-length cloth that decorates the round table in the corner. Under the drape happens to be an excellent place for permanent storage, too, as people who live in small apartments have long since discovered.

We have found that the best solutions to organizing come from thinking things through logically. We start by defining our need, and then fill the need in a way that pleases us visually. In addition to the many attractive ready-made gadgets that are available such as Lucite cosmetic holders, compartmented trays, and the like, you can "invent" organizers out of almost anything that pleases you. Carolyn's friend Ann seems to have a particular genius for coming up with such devices. In her tiny bathroom, she uses a bright green plastic flower pot for her lipsticks and other makeup. The pot adds a charming touch to the room. On her bureau she has a lovely hand-painted box that keeps all her current invitations and theater tickets in one place. Another box on the bureau, a decorative tin that she found in a little offbeat shop in New Orleans, contains the earrings and bracelets she wears most frequently. Ann's living room is small, too. Instead of letting magazines pile up on a table, she keeps them in an old copper washtub she was lucky enough to find at a barn sale. Ann proves the point that if you unleash your imagination and explore possibilities, there is no end to the number of ideas that will come to you.

I brought up the subject of how people get ideas one day at lunch with Robert Raymond. Robert manages the Brunschwig et Fils showroom in New York, the very prestigious fabric house, and his work brings him in constant contact with a pantheon of designers such as Mario Buatta, George Clarkson, Mark Hampton, Sister Parish, and Albert Hadley, as well as with many celebrities. Robert is noted for his imaginative resourcefulness. Invariably, his insights are an intellectual stimulus for me.

We had met by chance during one of these Tolstoian snow-storms that erase every taxi from New York's streets. I had been leaning into the wind for ten minutes, trying to make my way crosstown, when I decided to break the cold trek and stop in at a restaurant to warm up. It was a lucky decision, because there at a corner table was Robert, whom I had not seen in ages. He invited me to join him, and when we had caught up on each other's news, I brought up the question of how he gets decorating ideas for his own use.

Small Bedrooms

"I have lived in apartments in Paris, California, Boston, and New York," he told me. "The very first thing I do, the night I move in, is set up my bedroom. That is my private lair. The rest of the apartment may have nothing in it but wall-to-wall packing crates, but the bedroom has to be established as mine. I happen to be a night person, so I like dark colors and triple-thick window shades to block out the morning light. In my Boston apartment, I lacquered the bedroom walls navy blue, and installed Kelly green window shutters and carpeting. It was always dark and wonderful. Of course, I only used it at night. If I were a morning person and wanted it to look its prettiest by day, I would probably have used bright, sunny colors, like white and pale yellow. I like lacquered walls best because they reflect light and are washable. Lacquer is difficult to apply, though; it streaks, drips, and goes on in globs. I think it's best to have it applied by a professional.

"My apartment in New York is so cramped that my bedroom has to double as a work area, and I have had to give up the nighttime look that I find so luxurious. I have been very careful about the lighting just the same, because I still want it to look pleasing at night. Besides, New York apartments are so small that you do a lot of your reading and TV viewing in bed. I use bedside wall fixtures that don't take up table space, an up-light for my plants, and adjustable track lighting to illuminate my parade of paintings. I change the paintings often, because they are graphics that I create myself."

I asked Robert why he had used window shutters in his Boston apartment. He explained that shutters soften a room, and then gave me some useful views about window treatments. "If I had a printed dust ruffle and headboard, I would use the same print on the window, for a custom look. In that case, I would use a plain fabric for the bed cover, which would almost certainly be a quilt. Were I ever blessed with a high ceiling, I would use fabric from the ceiling to the floor; I love the vertical sweep. On a large casement window, I might use patterned fabric for side panels and a valance, with plain sheers over the window itself. I don't care for wall-to-wall traverse curtains, and anyway, that much window fabric would be overpowering in a small room. Roman shades are an interesting option, the ones made of pleated fabric that draw up to nothing. But if I had an unattractive window that takes up half a wall, I wouldn't try to make it interesting. I would treat the window as unobtrusively as possible, with horizontal or vertical louvered blinds the same color as the walls."

A Fantasy Bedroom

I couldn't resist; I asked, "What if you could have everything you ever wanted in your bedroom in place tonight when you get home from Brunschwig. What would it look like?" He leaped at the opportunity to indulge a favorite fantasy. "There would be chocolate-brown lacquered walls, with chrome track lights to spotlight the modern art on the walls. The bed, which would be queen-size because king-size is too big for the room and double is not quite as comfortable, would have low tables at each side. One would be an Early American blanket chest in dark pine, and it would be piled with books and magazines, and controls for the TV and hi-fi system. I'd have miniature speakers in the bedroom, too. They give excellent sound, and visually they are a big improvement over the early, unwieldy designs. On the other side of the bed I'd have a low Parsons table, which would have plenty of space for a plant or flowers, a tray of food, a pencil holder, scissors to clip magazines, notepaper, and a dictaphone. It would also hold a phone, and my calendar and address book. The bed itself would be covered with a down comforter, and I would have three different patterns of colorful sheets, so I could change them around just to cheer myself up. I'd use those big 24-inch European pillows, too; the department stores have cases to fit them now, so they are not the extravagance they once were.

"The lacquered-brown closet doors would have plain brown ceramic knobs, to replace the cheap metal discs or shabby, painted-over wood knobs that came with the apartment. My suits would hang inside the closet, but all my shirts, sweaters, and underwear would be folded on shelves. If there were no room in the closet to build shelves, I would use deep bookcases or plastic stacking bins. Between the folded linens, there would be cakes of expensive soap. Soap holds its scent longer than sachet, and when it begins to fade or I want a different scent, I can take it into the bathroom and use it for washing."

Apartment Light Fixtures

Robert completed his fantasy bedroom with furnishings that people usually think of as living room decor: sculptures that he likes, a chair so people can come in and chat with him, and his library of books, lining one entire wall. As he spoke of his books, it occurred to me that his earlier reference about the importance of lighting is something that people in rented apartments are apt to ignore. For some reason, they think they have to put up with the fixtures apartments come with, even though they rarely are in the best taste and hardly ever provide lighting that suits the room. I must have been in a hundred apartments in my day, and seen the same light fixtures in every one—inverted scrolled saucers on the kitchen and foyer ceilings, tiny chandeliers suspended from Spanish-Inquisition chains to show where dining areas are supposed to be, little frosted light bulbs over bathroom mirrors, and bare, glaring light bulbs somewhere in the closets.

You don't have to live with poor lighting. For a very small investment in your own pleasure, you can remove the landlord's fixtures, store them until you are ready to move out, and install your own replacements. In the dining area, you can cap the hole in the ceiling and use a standing or sideboard lamp instead. You can put a plain can-light or track lights in the foyer. And it is a simple matter to install inexpensive dimmer switches on the walls or lampcords, so you can adjust the mood of your lighting to suit the occasion. Another advantage of dimmers is that they conserve energy and reduce your electric bills when they are turned down low.

There is a wide selection of good-looking, efficient fixtures you can use in the bathroom that let you shave or put on your makeup accurately. I would suggest that you ask the electric company to give you a recommendation. Their experts' services are free, and they make house calls. Or else take your bathroom floor plan and measurements into a store that sells light fixtures, and go through their display for what suits you best.

When it comes to closets, I like the oversize, white-glassed globes that are decorative in themselves and that screw directly into existing sockets. You can add your own personal decorative touch for the light pull—perhaps a length of velvet, looped at the end so you can grasp it easily. Or faille gift-ribbon with something tied on the end for a handle—a whimsical bird intended as a Christmas tree ornament, a ceramic neck pendant, anything that captivates your fancy.

If you choose to change the light fixture in the kitchen, I think you will find that fluorescent bulbs are more efficient than incandescents. Incandescent bulbs throw heat, an element you do not need to add to a kitchen, and are less brilliant than fluorescents. In addition to ceiling light, I like fluorescent tubes underneath all the hanging kitchen cabinets so you can really see what you are doing when you chop celery, wash dishes, or sauté the beef for ragout.

Structural Changes

If you change the light fixtures in your apartment, you can take them with you when you move out, reinstall the landlord's fixtures, and leave the rental just as you found it. Walls, plumbing, and other structural elements are something else. Once they have been removed, there is no putting them back in place unless you are willing to spend great amounts of money. That is why structural changes are not permitted in most rentals. You can't blame the owners: they don't want to be stuck with a place that they won't be able to lease again because some innovative tenant has removed all the interior walls, or installed a Roman tub in the living room.

Portable Walls

A different sort of structural problem has emerged for renters lately, however: living spaces that are too large. There is a new wave of Americans who live in vast single rooms in converted lofts and other kinds of rehabilitated old business buildings. The challenge for them is to break the huge rooms into smaller living, bedroom, work, and kitchen areas without spending a fortune on the construction of permanent walls. Their solution: portable walls like the ones in the apartment of my friend David, an artist who lives in a loft in New York's Soho. He says, "I took one look and got depressed. The place had about as much charm and coziness as a bowling alley. My first impulse was to try to break it up by using furniture as dividers, to mark off separate areas. But at that point I owned only a few sticks of furniture, and didn't want to wait for the year or two it would take to acquire more. Besides, I am happier in small, snug little spaces. Then I read in a magazine about another loft-dweller who had built a series of portable walls that he could move around at will. If he tired of a space, let's say the dining room, or acquired a roommate and his needs changed, he could just pick up his walls and create a new room. The ideas fit me to a tee, so I rolled up my sleeves and went to work. First I figured out the size each wall should be and made frames out of two-by-four lumber. I attached legs at the bottom, the upside-down U's that you see on portable blackboards, so the walls could stand by themselves. Then I nailed quarter-inch thick beaverboard onto each frame, and painted the whole thing a soft rosy beige, which will be a nice, warm unifying background when I finish furnishing the room. I can always staple fabric onto the beaverboard when I feel like a change."

I told David that his false walls put him in a league with the celebrated artist Fleur Cowles, and her British industrialist husband, Thomas Meyer. They own an apartment in the Albany, a converted historic building in London's Piccadilly section that was originally designed for gentlemen of means and style. The rooms are generous, to say the least, with ceilings so high that they make furniture arrangements difficult. Fleur says that decorating their living room, which once was a ballroom, was a rich challenge. The room was such a colossus that the Meyers' furniture would have floated inside it and been lost. Fleur's solution was to build a box inside the room, with fake walls to give it human proportions, and a "lid" that dropped the 24-foot ceiling to a more pleasing ten feet.

While we were on the subject of portable walls, I gave David some other ideas for his. He had mentioned stapling on a print fabric; I suggested that he also consider a rich herringbone or tweed, or a solid flannel or felt. I think that texture adds richness to a room, and fabric has the added advantage of blotting up sound. David could take the fabric idea a step further, and make padded walls to gain a look of luxury for very little money and not much labor, either. With a staple gun in hand, he can tackle almost any decorating job he can think of.

Directions for padded fabric wall:

1. Cut fabric 3 inches wider and 3 inches longer than beaverboard area of portable wall.
2. Fold fabric back on all sides to form hem.
3. Staple or glue hem into place.
4. Cut large sheet of ¼ inch to ¾ inch polyester filling 1½ inches smaller than beaverboard panel. Cotton or foam rubber filling works equally well.
5. Staple edges of polyester filling to beaverboard.
6. Smooth fabric over filling and staple edges onto frame.
7. Optional: for a finishing touch, or to conceal staples if they show, glue a strip of fabric trim around border of fabric.
Note: Follow same directions to pad and cover portable screens or permanent walls. Substitute glue for staples, if desired.

Portable Closet Space

Converted buildings like David's and Fleur Cowles's are very much like the cramped apartments most of us are familiar with in one respect: they lack adequate closet space. One solution that I think is ideal when you are in rented, temporary quarters is to build or buy portable storage units. These are freestanding plastic or wood cabinets (often on casters so you can roll them around), fitted with poles for clothing and shelves for other possessions.

The first time I saw a portable closet was at the home of a friend in San Francisco, in one of those narrow, four-story townhouses that were built in the late 1880s as private homes and later converted into apartments. My friend, Virginia, lives on the second floor, where she has a living room, bedroom, bath, and small kitchen. Her living room opens directly off the stair landing, with no foyer and no coat closet to ease guests into the room. Virginia soon discovered that this was a problem, so she called in a carpenter and had him build a freestanding closet that also serves as a room divider and gives her a sort of foyer. She had the closet made of plywood, stained dark walnut inside and out, and made sure it was roomy enough to hold visitors' coats, boots, hats, and umbrellas. Then she placed the storage unit about five feet from the living room door, with one side butted against the adjoining wall and the side that opens facing the door. The five feet of space became her foyer, where guests could sit on a bench to take off their boots, and check their appearance in a mirror. The back of the portable closet, visible when you are seated in the living room, forms a nice dark-walnut background for one of Virginia's deep, flower-covered easy chairs.

For a long time I admired the ingenuity and good looks of Virginia's portable closet, and found myself so intrigued by the idea that I became obsessed with wanting a unit just like it in our house, even though we had no storage problem. I gave up when I realized that in order to create a solution, first you must have a need.

❧ ❧ ❧

9
HOW SOME OF THE WORLD'S BUSIEST PEOPLE CREATE MORE TIME FOR THEMSELVES

When I was in grammar school back in Columbus, Ohio, I had one of those homeroom teachers everybody seems to remember, a stout, white-haired woman who always wore burgundy dresses, dusty pink face powder, and an earnest, sometimes intimidating scowl of concern. She was a missionary type, dedicated to setting our young feet on the path of proper conduct. One of her favorite methods of instruction was to deal out homilies, the way amusement park machines give fortunes. Thinking back, I realize now how many of her sayings had to do with the passage of time. "Time and tide wait for no man," she would inform us. "A moment missed is lost forever." "There is so little time in which to do so much."

But everything she told us was absolutely true; most adages are. Over the years her sayings have served me well, especially when I have been tempted to "put off till tomorrow" what I really ought to do today. However, now that I have had the benefit of a few decades' personal, practical experience, I think I can add a useful truism or two of my own. One insight is that the secret of having enough time may be merely in learning to think things through and organize your activities. The other is to learn to recognize your own rhythms and let your personal needs guide how you use your time.

Your Inner Clock

Different people have different natural tempos to their lives. Some of us are morning people, and function best early in the day. Others are night owls who never really get going until the sun is well past midday. It doesn't matter so much whether you are a lark or an owl, the important thing is to know your own style and to work with it. I happen to be a fast starter. I am usually out of bed early in the morning and I plunge into the day bursting with energy. Morning is when I am at the peak of my efficiency, running on all cylinders. By midafternoon my vitality has wound down to a crawl, and I'm operating at about five miles per hour. It's a familiar pattern, and I know there is no use trying to alter the way I am. So I have learned to use my biological rhythm to best advantage. What I do is go into the office early and tackle the difficult projects right away. Any jobs that require thought and energy are on the early part of my daily agenda and I deliberately postpone until afternoon relatively mindless business details such as looking through trade magazines or answering routine correspondence.

On the other hand, Randy James, our senior buyer, is the exact opposite. Believe me when I tell you that trying to work with Randy at nine or ten in the morning is like trying to talk with a mushroom; he is that woolly and lifeless. By eleven, though, Randy has hit his stride and can do his sharpest thinking. What we have done is develop a system that meshes our best bands of time. For years we have made it a practice to conduct our joint work sessions between eleven and two when we are both feeling fresh and clear-headed. After lunch, Randy is supercharged, and goes to work on all the hard things that we've decided need to be done. At that point, I have begun to droop, so I go back to my office and take care of easy, less demanding tasks.

This working relationship lets each of us work without wasting time struggling over difficult tasks that we are too logy to accomplish quickly or well. And by taking that kind of drudgery out of business, it makes our days simpler and more pleasant. Part of that pleasantness also comes from the fact that, having developed work schedules that fit our natural body clocks, we

have abolished the guilt we might otherwise feel over not working at full speed all the time.

Dealing with Things
That You Don't Want to Deal With

This business of keeping compulsion in its place, of learning
not to stew about things that you don't absolutely have to take
care of this minute, can simplify your life to a remarkable degree.
A large percentage of the things we worry about really do not
have to be dealt with at any set time. We all have continuing lists
of phone calls we're supposed to make, thank-you notes to
write, reading we should do. If you stop to think about it, it
doesn't matter whether you handle every one of these tasks immediately, or deal with them tomorrow when you are in the
right mood. Almost always, you manage things much more effec-
tively when you work at your own tempo rather than according
to the clock on the wall. In the end, the trick to keeping up with
the list is to think in terms of definite rescheduling. The way I
reschedule is to shelve my correspondence and reminders in my
In box, which I check first thing each morning. Or else I make a
note on my calendar to take care of such and such on a certain
day. That way, I can forget about it, knowing I will be reminded
at the proper time.

There are interim stopgaps you can use, too, so you won't
leave holes that haunt you. Sometimes when I don't feel like
writing a letter to a friend or making a long telephone call, I'll
write a postcard to say that I haven't forgotten and plan to write
or call soon. It keeps us in touch, and lets me avoid the uncomfortable, choking feeling that I have bitten off more than I can
chew on that particular day. The postcard routine can be fun,
too. I like to stockpile postals that I pick up in restaurants and
museums in various cities throughout the world, and amaze my
friends with exotic sights when they least expect them. The postals make unusual birthday and get-well cards, too.

To Postpone or Not to Postpone

To each his own. Postponed action makes some people so uncomfortable they can't concentrate on anything but what they

are *not* doing. They are better off if they dive in and get the drudgery over with. As I have said, it's a matter of knowing your personal style, and functioning in the way that works best for you. Even so, I think that at some points we all need to stop and ask ourselves, "Why am I doing this? Is there a real deadline? Who created it? If it is not real, maybe I can change it." I had an experience very recently that is a perfect illustration.

It was one of those beautiful Saturday mornings in late summer, just perfect for a swim in the pool. But there I was, working away in the house because I thought I had to go through the tedious chore of getting my record collection straightened out before our friend Mimi Kilgore came in from Houston at one o'clock. Mimi is an art historian who is also interested in music of the 1930s, and I knew that we would want to listen to certain Gershwin and Cole Porter recordings in my collection. It had been on my mind that my collection had fallen into disorder and, to tell you the truth, I was embarrassed to have Mimi see the mess. But that pool was so tempting, I was torn. All of a sudden I saw how compulsive I was being. Something made me stop and ask, "Roger Horchow, what in the world would happen if you did *not* organize your records this morning? Do you really have to use up Saturday morning sorting records, or could you go for a swim and still give Mimi the pleasure of hearing the music she enjoys?" The answer was obvious. Of course, the records would be available even if they weren't in perfect order. I could relax and do what I really wanted to do that morning, and it wouldn't make a single bit of difference in the end. By going through the exercise of asking myself "Why?" I had put myself in charge of my own time instead of permitting some nameless compulsion to take over. I think the lesson is: we need to learn to edit our own lives and not cram our time full of useless, sometimes unnecessary activity. Otherwise you are apt to find yourself on overload, flailing around like a chicken without its head, trying to do everything at once and doing justice to nothing at all. Mostly it's a matter of sorting out trivia from what is important, so you can set priorities that make sense for you.

Know What Is Important

Trivia will take over if you let it. When Mimi Kilgore got to our house on the day I just described, I told her the story about how I had gone swimming instead of organizing the records. She understood perfectly, since she is a very busy person herself. Besides a full-time career of research, writing, and consulting on the arts, she teaches a course at the Contemporary Art Museum that people stand in line to get into. Therefore, she has gotten into the habit of questioning the projects she takes on so she can make the fullest use of her time. Mimi said that my story reminded her of the tale of the bride and the ham. She explained, "There once was a young woman who dreaded baking ham on Sundays because it meant that she had to spend twenty laborious minutes cutting three inches of bone off the end before she could put the roast in the oven. One day her husband asked why she always cut the end off a ham before she cooked it. The bride answered, 'Because that's what my mother always does and she is an excellent cook.' The next time he thought of it, the man asked his mother-in-law the culinary reason for cutting off the end of a ham. She told him, 'Oh, that's simple. I've never had a roasting pan that was large enough to hold a full-size Sunday ham.' "

Look for Options

Mimi's story makes a good point. Much of the trivia that takes up our time is just a matter of habit, with no reason for being. If we stop to think things through, we can usually find an option that gives us time for more of life's pleasures and eliminates a great deal of the drudgery. For example, for years we kept all our art reference books on the bottom shelf of the living room bookcase because that was the only shelf tall enough to hold them. It was literally a pain, bending over to lift a heavy volume every time one of us wanted to look something up. When we redid the living room and built a new bookcase between the living room and the sun-room, near where we do our reading, it didn't dawn on either Carolyn or me to change the system we had grown accustomed to. It took Lizzie, our resident efficiency expert, to point out that now we could move the art books and encyclopedias four shelves higher, and get at them much more easily. Lizzie had another suggestion. She said, "As long as you're at it, why don't we bring the photo albums down from upstairs and put them on the bottom shelf of the bookcase? Then we won't have to run up and down every time we want to look at them." I'm certainly glad that Lizzie spoke up. Her fresh point of view liberated us from a tiresome way of doing things that no longer made any sense.

You Have to Be in Charge of Your Time

It is my guess that Lizzie will always be one of those people who create a pleasant atmosphere for themselves and others because they can see the best ways to control their time and energy. She has a way of getting to the heart of the matter and acting decisively. I like to think that Lizzie learned some of her directness from Carolyn and me. Not that we were born knowing how to make the most of our time. We had to learn, like everyone else, that the busier you become the more you need to stay in control of your schedule. You know how easy it is to say yes to everything everyone wants you to do. And how pressure builds when you let yourself get in over your head. It could happen to us readily. Carolyn and I both serve on a number of committees and are constantly being asked to serve on more. We hate to say no. But even more, we hate to say yes, just to be nice, and then find that we have overbooked ourselves and really are not much help at all. Experience has taught us not to be impulsively agreeable or try to be good guys to everybody. We have learned to sleep on decisions and tell people, "I'll let you know on Wednesday." Or to explain to them, "I would love to work with you, and I think your project is really worthy. Let me review my calendar, to make sure I have enough time for the meetings and phone calls so I can give you the help you need. I'll call tomorrow and let you know."

Using a Calendar: Your Alter Ego

I couldn't live without a calendar to refer to. That's a personal idiosyncrasy. I'm sure there are many people who are far better organized than I who are able to carry everything in their heads. For me, it's write everything down, or else lose track. In the top drawer of my desk, where I can get to it instantly, there is a month-at-a-glance calendar that tells me every meeting, every trip and trade show I must attend. On top of my desk I have a daily calendar that lists my appointments, phone calls, and important errands. Some commitments are beyond my control: school board meetings, theater openings, convention trips, dates that originate with other people and that cannot be switched. Other entries are reminders of dentist's appointments, Spanish lessons, lunch dates, haircuts, and so on—movable events I can fit into my calendar at the times that are most convenient. It's by controlling the movable events that I stay organized. I know that if the dentist says to come in on Thursday the 12th and my day is already booked with appointments that cannot be changed, I can ask for another date. Nobody's feelings will be hurt and I won't be caught in a logjam. You almost always have choices. If somebody wants to confer with you at 9:00 A.M. and that is not your best time of day, all you have to do is find another mutually satisfactory time for your meeting. The thing is to make your needs known. I am always pleased when we have an out-of-town visitor who tells us what he or she would really like to do. It makes planning their time and ours so much easier. What I cannot stand is when you ask a person's preference and he or she says, "I don't care." The implication is that my concern has been wasted. I like people to respond as if my questions matter.

Tell People What You Want

I try to let people know where I stand. Last summer, for example, I spent a half day in Boston with my friend Bill Windle. Bill is a stockbroker by profession and a tour guide by disposition. He is always the one you can count on to organize a rich full schedule crammed wall-to-wall with delightful adventures. He had made plans for our brief visit, but gave me choices—he could either show me additions to the Faneuil Hall Marketplace, or else take me around to an exhibition of Judy Chicago's work. Bill said that he had already seen the Chicago show but would be happy to see it again if that was what I really wanted to do. I knew I would have other opportunities to see the show when it traveled and that Bill was apt to be bored by a second visit, so I told him I preferred to see the Marketplace. He was glad I had been definite about what I wanted to do and said, "This will be fun. There are always new places to see on the waterfront. Let's start by checking the shops and then have lunch at a great oyster bar I know. They serve oysters, all varieties." It happens that oysters are the only seafood I dislike, and I told Bill so. It was fine; he had another place already in mind. "There's a wonderful seafood restaurant right next to the oyster place where there are all kinds of fish and interesting salads. I think it would be a lunch we would both enjoy. Shall we go there?" We went, and it was just the right finishing touch for a very pleasant morning. Neither of us had been led into doing something we really didn't want to do, and we enjoyed our half day together to the fullest.

Freeing Yourself from the Tyranny of Trivia

I think people have more choices about how they will use their time than they realize. There is a lot of miscellany packed into each ordinary day that you really can move around at your own convenience. You just have to be flexible enough to be able to adjust time so that it serves you, rather than enslaves you. We have an aunt in our family who was completely tyrannized by time. Aunt Helen used to go crazy unless she paid each bill the day it came in. If she had a faraway look in her eyes when you talked to her, you knew it was because the hamper was half full and she was thinking she should be doing the laundry that minute. Helen must have averaged at least three trips a day down the street: to pick up a pound of butter because she might run out in a day or two, to go to the dry cleaner's because she had found a spot on her skirt, to buy a card for somebody whose birthday she'd just remembered. It never dawned on her that she could consolidate her miscellaneous errands—buy a couple of pounds of butter or a batch of birthday cards all at once, plan her time so she didn't consume each day repeating yesterday's maneuvers. It made me tired just to watch her ceaseless flurry and it wasn't much fun listening to her constant moans about how put-upon she was, with so much to do and never enough time for herself.

All that changed the winter Helen had to have an operation that required several months of bed rest afterward. It was one of the best things that ever happened to her. And, I might add, to the people around her. Helen's long recuperation forced her to change her style. She had to learn to organize the trivia of her life, to use alternatives, and above all, to free herself from time's insistent menace and the relentless mental pressure she had felt. She is so much more relaxed now, and fun to be with. She's more interesting, too, because she has reached out beyond her tight little island of trivia and become absorbed in new and more stimulating projects.

Systems for Handling Details

Helen likes to tell about her conversion from drone to free woman. "When I first came home from the hospital I was pretty washed out. Didn't have the strength to worry about paying bills or keeping up with the washing and ironing. As I began to feel better, I realized that these things had to be taken care of before they piled up and overflowed. I lay there and thought about how I would proceed without wearing myself out. Then as soon as I could get up, I took all the mail that had pyramided on my hall table and separated it into four stacks: Bills, Personal, Hold, and Who Needs It. You won't believe this, Roger—I didn't even open the bills. Just stuck them on my desk and made a note on my calendar to sit down and pay them all on the first of the month, the way my husband used to do. Actually he wrote checks twice a month, on the 1st and the 15th. Don't ask me why—I guess it made him feel better to keep current, the way I used to try to do. Or maybe it was easier for him to break the task into two short sessions rather than having to face a monumental production each and every month. In any case, I found that I like looking at bills just once a month. It means I never have to think about them in between, or break into whatever else I might want to do on the other twenty-nine or thirty days.

"Then I took the stack of personal mail and looked through

everything fast. The invitations that had to be answered right away, I took care of that afternoon. The letters that I wanted to answer in depth I put into a folder marked Correspondence, so I could write whenever I had the time and was in the mood. The Hold pile was a bunch of catalogs and magazines: things that I could pore through at leisure, then discard. The last pile, Who Needs It, went right into the wastebasket. These were circulars advertising items and services I couldn't use and fund-raising appeals for causes I didn't care about, like appeals for money to help a politician in some other state. You know . . . who needs it."

The Scarlett O'Hara Technique

At this point in her story Aunt Helen is apt to look astonished and flutter a hand to her hair. She'll declare, "I never thought I could live with myself if I put anything off till tomorrow. But you know? I think a little Scarlett O'Hara-ing is good for the psyche, as long as you're not totally lackadaisical and do attend to the important things on time."

Keeping Up with Reading Material

I always agree, and try to give Helen more ideas that will bolster her zeal. One time I teased, "Have you discovered the trick of reading everything without having to read everything?" She was way ahead of me. "I know exactly what you mean," Helen replied. "I used to wonder how on earth I was ever going to keep us with the endless flood of newspapers, magazines, and books that pours into my lap. Would you like to hear how I licked the problem?" I nodded, knowing full well there was no stopping Helen if I wanted to.

"Okay, first, the newspapers," she began, extending a forefinger. "I take the daily paper and one of the tabloids, so I can keep up on the gossip. All I do is scan the news headlines, because I know that the important events will be summarized for me in the weekly news magazines. If there's a local scandal or some other story that I want to watch unfold, I'll speed-read the paragraphs. I look at book and movie reivews only if they're about releases I think will interest me. The same goes for household hints and other chatter. Of course I check the baseball scores every day, and read up on how my favorite players are doing. That takes care of the newspapers."

Helen held up a second finger for point number two, unconsciously making a victory sign. "Next, magazines. I always turn to the index page first and circle the page numbers of articles I'm going to want to read. Then I flip through the magazine, taking in the ads and the general gist of each article as I go along. I stop and read whatever intrigues me, give a quick skim to pieces I'm only vaguely engaged by, and skip all the rest. Another thing, I've dropped my subscriptions to four or five of the magazines that I took for years. I found, when I really paid attention to what I was reading, they didn't mean a thing to me. Out! Anyway, I can always reorder them if I change my mind.

"Now as for books," Helen continued, stiffening a third finger to form the Scout's pledge. "I have become my own editor. Rather, I use book reviews to edit what I do and do not want to read, instead of trying to devour everything people tell me I simply must rush out and get. I tell you, Roger, my life is so much simpler ever since that winter when I wasn't able to run around. That illness was a blessing, because it made me stop and reevaluate what I was doing with my time."

It Pays to Go Fishing

Fortunately, Helen is in no danger of simplifying her life to the point where she has stripped away all the grace notes. She takes the time to be thoughtful about sending flowers and cards, and to telephone her friends often. And she knows how to squander an hour on purpose, whenever she needs to relax and recharge her batteries. As she puts it, "I go fishing, mentally. Just look at the treetops, or go out and take a walk or have lunch with a friend. Exercise, have a facial, go to a movie, or switch to some dumb job like straightening a bureau drawer—almost anything that changes the scenery and the rhythm of my life makes me feel better, I find. Peppier, too. That's what vacations are for, whether it's an hour's break from routine or a month in the

Caribbean. I've lost the guilty feeling about indulging in personal pleasure. Pleasure is a must."

Live Life to the Fullest

I have a principle about responding to pleasure: do it. Within reason, of course; you do have to be responsible for conflicting obligations. But the older I get, the more certainly I believe that we should grasp life's opportunities immediately, or else they may be lost to us forever. The moment when the fall foliage peaks is the moment to drive to the country and drink it in; next week it will have vanished. The filing you were going to do will keep, and your business appointment can most likely be changed. An exhilarating exhibit at the museum, an opening-night party, or a picnic just because it turned out to be a nice day may seem like ephemera or even frivolity when you think of all the solemn pursuits you could follow. But frivolity does not rule out the pursuit of accomplishment. And each is productive in its own way. I believe we should be receptive to both every day, and maneuver our time so we squeeze the most out of it.

Expanding Your Time

Carolyn and I are practically professional time squeezers. I think it's because we travel so much, and travel automatically means scheduling days and hours to milk the most out of them. Like the tour we took last fall. We were booked for a basic kind of buying trip in Europe: leave Dallas Saturday night the 18th, rest on Sunday, hit the showrooms and factories in Paris, Milan, and London Monday through Friday, and fly back home Saturday the 25th to get back to the office on Monday morning. Then along came temptation, and changed the colors of our plans. A friend called and said that he and his wife were going to be at a vineyard near Bordeaux Sunday the 26th, and if Carolyn and I would join them there, the four of us could stay overnight in their chateau and watch the annual grape harvest the next day. I started to answer that Carolyn and I had always wanted to see a harvest, but this was a business trip, and besides, we planned to be in the office that Monday. But then I thought, "Why not? We may never have another chance to see a *vendange.* The things I have to do in my office that day can be rescheduled, and what great difference will it make, in the grand scheme of things, if we add a couple of days to the trip? As a matter of fact, what if we add three days and come home by way of New York? Carolyn could go to New Haven and see Regen at Yale, while I could go to a Washington board meeting I thought I was going to have to miss, and visit with my mother, who lives nearby." We actually did just that: extended the trip just enough so we could do our work and have our pleasures, too. We maneuvered the time we had allotted so we could squeeze everything out of it that we liked, and I'm glad that we did. If we had put off those visits until we thought we could afford the time, we might never have had those chances again. You really do have to ask yourself, "Why not deviate from schedule? What will happen if I take everything this moment has to offer?" The answer usually is clear: "You will be living your life to the fullest."

How Some of the Busiest People Manage Their Time

It seems to me that is how most of the super-busy people I know live. Erica Wilson is one of them, and so is her husband, the furniture designer Vladimir Kagan. Erica runs her famous needlework shop, teaches, appears on TV, addresses women's groups and seminars, writes books and articles, creates designs for a number of manufacturers, and has a wonderfully rich personal life as well. You would think that she must have her days organized to the hilt, she gets so much done and has so much enjoyment. The truth is, Erica's idea of "organization" is nil. "I just take each moment as it comes and don't worry about the next one," she explains, with her typical relaxed, cheerful smile. "Vladi has a saying that we've cross-stitched onto a pillow: 'No amount of careful planning can ever replace dumb luck.' As far as I'm concerned, he is absolutely right.

"Planning things just isn't my style. I'm always late to everything because I think that time is elastic, and I say yes to every request and invitation. Somehow, though, everything gets done. I suppose I'm what you would call a deadline person. I find it good to be under pressure. A deadline forces me to stop working and reworking every design, or writing and rewriting every page of a book. It makes me finish up, once and for all. It's true what they say: 'Work expands to fill the time allotted to it.' The more time I have available, the longer I'll string out a job. I used to feel guilty about all the rewrites I did, until a publisher told me that practically every author in the world does the same thing. It's nice to know I'm not the only one, but I should remember the other saying: 'True wisdom is the ability to recognize your mistake when you make it the second time.' Vladi is more like that. He draws his designs in a single, quick stroke and if it's not right the first time, he throws it away and forgets it.

"Vladi is also different from me in that he is a morning person. He gets up in the morning and jogs for miles, while I am still trying to pull myself together. I never quite do. I really try, especially since I make so many public appearances and should present a proper image. However hard I work at it, things seem to fall apart on me. Like the time I was being interviewed on TV in Los Angeles. I very carefully assembled my wardrobe. A spotless, well-ironed blouse, a tidy jacket, the expensive skirt I had bought in London for the special purpose of presenting a fine public image. I got to the interview on time, the camera focused on me, and wouldn't you know? The hem of my skirt fell down, in full view of millions.

"Then there was the time one of the weekly magazines said they would like to photograph Vladi and me at home. The two of us went to work like a pair of beavers and tidied up every one of our disarrayed rooms. Except for the kitchen, which is an irreparable nightmare. The wallpaper is falling off in patches. There are old pipes sticking out of the corners. The sink and stove have needed replacing for years. Naturally, that is the room where the magazine people insisted on photographing us . . ."

Using Other People

Despite Erica Wilson Kagan's entertaining stories about how harried and scattered she and Vladi are, they are two of the warmest, most relaxed people I know. And the most hospitable.

Carolyn and I love to go to their parties, which Vladi usually organizes since he is the member of the team who is better at logistics. I think it is very nice when people who live or work together can lean on one another for balance. Most people have someone in their lives who takes up the slack. In our house, Lizzie is the savior who fills in the blanks for us when our memories go spotty. She is a walking computer, and the rest of us rely on her to remember all the things we forget. Like the time, not very long ago, when I absentmindedly forgot to leave a tip at a restaurant. When I got home and realized what I had done, I asked Carolyn to remind me to stop by the next day and repair my error. Actually I was passing my anxiety along to somebody else, but that's another story. Carolyn said she would be glad to remind me, but I noticed that she didn't write a note to herself and guessed that she would forget by morning. So I took out insurance by telling Lizzie, and she was the one who reminded me. Lizzie also always knows exactly where we left whatever it is we lose. She is the family Lost and Found Department, and our youngest daughter, Sally, is the Message Center. Sally remembers every telephone call that comes in and delivers each message verbatim, without so much as a note to remind her. To me this is remarkable. The only way I can keep track of things is to write everything down. Then my mind is free to get on with the day.

Where to Find Help

There are all sorts of ways you can lean on other people, and free up your time. Sometimes it means hiring a "go-fer" for cash, and sometimes you can exchange your time and effort for somebody else's. Most busy people say that they delegate all the nuisance jobs they can, which lets them spend their time and energy doing the things they think are more rewarding. Carolyn's good friend Janet Kutner is a master of the art of delegation. She has to be. Janet is art editor of the *Dallas Morning News* and Dallas correspondent for *Art News* magazine. Her work entails traveling the country to exhibits and museum conferences, reviewing books on art and architecture, and serving on committees. At home she is realtor Jonathan Kutner's wife, friend and hostess, and her third job is as mother to four school-age children. Janet says that her biggest problem in juggling her three careers is maintaining order in the Kutner's large suburban home. That's where her delegating prowess comes in. Janet has become expert at passing along detailed memos that tell everybody in her busy cosmos just what they should do to help out. She says, "I find that most people are willing to lend a hand to someone who is as busy as I am. They respect the fact that I have responsibilities to fill and cannot do everything myself. If our nine-year-old has to be at a soccer game at five, on a day when I'm working at the paper or away from home, I leave him a list that says:

ROBERT:
4:00   Sandwich and milk in the refrigerator
4:15   Call Mrs. Smith at 555-4545 to make sure she will
         pick you up at 4:30
4:20   Change into soccer clothes
4:30   Be out front for Mrs. Smith

"Or I'll leave lists for the housekeeper.

ESTHER:
Please clean the mirrors and picture frames.
Use spray starch on Julie's white blouses.
Market and fix dinner for 7:00. See menu # 4.

" 'Menu 4' refers to the notebook I made up last summer that gives the housekeeper two months' worth of menus and recipes to work from, and keeps us from being bored by repetitive meals. If I didn't have a housekeeper to run to the grocery store or escort the younger children to their games and lessons, I would certainly spend a few dollars and hire a teenager or somebody else to stand in for me. Or use the built-in help we have, now that Julie is old enough to drive."

Exchanging Time

Then there is the barter system—swapping favors with friends and neighbors. Carolyn and I use it all the time. If we're off on a week's buying trip, we'll ask a neighbor to pick up Sally at her soccer games. Then when we come back, we offer to reverse the favor and pick up the neighbor's children from wherever they happen to be. The point is, if you keep your eye on your objective—to save travel across town to the playground, or to save an hour at the supermarket—you will find a comfortable solution that lets you spend the time more usefully.

Asking People to Help You

There is another alternative to hiring or bartering—ask, as if you expect to receive. A friend of mine in Philadelphia goes through life asking people to carry his bundles, deliver his messages, drive him to this place or that. Sometimes they are absolute strangers, but his requests are made so amiably, as if he has every expectation that they will comply, people rarely even think of saying no. Another friend, an attorney in Louisville, has such a charming way of approaching her friends and staff that it never enters their heads to turn down her requests. She is an utterly delightful woman, very refined, who balances just the right quotient of elegance with expressions of personal interest and concern. You get the feeling, when you talk with Marion, that this is a woman who is accustomed to the best; she knows what is proper and what is not, and appreciates excellence in the people and things she surrounds herself with. You want to measure up. It is not uncommon for Marion to ask a colleague to shop for, say, a birthday gift for her mother—an errand she should, by all rights, do herself. Or else hire a shopper to do. And she has been known to say to an assistant, "My dear, you are the only person in the world who has the talent to organize my books. Would you go to my house this evening and do it for me? I'll be out, but I'll leave the key with the superintendent. Call me if there's anything you need." Then she is off in a cloud of black cashmere, leaving the assistant to race off after work, barely pausing to wonder how he or she got trapped into categorizing Marion's books—free.

Marion is not as high-handed as she sounds. In addition to the fact that she is conscientious and skilled, she does an outstanding job for her clients and goes out of her way to keep her staff happy. She never hesitates to entertain her secretary's visiting in-laws, and you can count on Marion to take care of your child on a Saturday, or send flowers when you feel out of sorts. Also, she uses good judgment in determining whom she asks to do things for her, taking into consideration the other person's ability, relationship, and whether she can "pay" for the filing or shopping with some other kindness.

Coping with Stores

You can hardly blame anyone for wanting to get somebody else to do their shopping. It has become an annoying, time consuming, effort-wrenching chore that seems to become more difficult with each passing decade. The leisure and the personal service that our parents enjoyed has all but vanished. Inventories and selections aren't what they used to be. Salespeople have disappeared, and electronic gadgetry has replaced them. We no longer have time to browse and ponder, or stand around while other people take forever with their purchases. On the other hand, the 1980s have made yesterday's dream technologies a practical, everyday reality. Nowadays you can order merchandise by cable TV, shop by mail, pay by credit card, even pay your bills by phone in some cities. And there is no doubt that more conveniences are on the way. You have to keep your eyes open and avail yourself of the constantly burgeoning new crop of marvels that make life simpler, let you cope faster. It's easy to miss out, the advances gallop by at such a dizzying rate. I have been traveling the world for years, yet I had no idea until just a few months ago that it is no longer necessary to stand in line for every shuttle flight. Somebody showed me the little machine they have in airports now that you click your credit card into, and presto, your flight is bought and paid for instantly. Away you go. Tomorrow I am sure they'll come up with another invention that will make the credit card machine seem archaic.

Shopping isn't all electronic magic. We still go to the store, look around, pause, and choose one item over another. Nor is shopping all drudgery, if you approach it in terms of shortcuts. My philosophy, whether I am shopping or attacking any other project, is always, "Take the easy way out, it saves time." You just need to know the tricks of the trade:

• To avoid standing in line at the cash register, write down the ticket information of the item you want—style number, size, price, color. Leave the store, go to your phone, and call in your order.

• To avoid waiting at the wrapping desk, ask the store to deliver. If they don't deliver, ask them to mail your purchase. If they say it's not their policy to mail, offer to pay for the postage and handling; it will cost less than your time.

• To avoid waiting for the customers ahead of you, shop at hours when the store is least mobbed. Usually that is as soon as it opens in the morning or at 6:30 to 7:00 at night, when the nine-to-five crowd has gone home and the late shoppers are still at supper. During a sale, the best time to shop is after the store has been open for three to four hours. There's a lull then. The early, rabid bargain-hunters have left, the lunch hour is over and the clerks have not yet become weary. Incidentally, if you only have lunch hours for shopping, see if you can switch your lunch hour to late morning or midafternoon, when all the other lunch-hour shoppers are at their desks.

• To save running around, plan your itinerary in advance and make a list. It may help to number your errands 1, 2, 3, and so on, in geographical order so you don't have to retrace your steps or zigzag like a jumping bean. I have noticed that Carolyn's lists usually end with the errands that entail heavy or awkward bundles, so she doesn't have to tote her burdens all over town.

Another simple device that can save you hours of time, miles of running, and an infinity of frustration is the advance check-up. Before you chase off to the florist, the bake shop, wherever you are going, call ahead and make sure they are open and have in stock what you need. Every place has its quirks and lapses. Some close on Mondays, some sell out your size before you get there, others send your favorite salesperson on vacation the very day you want to shop. It only takes a minute to pick up the phone and confirm whether the place is open, if it has what you want in stock, if the person who helps you will be around when you get there. In fact, you don't have to call every time. You can enter store hours and days in your telephone book or your home computer if you have one, alongside the name and address of the place. You can do the same with other people whose services you use from time to time: "Dr. Brown, children's dentist. Can call 8:00 A.M. Away every August." Or "Celeste, hairdresser. Closed Mondays. Eric for cuts."

Incidentally, whenever any of us has an appointment with a dentist, a doctor, a hairdresser, anybody whose appointment schedule is apt to run late, we always phone a half-hour before our appointment to ask exactly when he or she will be ready to take us. It saves an enormous amount of time we would otherwise have to spend sitting around in waiting rooms. Just in case, though, we have learned to bring reading matter, office or homework, or handwork with us, so that if we are stuck in a waiting room, we can use the time pleasantly. There is rarely an occasion when you have to be irritated because somebody else is running late, as long as you are prepared to take advantage of the extra time on your hands.

I can't remember when it was that repair and delivery people showed up at our house when they said they would, but I know perfectly well that these days if the TV or washing machine doctor is supposed to arrive at 10:00 A.M., whoever is waiting had better block out the next few hours for leeway. And had better telephone the company that morning, too, to confirm whether our house is indeed on the route ticket.

Everyone sighs, "Life has become so complicated," and they are right. They just neglect to add that there is a multitude of easy ways to uncomplicate it.

Shopping Lists

I have one final tip about how to shop when you have no time for shopping—use lists. Lists keep you on track. They are your memory, your caretaker, the friend that tells you what you went out for in the first place, so you don't have to make duplicate trips.

If they held a contest for world's champion list-maker, I am sure Carolyn would win in a walk. Hers are as neatly compart-

mentalized as an architect's blueprints. She says the reason she
is so good about keeping lists is that she is essentially lazy and
refuses to make any more moves than she has to. That's a perfectly valid reason; I have heard it said that half of the population scurries the way it does to justify the guilt of wishing to just
lie down and sleep. But I know Carolyn, and she is essentially an
orderly, well-organized person. That is her nature, and she
couldn't change it any more than our Labrador could turn into a
lap dog. What's special about the way Carolyn sets up her lists is
that they are like a miniature, portable filing system. She keeps a
To Do notebook in her purse at all times. Hers is leatherbound,
with two pads of paper, but she could just as well use one of
those inexpensive little spiral-bound notebooks that you can
buy in drugstores or the five-and-ten. One side is headed Today,
and it has items like groceries, nail polish, the dry cleaner's, and
appointments. The other side says Sometime, and it reminds her
of the things she can do when she is in the right neighborhood—buy extra wineglasses, film, a blue handbag. Carolyn
says that there are items on her ongoing Sometime lists that take
care of themselves. She has got through a whole season in great
style without ever buying the blue handbag she once thought
was a wardrobe must. It just proves that nothing in this world is
etched in stone, including a listmaker's lists.

I know somebody whose lists are in fact graven, if not on
stone, on whatever she can get her hands on at the moment a
thought flies into her awesomely productive head. Tish Baldrige
juggles so many projects and has so many ideas at one time, she
is forever scribbling notes on every improbable surface. The
backs of restaurant matchbook covers or unused checks, the
back sides of campaign buttons or the flaps of used envelopes—
whose backs are already covered with lists of twenty-three
things she must do instantly. One morning in New York I took it
upon myself to stop in at her office, expecting to see the dazzling
filing system into which each of these memoranda are dropped. I
saw chaos. Yet I know that everything on her blizzard of lists
gets done superbly. Mystified, I sat down to ask by what sleight
of hand she accomplished her multiple miracles. "I suppose by
two o'clock you will have that overflowing In box cut down to
size," I suggested. "Impossible," she replied. "I'll simply swoop

up the whole thing, basket and all, and take it home with me and deal with it after dinner. And if you ask me what I will tackle first, the answer is 'Everything.' I am hopelessly unpriority-conscious and treat trivia with exactly the same importance that I treat everything else. I can organize other people, though. I spent years seeing that my bosses met their priorities without a hitch. When I worked for Jackie Kennedy, Claire Luce, and before that, Evangeline Bruce, they got sheets of paper from me every morning telling them exactly what they must do that day and what time to do it.

"Chaos is normal for me and I'm too busy to change my style. I think it's the energy I was born with. That's a gift, you know; people have it or they don't, and I have always had it. It goes hand in hand with the fact that I have an affirmative attitude. Today, for example, I have to get out a magazine column, rewrite a chapter for my next book, attend a committee meeting, and direct nine of the other enterprises I'm involved in. I'll concentrate on each thing as it comes along, and it will all get done. I know that I can do whatever I have to do. Not as magnificently as possible, but as best I can."

I asked if there were some way people who weren't born with copious energy could develop greater staying power. She thought for a moment and said, "The secret of not getting tired lies in not thinking of all the things you have to do. Otherwise you feel so pressured that you don't complete your agenda, and you wind up feeling more and more upset. I have another secret that I'll confide in you. I do get tired. I'm a very early riser—five-thirty or earlier—and around four o'clock I begin to fade. When I leave the office I sprint headfirst into another kind of activity. Usually I stop and market, then get home and preside over the children, talk with my husband, check on the laundry, and that sort of thing, set the table, fix dinner, and then maybe put in some time at my typewriter at home. Sometime in between, I give myself the greatest picker-upper in the world—a hot bath, replete with all the sybaritic oils and bubbles and moisturizers I can crowd into the tub with me. After that, I am ready to do anything—go out to dinner, go to sleep, or write that impossible letter that I've been putting off all week and now have the courage to conquer."

How One of the World's Busiest Businessmen Handles His Time

Andrew Melton, chairman of the mammoth Wall Street brokerage firm of Dean Witter Reynolds, displays a considerably different style. His is understated, systematic, and thoroughly orderly. "You have to be low key and predictable when you are an executive in a large service business like this one," he says. "There are 9,600 people who work for this firm and it is their nature to be entrepreneurial, aggressive, sometimes emotional. So it pays for me, as the person on the top, to be fairly pragmatic."

You would expect Andy Melton's days to be long and full. They are. He is up and ready to comb the *New York Times* and the *Wall Street Journal* the instant they hit his apartment door at 5:30 in the morning. By 7:30 he is at his desk getting set for another ten-hour day. This does not strike him as extraordinary. For one thing, his right-hand assistant vice-president Eileen Costello, works twelve hours a day, lunches at her desk, and loves every minute. Neither of them ever thinks about the word "tired."

However, Andy only sounds like a superman. He recalls the time when stretched-out days nearly did him in. "Years ago, when I first began to travel to Brazil, the people I was there to do business with would pick me up at eight in the morning. I would go through my day's appointments and then we'd meet for dinner, Brazilian time, about eleven o'clock at night. Then they'd drive me back to my hotel and drop me off at two or three in the morning. After a few days of this, I was run into the ground and marveling at their stamina. I didn't realize for a long time how they did it. Then it became apparent. The people who picked me up at eight in the morning were a whole different troupe from the ones who dined and dropped me off at night. I was the only one who was going fourteen hours a day! They had what people in Rio call the Carioca spirit—knowing how to pace yourself.

Getting Away from It All

"The way I pace myself and recharge my batteries is to pull the curtain on weekends. Every Friday I fly to our home in Palm Beach, or else to Vermont."

Allowing Leeway

Andy says that probably the most valuable part of his working day is from 7:30 to 8:30 in the morning. "You can prepare for everything that's coming, in those quiet hours. The worst mistake people make is when they are not reasonable in their expectations of what they can accomplish in a given period. As a result, they schedule themselves so tightly, they get into a knot and cannot do anything well."

System for Saving Time

Just about everybody who crosses Andy Melton's threshold receives a gift of the book that is the company's bible. It's a self-help book by a time management consultant, and the two big messages concern dealing with paper and setting priorities. In the case of the chairman of the board, it takes two to control the flow of paper—one to throw nearly everything away, the other to rifle his wastebasket every day and resurrect what she knows he will be looking for later on. Her method is straightforward as for priorities, the general gist of the advice is to "look at the big picture. Analyze what the job entails. Decide what steps have to be taken to reach the goal. Write each step down in the sequence it should be taken. Then do it."

The Effortless Look

It occurs to me that both Carolyn and her mother function very much that way, but on a less formalized basis. And that no matter how much they have to do, neither of them ever appears ruffled. Both women have earned reputations as marvelous hostesses, and I think I am in a position to say that they deserve all the applause they receive. I am also in a position to know what goes on behind the scenes—how they are able to run their homes so smoothly, to appear utterly effortless at all times, and to be genuinely relaxed no matter what. Their secret, which I have overheard Carolyn discuss with our daughters, is always to think things through ahead of time, with the other person's comfort in mind.

I remember when Carolyn was helping Regen set up the first teen party where she was the hostess. Regen wasn't sure what to do or how to begin. Carolyn told her, "Put yourself in your guests' shoes. Go through their motions in your mind, figure out what they will need, then take whatever time you have to to prepare everything in advance. If you get all the dirty work and the obstacles out of the way, you'll have nothing to do the night of the party but be calm, cordial, and join your friends in having a good time."

Regen needed to be walked through the specifics, so Carolyn said, "First, figure out what you are going to serve for food and drink. Make a marketing list. Give yourself a timetable for when you will cook your casserole or fix the punch. Pick out the serving dishes you'll want, so you won't be scrambling at the last minute. Next, imagine what will happen when your guests come in. You will have to tell them where to hang their coats. Then they'll come into the living room, and what's the first thing they'll want—a drink, some snacks? Make it easy for them. Beforehand, set out everything you think they will ask for where you can get at it handily. Will they want music? Before the party, take a few minutes to stack up the records that you think will set the right mood, so they won't have to wait in silence while you go through your collection. See what I mean?"

Regen did see, and her first party was reported "a smash." They laughed and partied for hours, and I was sure that not one of the gang had even an inkling of the backstage preparations that had gone into their evening's pleasure. Regen was thrilled with her success, and the next day she said to me, "When I was little I used to think people loved to flock to this house because it's so attractive. But I know differently now—it's because Mom is so thoughtful and always takes time to think about the pleasure of each person who enters it."

Carolyn smiled when I reported Regen's comment to her. "I used to say the very same thing about *my* mother," she mused.

10
TRAVEL:
DELIGHTS AND
DISCOVERIES

Whenever we show one of the Astaire-Rogers or other 1930s musicals that are a mainstay of my video cassette collection, I marvel at how well those movies wear. None of us in the family, not even the teenagers, seem ever to tire of the glamorous costumes and sets, the glittering dialogue, the elegant scores and dance routines. For ninety cheerful minutes we can escape real life and imagine ourselves, fashionably top-hatted or chiffon-gowned, treading silken paths in a world filled with rainbows. The films are fairy tales, and I think we all have a need to believe in them.

Certain scenes cling to my mind, and I have noticed that they often involve travel. Sometimes the setting is a ballroom-size stateroom dense with champagne, flowers, and huge steamer trunks that invisible maids tend while the tenor and tap dancer frivol. Impeccably tailored gentlemen at great railroad depots have but to snap their fingers, and droves of porters race forth to whisk away dozens of gleaming leather valises. In the hotels, graciousness is the unvarying order of the day. Everybody is carefree. No wonder we feel a nostalgia for yesterday, when "getting there" really was half the fun.

The New Kind of Travel

Of course, travel remains what it has always been: a stimulating and gratifying experience. I am afraid, though, that nowadays stylish and leisurely transportation exists mainly in film. The act of getting from one place to another too often is an endurance contest fraught with the anxieties and tensions of long lines and delays, overbooked reservations, lost baggage, crowded spaces, and physical discomfort. Even those of us who travel a great deal find that things get out of hand with exasperating regularity. Part of the problem is that more people travel than ever before, and the other part is that the helpful assistants of yore have been replaced by impersonal computerized services. Even room waiters are hard to find. We have entered a do-it-yourself era in travel, and the message is if you want to enjoy yourself, you have to know your way around.

Travel Agents

Perhaps the first step is to find people who can lessen the strain for you. I have found that travel agents fill the bill; a good one is as invaluable to me as a pair of good walking shoes. I can let him or her handle all the bothersome details: plot complex itineraries, synchronize interairline and hotel connections, make reservations for me at the right places. What is more, a travel agent's services are free. As you probably know, agents are paid in commissions from the airlines, hotels and other suppliers they represent.

I wouldn't bother to use an agent to book a simple trip: say a flight from Dallas to Los Angeles or from New York to Miami. It is easier to just phone the airline and get in touch with a hotel myself. But if there are any complications involved—an interairline connection or an overnight stay between flights—an agent is much better equipped than I to work out the itinerary. Large agents, especially, have the computer connections that plug into the computerized reservations system hotels and airlines use, and are up-to-the-minute on current flights and room availabilities, services that save me time, money, phone calls, and errors. In addition to computer connections, I look for agents who have personally been to the places Carolyn and I are thinking of visiting, and whose ideas of "de luxe" and "economy" match ours. To illustrate—there is a beautiful hotel in Acapulco where I wanted to take the family one Christmas, and our agent advised us to go elsewhere. He had been there himself, and knew that the management did not care to have children around. Also, this particular agent has taken care of us long enough to know our needs and our tastes. He understands that we want the best hotel we can afford, and that we like to live at least as well as we do at home. We talk the same language by now. When we say we would like "simple accommodations," he knows that we mean a nice room in the medium-priced range, and not someplace where "simple" means the bathroom is half-way down the hall. If we were talking with an agent whose standards we were not familiar with, we would make sure to spell out precisely what we are looking for.

I look for attention to detail. If I discover that an agent has booked me on a nonexistent flight, because he hadn't noticed that the flight was cancelled from the schedule a week ago, I would drop that agent instantly. One careless error means there probably will be more. I also look for an agent who is good at getting me the best there is for the money I spend—the flight least apt to be crowded, rather than the one packed solid with group travelers, the airport closest to my destination, hotel services such as airport limousines that you get at no charge, if somebody knows enough to ask for them.

Choosing a Destination

You cannot expect an agent to recommend where you should go if you are undecided or cannot be specific about your wants. If you don't know whether you would prefer London or the Caribbean for your vacation, you had better do some personal research and make your own choice.

People who have a good instinct for travel research do the following:

1. They talk with friends whose interests parallel their own.

2. They read magazine articles by writers they have come to trust.

3. They ask themselves what is the real objective of their trip—whether it is to be alone and rest, to meet people, to see great museums in historic sites, to do something they have dreamed of and cannot do at home.

Caskie Stinnett, the sophisticated writer about privileged dining and travel, once told me that his objective in travel is to live out his fantasies. He added that as a career traveler, he is in a somewhat different position from most people. He has traveled so much that he now looks for things the rest of us do not—mainly, adventure. I asked Caskie to describe some of the fantasies he has carried out, and his answer told of dreams come true.

"I once spent the best part of a winter day locked up in Elsinore Castle, by special request. Elsinore is where *Hamlet* was set, and I wanted to transpose myself into the legend. It was out of season and the castle was closed, but I told the keeper if he would just let me inside and lock up again, he could go away and do whatever he liked. I nearly froze to death, but I lived out my fantasy.

"I have traveled to New Guinea because I wanted to see relics of the Stone Age and learn how a family lived then. I have endured a harrowing but exciting experience in a jungle looking for a village of Indians. I have taken the Orient Express from Paris to Istanbul, even though flying would have been quicker, because I wanted to see what the fabled luxury train was like. And I have looked out of a train window, seen a little hillside village that captured my imagination, got off, and spent the night there. I have never regretted any of my recklessness."

Since Caskie qualifies as a man who has adventured almost everywhere, I asked him to tell me a few of his favorite places. Without hesitation, he reeled off a list.

"I think Scotland is the most beautiful country in the world, and the island of Java is beautiful, too. Italy captivates me, the sweet sadness of it. Switzerland is beautiful, and the most European nation in Europe. They speak French around Geneva, German in Zurich, and Italian down around Lugarno. As for cities, I think London is the last male's city in the world, Washington is pretty but dull, and New York is gritty and tense.

"To me, all seasons are wonderful, but I prefer spring. The Italian word 'primavera' really says it: first green. I love to ride on a train, especially in the rain. The Blue Train in South Africa is a sheer delight. What I do not like are beach hotels that try to discourage ocean swimming, mountain cable cars, and the atmosphere of gambling casinos. I also have a rather low opinion of the operetta royalty that you find in some of the little European countries.

"I think the best airport in the world is at Kuala Lumpur, the capital of Malaysia. The next best is Frankfurt. In the U.S., Tampa is a very nice airport and Miami is perfectly dreadful. The airport I hate the most is San Juan, and next to that, the chaos at some of the departure gates at New York's Kennedy airport.

"If I were not a professional traveler, I would travel a great deal less than I do, and I would try to go to Europe once a year. I probably would not go there on a package tour, although there is nothing wrong with them; package tours are simply not to my adventuresome tastes."

Package Tours

Personally, I like package tours. They are a good way to beat today's tight money problem, and people in the travel business tell me they are dominating the field these days. Some resorts, such as the Canary Islands, are actually the creations of package tour operators. The Canaries have everything people look for—a sunny, temperate climate, golf courses, and accessibility to both Europe and the U.S. All that was missing before was guest accommodations, so the tour operators built large hotels and created the ideal resort. Mombassa, in Kenya on the Indian Ocean, is another package tour creation. Five years ago nobody ever heard of the place. Now it has huge hotels that are filled one night with West Germans, the next night with Canadians, the next with Americans.

It is easy to understand why package tours appeal to people who are concerned about foreign languages—although sign language works almost everywhere in the world—and who like having everything done for them, from the logistics of transportation to hotel reservations, vans from the airports, baggage handling, and the company of people they know. Personally, what appeals to me most is that I can get a reservation during a busy season, and that I can get a terrific bargain and then go off on my own.

For example, I might sign up for a package week in Puerto Vallarta at $700, which includes transportation, hotel room, and meals. Let us say that is $500 less than if I made my reservations independently. Now I have the option to use the $500 to upgrade my room, spend a few days in another town, hire a driver, charter a sailboat, or whatever else I choose to do on my own. My only restriction is that I must travel on the date offered by the package operator. At that, I have flexibility. I can call several different travel agents, for different dates and perhaps different trips. Many agents specialize in the kinds of trips they offer. Agent A may offer wine tours or ski weeks. Agent B may feature nature trips, to see the foliage change in New England or the moss hang in Natchez. Agent C may offer low rates to Las Vegas, the Bahamas, and other gambling destinations. I don't have to watch the leaves change or gamble when I get there, I can tailor my bargain-rate vacation to suit my own tastes. And, as I have pointed out, there will be people to help get me through the airport lines and baggage-claim confusion.

I spoke with another famous and experienced traveler, Horace Sutton, to ask his opinions about contemporary travel. Horace is the travel and editorial director of the *Saturday Review*, writes a syndicated newspaper column, and has authored a number of travel books. His office testifies to his profession. It is a forest of trophies from his travels all over the world: paintings from Bali and Fiji, ceramics from Valleuris, Chinese inlaid boxes, French paperweights, drawings of dancing girls from Angkor Wat, and dozens of reporter's notebooks bearing exotic labels.

Airline Club Lounges

When we discussed difficulties at airports, Horace spoke about joining airline clubs, as a way to avoid crowded waiting rooms. "One of the perks of my job," he said, "is that I am invited to use club lounges as a guest of the airlines. They are comfortable places to wait. But most people have to pay a membership fee to each airline club they want to use. It can add up. I think clubs are valuable to those who travel a great deal and frequently use the same airline."

As Horace spoke, I made a mental note that an airline club membership would make a handsome Christmas gift for a constant traveler who would appreciate having a phone at his disposal between flights, perhaps a drink or a snack, and an attendant to help out if he wants to alter his tickets. Sometimes you get even more than that. I was recalling a most unusual airline club experience some friends of ours experienced, and went on to tell Horace about it.

A couple from Washington whom we know, Joan and Steve, arranged to go to Europe, to which they had never been. They were elated, and made elaborate plans to ensure that they would have the trip they had dreamed of for years. To start things off with flair, Steve arranged through connections to use the airline's VIP lounge. There he and Joan sat back in upholstered comfort to wait for their 9:00 P.M. flight, while background music played and attendants kept filling their glasses with complimentary champagne. They were reveling in sybaritic splendor when suddenly Joan had an odd feeling. In a flash, she knew what it meant. She checked her watch and sure enough it said 9:15. They had been VIP'd out of the only flight of the day. She went into a tailspin. "Won't you put on another plane? I heard that when Lillian Hellman got left behind, they put on an extra plane just for her. What are our rights?" The attendant explained that Miss Hellman's mishap had occurred when she was London-bound from Paris, and other aircraft were available. There simply were no extra planes to be had in the present situation. But it was good that Joan spoke up instead of meekly submitting to her plight. The airline recognized the problem and said they would be happy to put her and Steve up at any hotel they chose, and pay all their expenses until flight time the next night.

At that point, Joan's sense of humor took over and she saw that the impasse was comedic. So she and Steve accepted the offer gracefully and checked in at the finest hotel in town. She describes the unexpected twenty-four-hour layover as a delightful preface to their European adventure.

"We slunk into the hotel like a pair of Brink's bandits, hoping we wouldn't run into anybody we knew. It would have been too embarrassing, after the fuss we had made about our trip, the send-off parties and the farewells. We went right up to our suite, no less, and ordered a divine room-service dinner. It was a luxury we had never indulged in before. The next morning, we thanked our stars that we had toiletries and an overnight change of clothes with us in carry-on bags, since our check-through luggage had already flown to Europe on the nine o'clock flight. As we dressed, I remembered that a nearby museum had an exhibit of Paris architecture. Steve agreed that would be a perfect prelude to our trip, so we taxied over and spent three fascinating hours. When we finally did get to Paris, we felt familiar with every red rooftop and historic avenue.

"After the museum we had a long, lovely lunch at one of our favorite restaurants, then walked through a historic part of town that we wanted to know better. We went back to the hotel to rest and clean up, and before we knew it, it was time to go to the airport again. This time I assure you there was no mix-up. The airline manager personally escorted us to the plane and the pampering never stopped. They flew us over first class, even though we had paid only for coach, and when we got to the Paris airport a limousine drove onto the field, picked us up at the plane steps, and whisked us straight to our hotel without even a stop for customs. Our bags were waiting in the lobby and the staff had been alerted to our Very Important Arrival. I loved every bow and curtsy: it was a wonderful introduction to Europe. I say, give me a so-called calamity every time, I'll show you how to turn it into a glorious opportunity."

Horace chuckled at the story and said, "Perhaps the best advice to give people is, learn to roll with the unexpected."

Overcoming the Problem of Lost Baggage

To which I would add: learn to *expect* the unexpected. Even first-timers Joan and Steve were unrealizingly prepared for an upset in their plans. They had packed carry-on survival kits. I think nearly everybody knows by now that the problem of lost baggage is as common as head colds. Most travelers have devised ploys to keep their risks to a minimum. Magazine editor Richard Kagan says he seldom checks anything through. He gets by very nicely with just three bags—one that fits under his seat, a shoulder bag that can go into the overhead compartment or else stay on the floor at his feet, and a hanging suitbag. With a coat over his arm, he is all set for three well-dressed weeks on the Continent. Since Dick's job sometimes takes him to dressy scenes, he has devised a way to attend black-tie affairs without carrying the extra bulk of a tuxedo. Instead, he packs a black worsted summer-weight suit (which can also be worn in the daytime), a cummerbund, a black bow tie, a good point-collar white shirt, a pocket handkerchief, and black shoes. "Earl Blackwell, the publisher of *Celebrity Register,* uses the same travel trick," Dick told me. "I discovered that when we ran into each other at an embassy reception in Washington and found that we were almost identically dressed."

Traveling Light

Dick says that the women writers he works with share his attitude about traveling light. Their packing lists often include no more than a couple of skirts and a suit with several different blouses, an unwrinkleable "everywhere" dress, and a dressy belt, scarf, or costume jewelry to change daytime outfits into evening wear. They seldom travel with real jewelry—it is too apt to be stolen. When they do take it, they never pack it in a suitcase or leave it in a hotel room. They wear it, or put it in the hotel safe. Most professional women say that comfortable shoes, a hair dryer, and their work equipment are much more important to them than toting tons of chic outfits. They theorize, correctly, that with porters a vanishing breed, you are most mobile when you can handle your baggage yourself.

Packing Tricks

Carolyn and I have both developed packing tricks that make travel easier. She packs her clothes on their hangers, to hasten the job of unpacking and to assure that she will have enough hangers when we get to the hotel. Hotels are frequently stingy in that respect, and they hardly ever have the variety of pants, skirt, and dress hangers she prefers. My own method is to use just one fold-up carryon whenever I can with a plastic insert organizer so I can get at my sweaters and socks easily. I pack a minimum of shirts, because most hotels can launder and return shirts the same day. If the trip is extra long or involves a change of climate, I roll and fold more clothes in a second bag—a duffel or parachute type that collapses to nothing and weighs less than a cloud. I have found that these bags sometimes rip, so I have learned to carry a small roll of adhesive tape with me, just in case.

I use another strategy when Carolyn and I go on a very long trip—a few weeks to a resort or to Nantucket for the summer. To avoid the crush at the baggage claim, we pack our belongings in laundry boxes or cartons and ship them ahead by parcel post a week or ten days before we leave, as we also did when Regen went off to college.

Packing for a trip is a game of outwitting the system. Those of us who travel frequently have developed certain procedures that become all but automatic. Here are some of the rules we have tested and proved:

• Use luggage tags and include the name of the hotel where you are going. On return trips, use your office rather than your home address, or just the name of your city, so possible house robbers cannot ascertain that you are away.

• Keep a bright-colored length of yarn or ribbon tied to the handle of each bag, so you can spot your luggage quickly when it comes off the carousel.

• Leave your luggage key inside the bag between trips, so you can find it without pawing through every bureau drawer in the house.

• When you have several short stays on your schedule, pack your boots, fold-up umbrella, and other rarely used items on the bottom.

• Wedge hosiery, film, Kleenex packets, and various small articles into shoes, in corners, and miscellaneous spaces.

• Use plastic bags instead of tissue, to prevent wrinkles, and to hold nylons and assorted loose objects, for laundry and wet bathing suits.

• Between trips, keep a toiletries kit packed and ready to go. Use sample-size products in plastic containers: your favorite brands of shampoo, toothpaste, face soap, body oil, sun lotion, aspirin.

• Keep a written list of emergency supplies to pack:

> Extra battery for travel alarm
> Extra shoestrings for tennis shoes
> Extra pills and refill prescriptions
> Extra eyeglasses
> Immersion heater or travel pot, instant coffee, dehydrated
>   soup and spoon, for do-it-yourself room service
> Corkscrew, can opener
> Miniature clothespins and nylon line
> Small sewing kit
> Scotch tape to mend hems, repair maps, and perform other
>   odd jobs.

Carolyn also keeps a list pinned up inside her closet of certain items she should remember to pack for each trip:

> Pantyhose
> Nightgown
> Robe
> Travel slippers
> Silk undershirt for warmth without bulk
> Sweater
> Scarf
> Belt
> Hat, long-sleeved shirt, and bug spray for the beach
> Notebook
> Checkbook
> Stamps
> Addresses for postcards home
> Address book for the place we are going
> Our doctor's and lawyer's phone numbers
> Camera

The list may seem prosaic but Carolyn says that even when she has plenty of time to think about what to pack, there is always a chance she will overlook a basic necessity. Carolyn has also given some thought to what she needs to stay fresh and comfortable when she travels, and her list of personal necessities includes a small white-noise machine and an eye mask. Experience has taught her that if she gets a good night's sleep, she is ready for anything the next day.

Traveling with Children

Experience has made Carolyn an expert at traveling with young children, too. It seems to me that she spent years shepherding three small daughters into airplanes and automobiles, but I have no recollection that we were bothered by the usual demands of young children: "How much farther do we have to go?" "When do we get there?" "Why can't I get out and play?" Thanks to Carolyn's thoughtfully prepared travel kits, they were always kept busy with coloring books, word puzzles, pocket-size games, cards, books, pencils, and note pads. We used to travel with food, too, to keep their stomachs settled and to provide another occupation. Carrot and celery sticks, apples and bananas are good for munching and don't make you thirsty. With a plastic storage box filled with crackers, a thermos of juice and Handiwipes for instant cleanups, our children were satisfied for hours.

Even without children along, Carolyn and I often travel with peanut butter and cheese crackers. They are satisfying and take the place of a meal if we are on a train or air flight where the food is impossible.

Airline Meals

Airline meals apparently irk a great many people, although there is no reason to think you are locked into them. You can phone some airlines twenty-four hours in advance and order one of the special meals they offer: kosher, salt-free, or another menu that appeals to you. You can eat before or after the flight instead of on board. You can brown-bag your own food, as Jean and her writer husband, David Halberstam, did when they flew to Europe on their honeymoon. They had a catering shop fix a box lunch of pâté, French bread, sliced chicken, salad, and pastries.

All they needed to round off their epicurean feast was wine and hot coffee from the plane's galley.

"Brown-bagging" is a term everyone understands, but I have yet to see anyone bring aboard a meal in a plain brown paper bag. Instead, people use everything from pastry boxes to status-label shopping bags. I once heard an amusing story about Mary Lou Whitney and her penchant for carrying meals aloft.

She and her husband, Cornelius Vanderbilt Whitney, often are airborne en route to one of their six homes. They are confirmed "brown baggers," with their meals usually contained in a paper bag from one of the prestigious stores where Mary Lou shops. Apparently at one point she let it be known to a newspaper reporter that she used small Tiffany bags for meals. The smart people at Cartier's read that and promptly messengered her a dozen of their large bags "for your long trips" and a dozen small ones for short trips. I wonder if airline food would taste any better if it came in bags from Fifth Avenue!

Another of my favorite food stories involves some delicacies that were actually checked through from Los Angeles to New York. It wasn't a meal, but an insulated plastic case filled with masses of homemade Mexican hors d'oeuvres. A friend of ours was taking the food to New York as a gift for her homesick nephew. Maureen had frozen dozens and dozens of her specialties—tamales, chili rellenos, and a variety of other delicacies, and packed them in dry ice inside an insulated container so they would keep during the flight. When the plane landed in New York, she hurried to baggage claim and got there just in time to see her case hit the carousel—and blow up, spraying the airport with hors d'oeuvres. The dry ice had burned sufficiently through the plastic so the case could not withstand the impact. It's lucky her nephew wasn't homesick for fresh California eggs.

Making the Most of Your Hotel

One aspect of travel about which I feel strongly is hotels. We have all been in hotel lobbies where we have overheard guests screaming their heads off at room clerks for bigger rooms or faster service. Their bullying usually gets them nowhere.

Hotels are in business to serve you, and you should ask for the things you want pleasantly but firmly. You are paying for them, and there is no extra charge for asking: the trick is to know what you are entitled to. A room that pleases you, for one thing. When the room you are assigned is not to your liking, it is your privilege to ask for a different room. In our case, since Carolyn is a light sleeper, we always ask for a room away from a noisy street or alley. And since we travel so frequently, we keep notes of specific room numbers that have pleased us because they are quiet or spacious. Then, next time we call that hotel for a reservation we can ask for the exact room we prefer. On occasion, we have been assigned rooms that we didn't like and when we asked for another, were told that the hotel was sold out. We know that hotels are not usually sold out, and that employees are sometimes too busy or lazy to show us something else. So we ask very nicely, and without making any accusations, if the room clerk or manager will please look one more time? Almost always they find us a room that we like.

If you assume that the person you are speaking with is happy to help you, and realize that a pleasant attitude can break down even the crankiest of curmudgeons, you can almost always get what you want. Would you like a bed board to firm up a soft mattress? Call the housekeeper, or ask the bell captain whom to call, or check the list of service numbers posted in your room. Do you need a button sewed on, an adapter for your electric razor, a stronger light bulb, more towels? Ask; they come with your room. Be pleasant and firm, without being folksy. "Room service? I called a half hour ago. Would you check on my order, please," or, "When you get a chance would you please bring me the newspaper I asked for with breakfast." Of course, you have to be realistic. If you have checked into a hotel that is stacked to the gunwales with conventioneers, you have to expect room service to be overburdened. To make life easier all around, why not order your evening drink and sandwiches in the morning, so room service can schedule you ahead of the evening flurry of calls.

More Tips on Getting Good Service

I have found that in addition to the expected tip, "Thank-you" is one phrase that nobody ever tires of hearing. Whether you are talking to a waiter, a desk clerk, or your husband or wife, you cannot say thank-you too often. When in doubt, my advice is to say thank-you anyway.

On the subject of tipping, something that people ask me about all the time, there simply is no universal rule. Tipping practices vary considerably from city to city and from country to country. All I can tell you is that, in general, the tip for average service is twelve to fifteen percent, the tip for de luxe service is twenty percent, and in some places tips are included in bills. When you need to know what the specific local practice is, I think the best bet is to ask somebody who lives in the place you are visiting, or else consult an up-to-date travel guide.

Travel Guides

Horace Sutton says he likes a combination of the Michelin Red and Green travel guides. They tell you where to stay, where to eat, what to see, and provide historical background. He cautions about guides that are unreliable, and apt to omit a small but gorgeous hotel in Monterey, or the charming old New England village that is off the turnpike. In most cases, though, the established guides' street maps and notes about interesting sites are well done, and a valauble aid when you are deciding which hotel location best suits your needs.

Local Transportation

Access to local transportation is especially important when you travel on business. I look for hotels that always have plenty of taxis lined up at the door, so I don't have to worry about how I will get to appointments on time. If I am in a city where mass transit is scant and taxis, too, I hire taxi drivers by the day to take me to my various appointments or to go sight-seeing. If I can't find a taxi driver to hire, I ask the bell captain or doorman if he knows somebody who would like the job. I usually save money in the long run because it costs less to hire one driver for a day-ful of stops than to use a different taxi for each trip. Besides, he does the waiting, not I. Of course, if I have only one or two calls to make, or my trip involves distance driving, I rent a car and drive it myself. Otherwise I prefer to let somebody else figure out strange street routes, find parking spaces, and deal with local traffic regulations. And if I am lucky enough to hire a knowledgeable driver, he can help me to learn the fine points of the city, as well.

Sight-Seeing Techniques

I also like to use sight-seeing buses, not for transportation but to get the lay of the land. Carolyn and I nearly always take one of the half-day guided bus tours when we go to a new place. Then if we see something that interests us we can go back on our own. We use the same system to cover museums, cathedrals, historic buildings, and other tourist meccas—the quick guided tour first, to give us an overview, then a return visit for in-depth inspection of the areas that interest us.

I must tell you that the technique did not come to us in a flash because we are such clever people; it came to us because we are parents. Carolyn and I learned, two or three daughters ago, that you cannot drag exhausted, impatient children through a museum while you stop to examine every painting. You have to give them short, brisk visits so they can look around, then move them on to someplace else before they become fidgety. Well, grownups are subject to fidgets, too; neither Carolyn nor I want to spend hours studying every piece of art in a museum. We just like to look at those that really interest us. So we have adopted the preliminary overview method as a way to edit our sight-seeing ventures into rewarding and pleasant experiences.

How to Get a Sense of Place
Through Personal Discoveries

Traditional points of interest for tourists are a must. I would not like to miss out on seeing anything that reflects history, or that is so beautiful it has withstood the test of time. So I combine the standard points of interest with personal discoveries that you make by exploring on your own. You are apt to run into pleasures you never anticipated, besides. The key is to keep your mind open and not to schedule your time tightly. I always like to leave free time, even on business trips, so I can prowl around off the beaten track: away from the hotel, away from the monuments, away from the famous tourist restaurants. If there is a bus or streetcar in town you are sure to find me riding it to the end of the line. Then, on the return trip, I will get off at some residential section that looked inviting and wander around. I have explored San Francisco, New Orleans, Boston, Milan and other towns by streetcar, and sometimes my wanderings have taken me to little cafes where I have fallen into conversations with wonderful, friendly people I never would have met if I had stayed on the tourist path.

You get a sense of the rhythm of a place, too, when you move around casually, listen to people, learn their concerns and their interests. If I had stayed close to my hotel in Milan, I would not have known the real Milan—a city of energetic, hard-working cosmopolites who are intensely interested in their theaters, restaurants, and museums. I learned that San Francisco is a slower-paced city, with plenty of time for hospitality to strangers and a pulsebeat that has a noisy, hippie quality. Boston is like madras plaid—college kids in a tearing hurry interwoven with the mature population's more reflective historical perspective. Even the architecture and the storefronts reflect Boston's two points of view. In fact, architecture provides good clues to any city's past and present—another reason to get away from your hotel and look around. I am thrilled that I have had the opportunity to see the antebellum mansions in the countryside miles beyond touristy New Orleans, the stolid farmhouses and factories outside Shanghai, the ancient houses and modern high rises in Tokyo's suburbs.

You can get another good index to the culture of a place if you make it a point to seek out local restaurants. In addition to finding new pleasures for your palate, it makes you feel more as if you are a part of the region, to dine as the natives do. The cuisine, the setting, the local customs become memories you can take home and treasure the rest of your life. Whenever Carolyn

or I think of Sevilla, we remember, besides the river and the Al-
cazar, the late afternoon *tapas* that we savored with our wine in a
small, blue-tiled bar we discovered by chance on a winding side
street. And the leather-goods shop next door, where Carolyn
bought me a pair of gloves and I bought her a handbag. Then
there was the time in Tucson, when we decided for no reason at
all to drive out past the famous mission church. There wasn't
much to see and we were about to turn back when we came
upon a lonely roadside diner. We decided to stop for coffee, and
went on to find a warm, happy room crowded with neighborhood families out for a modest Sunday dinner. We were
tempted by a local specialty, wheat tostadas, and ordered them.
We had never tasted tostadas made of wheat before, and found
them delectable. We complimented the owner, who was also the
chef, and before we knew it she and her husband sat down at
our table and gave us their recipes for tostadas, chimichangas,
another Tucson specialty, and a dessert called sopapillas that we
had heard every child in the room clamor for.

An inclination for spontaneity has taken me to a lot of offbeat
places and spawned many wonderful memories. I cannot imagine Greece without thinking of the sidewalk cafe in Athens
where I first tasted ouzo. Tokyo is synonymous with the saki I
sipped at a hillside picnic, with people I had met just the day
before at a business associate's party. Closer to home, I remember Maine for the fresh fish chowder so thick it all but bent my
spoon, and for the sturdy, weather-wise fisherman who served it
to us. Carolyn and I met the fisherman by chance when we wan-
dered into a barn sale looking for old weather vanes. Somehow
we fell into conversation with the man, and it seemed perfectly
natural for him to invite us to his home after the sale.

Making the Best of Misfortune

There is no doubt in my mind that you should seize every
travel opportunity you can. Sometimes, though, it is opportunity
that seizes you. Friends of ours from Atlanta, Ellen and Dan, told
me about an adventure that was forced on them in Paris, the year
the Hong Kong flu epidemic hit Europe. Ellen explained that
Dan must have been incubating the virus, because he came

down with a severe case two days after they arrived. Ellen, who hadn't uttered a word of French since she graduated from college in 1959, said she didn't know what to do. Her French was rudimentary, and she couldn't understand the telephone operator at the small hotel where they were staying. Finally, she went to the lobby and managed to communicate with the concierge. "C'est mon mari: mal, très mal. Au secours, s'il vous plaît," she wailed, mispronouncing every syllable. By pointing to her wedding ring, "Mon mari, my husband," and clapping her hand to her brow, "Mal, très mal, very bad," she got her message across. "Au secours ... help, please." She may have been inaccurate but the concierge caught on and told Ellen how to take Dan to the American Hospital. At the hospital, a doctor told her to keep Dan in bed at the hotel, feed him aspirin, fruit, and bottled water, and he would be better in three days.

"Now came the real test," Ellen continued. "I had to find a neighborhood chemist, do my marketing, and spend the next three days in Paris without Dan by my side to share experiences, deal with subways and headwaiters, figure out how much a franc is in dollars ... all the things he usually takes care of.

"I figured I should also take the list of places we planned to see and make a loose schedule for myself. Solo or not, I certainly wanted to see the famous avenues, the Left Bank, and all that. However, I am not as interested in art as Dan is, and since I had only myself to please, I crossed off all the galleries and museums on the list, except for the Louvre and a few others whose architecture and history truly excite me. But what made my pulse really go crazy, between you and me, was the idea of shopping in Paris with no impatient husband to rush me on. Hot dog!

"I knew a dozen shops I was dying to caper through, and found many more wherever I went on my solo tour of beautiful Paris. Francs and dollars were not a problem, even where the exchange rate was not posted. We had changed our American dollars into French currency at an airport bank when we first arrived, knowing that hotels and shops give poorer rates and sometimes charge a handling fee. I had traveler's checks from my bank at home, I had my credit cards, and to sew things up, I had Dan's pocket-size calculator in my purse so I could figure conversions instantly when I had to."

Ellen made the most of her unexpected three days alone. Somebody with less vitality or imagination might have thrown up her hands when her traveling companion became ill, and sat around in the hotel room instead of getting out and discovering new experiences.

Gifts for Strangers

Something I always have on my mind when I travel is what gifts to buy for business acquaintances and friends. Since I meet so many people who entertain me in their homes, I usually tuck small things into my bag before I leave home: nice handkerchiefs, American phonograph records, Texas jewelry, or tee shirts for youngsters. The gifts vary according to the custom of the country I am visiting. In Japan it is customary to bring cookies as house gifts; in Germany, people bring flowers. Of course, I don't pack cookies or flowers in my luggage. I pick up fresh things at local shops, and other kinds of house gifts as well. Actually unless you travel as constantly as I do, it is probably better to shop locally than to bring gifts from home. Customs change all the time and a store clerk may be able to inform you that last year's *de rigueur* ball-point pen is no longer the most desirable gift; this year the Japanese much prefer to receive American perfume, or something else that has become precious.

Meeting People

Occasionally, despite all the traveling I have done and the many business connections I have throughout the world, I find myself going to a city where I don't know anybody who invites me into a home. That doesn't bother me because, as you know, I like to go off and explore on my own. Besides, I am a fairly talkative fellow, and I find that if I want to meet people I just have to make myself accessible to them. Impromptu friendships are sparked very readily, and you have no idea how many of my friends I first met in a bar, or a store, or in an airplane waiting room.

Sometimes, however, I like to set up a situation so I will be sure to have somebody to call on for advice, or to share lunch or dinner with. I felt that way the first time I went to Tokyo. So I told everybody I knew in Dallas where I was going. So many people travel to so many places these days, practically everybody I spoke to knew someone there, or else knew someone who knew someone else. When I felt confident that the recommendation would be a good one, that I would meet somebody on my wavelength, I asked my Dallas connection to write ahead and make a preliminary introduction for me. I would be imposing if I telephoned somebody who has never heard of me, or who may have some reason to not want to see me. It puts them on the spot. Besides, Japan and other Eastern countries are more formal in their manners than we are. They would be displeased by the casual Western style of getting right down to business, "Hello there, I'm in town for a few days and so-and-so gave me your number. How about if I drop by?"

I am sure no one would be that outrageous, for there are ways to call without the benefit of a previous introduction that permits the other person to back off gracefully. One way is to mention the name of your mutual friend—be sure it is a valid connection—and throw in a reminder in case the person can't quite recall whom you are talking about. "My name is Roger Horchow. I'm from Dallas, Texas, and I'm in town for a few days on business. A friend of mine in Dallas, Mary Jones, suggested I call you while I am here. You probably remember Mary as the tall, pretty architect whom you met at the party the Smiths gave when your book was published in the States. Is this a convenient time to speak with you?"

The second key is to open up the opportunity for a little conversation, to give the other person a chance to find out if you sound like somebody he or she would like to meet. The best way is to ask a question, so they will have something to respond to.

YOU: I wonder if you could tell me of a good seafood restaurant in town?

THEY: Oh, yes indeed. We have several that we are very proud of. There's Brown's, on the waterfront. It's quite large, but good. White's is a landmark in the financial district of the city. Businessmen like to go there for lunch. And then there is Black's, very informal, with paper plates and the world's best french-fried potatoes.

YOU: Thank you. I'll be sure to give at least one of them a try. Perhaps I can go to White's tomorrow, while I'm downtown. Do I need a reservation?

THEY: Yes, it's a popular spot. You should call them in the morning, to make sure you have a table when you want it. Would you like me to look up the number for you?

YOU: You are kind to offer, but I have a phone book right here so please don't bother. Tell me, have you seen our friend Mary lately?

By this time you have caught the timbre of one another's voice. "They" can now decide whether they want to keep the conversation rolling with chatter about Mary, and then go on to invite you to their home or another meeting place. Otherwise, you have made it easy for them to tell you how nice it was of you to call, and please not to hesitate if there is anything else they can do for you. You have let them off the hook in the nicest possible way.

In any case, whether you connect or not, it is a courtesy to report back to the mutual friend who paved the way for you. Whenever I am in the position of being that "mutual friend," I like to learn the results of my efforts.

Traveling Alone

Several of our women friends who travel alone on business have told me that they often have no one to call and are at a loss for something to do after business hours. They are not accustomed to going to public places by themselves and talking to strangers. I tell them that they don't have to worry. It is perfectly acceptable these days for anybody, man or woman, to be seen alone in public and to talk with people without a formal introduction. I am often faced with a lonely evening myself, on business trips, and I never think twice about going alone to restaurants or cocktail lounges where I know I will meet friendly people. Or I can talk to the bartender, if the fellow on the next stool is a bore. Or I can just sit there and listen to other people talk. I can entertain myself for an entire evening by stopping at four or five different bars, just to see what they look like. I might try the hotel lounge, a roof garden, a restaurant bar, and a lounge that I have heard about in my travels. It's a good little tour and an interesting project, even when I don't find people to talk to. And nobody minds that I sometimes order plain soda or tonic instead of something alcoholic. I know my capacity, and five drinks in succession would stand me on my ear. That is not my idea of fun.

Cruise Ships

Unfortunately, the magnificent luxury liners that were once the only link between continents have disappeared as a mode of transportation. All is not lost, however. The good news is that even though midnight sailings and bubbling champagne have given way to fast jet crossings, short cruise vacations have become more popular than ever before in travel history.

Besides the fact that they are relaxing and fun, one of the major attractions of cruise ships is that you know in advance what the cost of your vacation will be. You can go from the West Coast to Mexico or Hawaii, or from the East Coast to Bermuda or the Bahamas, and know before you leave home exactly how much you will spend for transportation, accommodations, meals, and tips. That is quite a bit easier for most people to manage than flying off to Italy, for example, and discovering that they have to spend more than they budgeted for because the bottom just dropped out of the American dollar.

Travel by Train

The big trip of 1980, the experts tell me, was cruising the Nile. Then came the year when "everybody" went to China. For me, keeping up on the latest thing in destinations is not terribly important; what tantalizes me is the trip I have never taken. That is why my current travel ambition is to see a continent by train. Not any old train, but one of the gracious, stately trains that most of us have read about and never ridden. I have sampled a little of the superb service on T.E.E., the Trans European Express; I want to ride it end to end. I must try the futuristic new German train that works by magnetic levitation and whizzes along at 250 miles an hour. I cannot wait to ride the Orient Express that goes from Paris to Venice. It is owned by my London friend, Jim Sherwood, who also owns the Cipriani hotel in Venice. Then there is the Blue Train in South Africa that Caskie Stinnett says is the most luxurious in the world. He also told me about the wonderful new Empire Builder that goes from Chicago, through Glacier National Park, to Seattle. That train operates only in the West because its double-deck coaches do not fit into Eastern railroad tunnels. The other American luxury train I am eager to ride is the Twentieth Century Limited. Jim Sherwood, of the Orient Express, is bringing it back to life, complete with the leisurely splendors of the past—meals served by white-coated waiters, starched tablecloths, comfortable beds, attentive service, and mile after mile of effortless transportation. That is my idea of traveling in style.

♨ ♨ ♨

Appendix—Recipes

AUDREY WERTHEIM'S
ALL-TIME STANDBY BUFFET (*Page 23*)

Polynesian Chicken (Glazed chicken and pineapple—serves 8)

8 medium-size chicken legs and thighs
4 chicken breasts, halved
Garlic salt and medium-ground pepper to taste
2 medium-size green peppers
1 can (12) round pineapple slices in heavy syrup, drained; reserve separately ⅓ cup syrup
1 can button mushrooms without stems or 12 medium-size
  fresh mushroom caps sliced
1 lb. bag whole blanched almonds
1 lb. box dark brown sugar

Place chicken parts in 10 × 15 baking pan. Season heavily on
both sides with garlic salt and pepper to taste. Core and slice
green peppers and place on top of chicken. Top with symmetri-
cally arranged pineapple rounds. Tuck mushrooms around
chicken and sprinkle almonds around pan. In saucepan, melt 1
lb. dark brown sugar in ⅓ cup reserved pineapple syrup to make
heavy glaze. Coat chicken with glaze. Place in preheated 450°
oven and bake 1 hour, basting occasionally until sugar syrup
begins to glaze. Serve on large platter garnished with watercress.

Golden Rice (serves 8)

½ cup sweet or salted butter
3 cups long-grain rice
4 cups chicken stock or 4 packets MBT Chicken Broth dissolved in 4 cups hot water.

Place butter in 4-quart oven-top casserole over low heat and melt (do not brown). Add rice and sauté for about 5 minutes until browned. Pour in the broth and cover. Bring to a boil and immediately reduce to simmer. Cook until all the liquid is absorbed by the rice and perforations begin to appear in the rice. Remove from stove and cover with a dry towel for 10 minutes. Serve warm.

Mandarin Orange-Watercress Salad

1 head leafy garden lettuce
2 bunches watercress
4 scallions, bulb ends only, chopped
1 large can mandarin oranges, drained.

Tear lettuce into bite-size pieces. Toss lettuce, watercress, and scallions. Place greens on salad plates. Arrange orange segments around salad greens. Drizzle with Mandarin Salad Dressing.

Mandarin Salad Dressing

1 cup red wine vinegar
½ cup canned mandarin orange juice
½ cup olive oil
¾ tsp. salt
¼ tsp. white pepper

Place ingredients in a small capped bottle and shake well. Chill before serving.

MARILYN HORNE'S
GLORIOUS GREEK SUPPER (*Page 23*)

CANAPÉS
Taramasalata (Red caviar canapés—serves 8 to 10)

3 slices white bread, crusts removed, soaked in water and squeezed dry
5 ounces tarama (red fish roe)
1 cup olive oil
Juice of 1½ lemons
1 T. red wine vinegar
1 to 2 T. water, if needed
½ onion, grated (optional)

With an electric mixer or blender, thoroughly blend the bread and tarama. Slowly add the olive oil blending at a medium speed; add lemon juice and vinegar, blending at a higher speed. If needed, use water to smooth mixture. Add grated onion and whip at high speed. Serve with triangular-cut pita bread, mini-rounds of party-size pumpernickel, ¾" thick French bread or water biscuits.

Saganaki (Fried cheese canapés—serves 4 to 6)

½ lb. kasseri cheese
2 T. butter
Juice of 1 lemon

Cut cheese into triangular bite sizes. Melt butter in a saganaki (shallow two-handled pan) or frying pan. Fry cheese on both sides until crusty. Squeeze lemon juice onto cheese. Serve on platter garnished with lemon wedges, parsley, and decorative toothpicks.

ENTRÉE
Sinagrida Scharas Ladolemono (Grilled red snapper with lemon oil sauce—serves 4)

  1 whole 4-lb. red snapper with head and tail
  Salt and fresh-ground pepper to taste
  2 T. oregano
  1½ cups olive oil
  Juice of 1½ lemons
  Sprigs of fresh parsley
  6 rosebud-cut radishes

Preheat broiler to 450°. Starting at base of head, make incision down to the tail on both sides of the fish. Rub fish inside and out with salt and pepper. Brush with olive oil and place on grill. Cook approximately 15 minutes on both sides. Test for ideal moisture by lifting small section of fish from incision. Place on hot ovenware platter and sprinkle oregano from head to tail. Cover with a sauce of olive oil and lemon juice, blended until creamy white. Garnish with sprigs of parsley and rosebud-cut radishes.

Nico's Favorite Tzatziki (Yogurt cucumber salad—serves 4)

  6–8 cloves minced garlic
  ¼ cup red wine vinegar
  ¾ tsp. salt (optional)
  2 cups plain yogurt
  1 cup sour cream
  1 long cucumber, pared and sliced thin
  2 T. finely chopped dill or parsley

In glass mixing bowl, mince garlic into red wine vinegar; add salt. Mix in yogurt and sour cream; stir until mixture is smooth and pale pink. Place cucumber in glass or earthenware salad bowl. Cover with mixture and toss lightly. Garnish rim of bowl and center with parsley or dill. Refrigerate until served.

DESSERT
Frouta Freska Macedonia (Macédoine of fresh fruit—serves 6 to 8)

Fresh peaches, pears, apples, seedless grapes, melon, canta-
loupe, bananas
Granulated sugar
6 to 8 tsp. Cointreau
6 to 8 T. thyme-flavored honey
1 cup finely chopped blanched almonds and walnuts, com-
bined

Using a sharp paring knife and a melon-ball scoop, cut fruit into
bite-size pieces. Place in bowl. Sprinkle with sugar and mix in
Cointreau. Chill. To serve, ladle into frosted champagne glasses;
top with tablespoon of honey and generous dusting of nuts.

Kourabiedes (Butter cookies—approximately 50)

2 cups softened sweet butter
2 cups confectioners' sugar
2 egg yolks
2 T. fine cognac
5 cups sifted all-purpose flour
½ cup salt
1 tsp. baking powder
1 tsp. vanilla extract
50 whole cloves

In large bowl, cream butter until fluffy. Gradually add sugar, egg
yolks, and cognac. Sift flour with salt and baking powder and
beat into mixture. Blend in vanilla extract and knead into a soft
buttery dough. Shape into crescents on buttered baking sheets.
Place clove in center of each cookie. Bake on center rack at 350°
for 15–20 minutes or until cookies are golden brown. Place
cooled cookies on bed of confectioners' sugar; top with sifted
sugar.

CAROLYN'S
BASIC BACKYARD BARBECUE (*Page 36*)

Guacamole

3 medium avocados
1½ tomato, chopped
Juice of 1½ lemons
¾ of medium onion, chopped

Mix together and salt to taste. Serve with Tortilla Chips.

Barbecued Spareribs for 6

5-6 pounds spareribs (have the butcher cut them in 2-3 rib portions).

Salt and pepper ribs and place in a lightly covered roasting pan. Bake at 350° for 45 minutes. Pour off all fat and then coat ribs heavily with your favorite barbecue sauce. Grill over hot coals about 15-20 minutes until brown and glazed.

Gertie's Jalapeño Rice

4 cups cooked rice
¼ lb. butter or margarine
1½ cups sour cream
8 oz. Cheddar cheese, grated
4 Jalapeño peppers, chopped
Salt and pepper to taste
2 T. Parmesan cheese

Mix all ingredients together. Place in 2-quart casserole. Sprinkle Parmesan cheese on top. Dot with butter. Bake at 375° for 45 minutes.

Raw Vegetable Salad for 12

    1 lb. asparagus cut on diagonal
    1 bunch cauliflower, cut in small flowerettes
    4 stalks celery, slivered
    2 zucchini, sliced thin
    4 yellow squash, sliced thin
    1 cup Brussels sprouts, cut in half
    1 lb. sliced raw mushrooms
    1 cucumber, sliced thin
    4 green onions, sliced
    6 radishes, sliced thin
    6 cherry tomatoes, cut in half
    Sherry French dressing

Put asparagus, cauliflower, celery, zucchini, yellow squash, and Brussels sprouts in colander. Pour boiling water over. Drain and cool. Add mushrooms, cucumber, green onions, radishes, and tomatoes. Pour dressing over and refrigerate 1 hour, then drain off dressing.

Sherry French Dressing

    1 egg
    1 tsp. sugar
    2 tsp. salt
    2 cups salad oil
    2 cups olive oil
    ½ cup vinegar
    ½ cup sherry
    2 cloves garlic

Mix egg, sugar, and salt. Add oil and vinegar. Then add garlic which has been barely crushed.

Mrs. Taylor's Three Fruit Sherbet

Allow ½ gallon pineapple sherbet to soften. Mash 3 or 4 ripe bananas. Add bananas and 1 cup fresh orange juice to sherbet, using potato masher to mix thoroughly. Put into freezer.

Oatmeal Chocolate Chip Cookies

1 cup butter or margarine
2 cups brown sugar
2 eggs
2 tsp. vanilla
½ tsp. salt
1 cup flour
3 cups rolled oats
One 12-oz. pkg. semisweet chocolate bits

Preheat oven to 350°. Cream butter and sugar. Add eggs, vanilla, and salt. Stir in flour and oats. Add chocolate bits. Drop in small mounds onto greased cookie sheets. Bake 15–20 minutes.

INDEX

Memo

From

BOB BARNHILL, SR.

To

BARNHILL & ASSOCIATES, INC.
(301) 377-5952
6607 Weymouth Court
Baltimore, MD 21212

Memo

From

BOB BARNHILL, SR.

To

BARNHILL & ASSOCIATES, INC.
(301) 377-5952
6607 Weymouth Court
Baltimore, MD 21212